Helion & Company Limited
Unit 8 Amherst Business Centre
Budbrooke Road
Warwick
CV34 5WE
England
Tel. 01926 499 619
Email: info@helion.co.uk
Website: www.helion.co.uk
Twitter: @helionbooks
Visit our blog http://blog.helion.co.uk/

Designed and typeset by Farr out
    Publications, Wokingham, Berkshire
Cover designed by Paul Hewitt, Battlefield
    Design (www.battlefield-design.co.uk)
Printed by Henry Ling Ltd, Dorchester,
    Dorset

ISBN 978-1-911628-07-1

British Library Cataloguing-in-Publication
    Data
A catalogue record for this book is available
    from the British Library

We always welcome receiving book
proposals from prospective authors.

CONTENTS

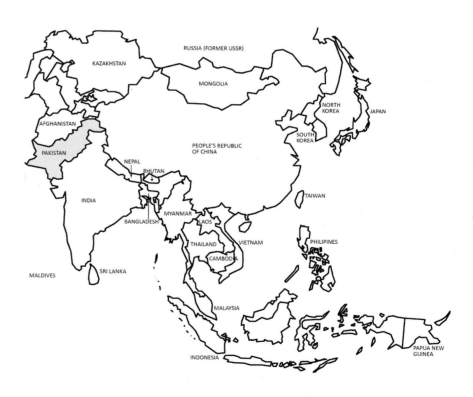

Note: In order to simplify the use of this book, all names, locations and geographic designations are as provided in *The Times World Atlas*, or other traditionally accepted major sources of reference, as of the time of described events. For reasons of simplicity, genuine designations for Soviet/Russian-made weapons used in this book are mentioned once, and then their ASCC (or 'NATO') codes are used instead.

ABBREVIATIONS

ADC	Aide de Camp
AFV	armoured fighting vehicle
AGRP	Army Group Royal Pakistan Artillery
AM	amplitude modulated
AP	armoured piercing
APDS-FS	armoured piercing discarding sabot – fin stabilized
APU	auxiliary power unit
ARV	armoured recovery vehicle
ATGM	anti-tank guided missile
AVLB	armoured vehicle launched bridge
AWOL	absent without leave
BOQ	Bachelor Officers Quarters
BRBL	Bhambanwala Ravi Balloki Link
CBI	China Burma India
CIH	Central India Horse
C-in-C	Commander-in-Chief
CO	Commanding Officer
DSO	Distinguished Service Order
DZ	drop zone
EICO	Emergency Indian Commissioned Officer
EME	Electrical and Mechanical Engineers
ERE	Extra Regiment Employment
FC	Frontier Corps
FMF	Foreign Military Funding
GGBG	Governor General's Bodyguard
GHQ	General Headquarters
GMC	General Motor Corporation
GOC	General Officer Commanding
GSO	General Staff Officer
GSP	General Staff Publication
HE	high explosive
HEAT	high explosive anti-tank
HF	high frequency
HIT	Heavy Industries Taxila
HRF	Heavy Rebuild Factory
HVAP	high velocity armour piercing
IAC	Indian Armoured Corps
IC	Indian Communication
ICO	Indian Commissioned Officer
IDSM	Indian Distinguished Service Medal
IMA	Indian Military Academy
INA	Indian National Army
IPS	Indian Political Service
ISI	Inter-Services Intelligence
JCO	Junior Commissioned Officer
JTA	Junior Tactical Armour
KCIO	King's Commissioned Indian Officer
KEO	King Edward's Own
KPT	Khairpur Tamewali
KSA	Kingdom of Saudi Arabia
LAD	Light Aid Detachment
MAAG	Military Assistance and Advisory Group
MAP	Military Assistance Program
MBT	Main Battle Tank
MC	Military Cross
MES	Military Engineering Service
MGO	Master General of Ordinance
Mk	Mark
MOD	Ministry of Defence
MPML	Manual of Pakistan Military Law
MS	Military Secretary
MS&B	Muslim, Sindhi, & Baluch
MTO	Mechanical Transport Officer
NCO	Non-Commissioned Officer
NWFP	North-West Frontier Province
ODRP	Office of Defence Representative Pakistan
OP	observation post
OR	other ranks
ORBAT	order of battle
OTS	Officer's Training School
PAIFORCE	Persia and Iraq Command
PAKBAT	Pakistan Battalion
Para	parachute
PAVO	Prince Albert Victor's Own
PBF	Punjab Boundary Force
PHV	Peshawar Vale Hunt
PIFFERS	Punjab Irregular Frontier Force
PMA	Pakistan Military Academy
POW	prisoner of war
QRF	quick reaction force
R&S	reconnaissance and support
RAC	Royal Armoured Corps
RTC	Royal Tank Corps
RDH	Royal Deccan Horse
Recce	reconnaissance
RFA	Royal Field Artillery
RHQ	regimental headquarters
RIASC	Royal Indian Army Service Corps
RIMC	Royal Indian Military College
RPG	rocket propelled grenade
RR	recoilless rifle
RSO	regiment signal officer
SDM	Squadron Daffadar Major
SSG	Special Services Group
STO	Squadron Technical Officer
TAS	training advisory staff
TDU	Tank Delivery Unit
TEWT	tactical exercise without troops
TM	technical manual
TO&E	table of organization and equipment
TPP	time past a point
TSIC	Temporary School for Indian Cadets
VCO	Viceroy's Commissioned Officer
VHF	very high frequency

FOREWORD

History is a teacher. Wise nations learn from the battlefield errors with an open mind. They examine their performance in combat critically, objectively, and analytically to ensure that the mistakes made in the past are not repeated again. Wartime mistakes can be very costly in men, material, and professional reputation. Pakistan's open society takes professional operational errors seriously, and takes steps to correct them in peacetime training. Those who sweep their mistakes under the carpet face a grave risk. As professional soldiers, we should never forget that history has the habit of repeating itself. Karl Marx claimed that one should understand history in order to make history.

Soldiering is a noble profession. It demands dedication, devotion, and the development of mind and soul. People in the military profession pay the supreme price for the pride and glory of the motherland. They shed their blood and die with their boots on, to enable their countrymen to live with honour, grace, and respect. Cavalry officers and men have played their full part in the pleasant and arduous history of their country. The 'Charge of the Light Brigade' lives in history. It is a shining example of bravery and dedication despite its heavy cost. The horse era of the past has since been replaced by mechanised warfare. Gone are the days of the famous cavalry charges of the yesteryears. The roar and thunder of the advancing tank-led mechanised columns in the modern battlefield has revolutionised the art of modern warfare. Despite the quantum jump in the style and technique of warfare, the cavalry spirit remains unchanged. The cavalry charges have now been replaced with the sudden shock and the terror effect of deep thrusts made in the heart of the enemy by the mechanised tank columns. This impact is as devastating as was the cavalry charge. Death is the fate of all human beings but soldiers sacrifice their lives in the battlefield for a national cause that is sacred and noble. Macauly writes:

And how can man die better,
Than facing fearful odds
For the ashes of his fathers,
And the temples of his gods

Are commanders born or made? This debate is educative. Alexander maintained that commanders are made (with time and effort). "My soldiers follow me not because I am brave but because I am well read", said Napoleon. Disraeli maintained that men govern through words. This depicts the eminence of education. Liddell Hart was a captain but his writings are a source of knowledge for generals. The lessons of history are boldly engraved on the walls of time. Every military leader should be well educated. He should be professionally groomed and be ready to pounce on the fleeting opportunities that occur in war. A commander who seizes such a chance ends up in fame. Those who fail to utilise such chances usually end up as the losers.

I joined 11th Cavalry (FF) as a second lieutenant in 1949. The early days of joining the regiment remain fresh in my mind. I was advised to read regimental history and Mess Rules and acquire knowledge about the silver displayed in the officer's mess and the paintings and photographs hung there. Our senior subaltern, Sadiq Ali curtly stated that an officer is late on parade only once in life – the day he is dead. He also arrogantly claimed that a second lieutenant is the lowest form of humanity who should better be only seen, not heard. The ground rules on drinking were ambiguously clear. Drinking may be a sin I was told, but it is not a crime in the country. Drink if you may but clear your mess bills every month.

Ali Hamid's book is rich in thought and content, and richer still in history. It is an excellent effort for which the author deserves praise. Well done Ali! You have risen to the occasion. The Armoured Corps will remember your efforts. So will the Pakistan Army. This book fills in a wide gap that existed in the history of our army. Nature has located Pakistan with a neighbour who is bigger in size and richer in power potential. It is therefore important for all soldiers, sailors, and airmen in Pakistan to maintain a professional edge in their quality to a military effort. This pleasantly readable historical record should be a "must-read book" for all officers of the Pakistan Armoured Corps in particular and the Pakistan Army in general.

General (Retired) Khalid Mahmud Arif

PREFACE

Maj Gen Ali Hamid has done something that was long overdue. He has compiled a fascinating, and extremely well researched and documented history of the Pakistan Armoured Corps. Writing any history is a difficult undertaking and putting together a history from documents, letters, photographs, and interviews is a truly monumental task. Ali has accomplished this with great skill. The historical journey detailed by him is studded with his insightful comments, most interesting anecdotes, and some great photographs.

The author quite appropriately takes as his starting point the mechanisation of the Indian Cavalry in 1938 because this process started the evolution that led to the Pakistan Armoured Corps. As he rightly stresses, mechanisation was not just re-equipping and training, but it meant changing mind-sets. To a moderate extent, the credit for this is attributed to General Frank Messervy of the 13th Lancers who was the Major General Armoured Fighting Vehicles in India and later the first commander-in-chief of the Pakistan Army. Interestingly the

first commander-in-chief of the Indian Army, General Roy Boucher, was also from the 13th Lancers!

With a great insight, Ali Hamid points out the fact that in spite of inheriting a small cadre of mostly inexperienced but dedicated officers, the Pakistan Armoured Corps very quickly moulded itself into a cohesive and credible fighting force. In the decade of the 50s and early 60s, the Regiments finally found locations that suited them logistically for operations and training. This was also the period in which the Pakistan Armoured Corps became an all-track force first on Shermans and M36B2s and later on state-of-the-art Pattons that came under the US Military Assistance Programme. This gave Pakistani armour a decided edge over the Indian Armoured Corps. In both the 1965 and 1971 Pakistan-India Wars, the Pakistan Armoured Corps played a major role and this has been faithfully and objectively noted by Ali.

After the wars, there was introspection, expansion, new operational thinking, and a shift to Chinese tanks. This entire evolutionary process has been covered in the book right up to the present-day status of the Corps. Ali Hamid has also covered the foreign deployments of the Armoured Corps and has given a great description of the training procedures, doctrines, and the culture of the Armoured Corps as it existed at Independence and as it has evolved subsequently – 'an interesting fusion of strong regimental identities set within the larger structure of the Corps.'

I had the privilege of knowing Ali's father, the Late Maj Gen Syed Shahid Hamid and Ali has certainly inherited his father's remarkable language and writing skills so the book he has produced for us is excellent. For Ali, the diehard Armour man that he is, this must have been a labour of love, and as for us, we must acknowledge with gratitude the great service he has rendered for our Corps. I also appreciate the assistance provided to Ali by the Armoured Corps Directorate, the Centre and School, as well as the valuable and ready input by the serving and retired officers of the Corps.

General (Retd) Jehangir Karamat

AUTHOR'S NOTE

This book is not a history of the armoured regiments of the Pakistan Army, but of the Corps of which they form a part; its culture, organisation, doctrine, equipment, garrisons, and a myriad of events and personalities that together portray what and why the corps is today. It spans 95 years, beginning with the mechanisation of the Indian cavalry and concludes around 2015. The four years it has taken me to compile and publish this history have been a labour of love for two reasons. Firstly, it repays to the armoured corps in a small way all that I have gained from it. Secondly, it is a sequel to a book that my father the Late Maj Gen Syed Shahid Hamid wrote on the cavalry of the British India Army titled *So they Rode and Fought*.

Very broadly the history of the Pakistan Armoured Corps can be divided into four segments: the pre-Independence period which commenced with the mechanisation of the Indian cavalry, the post-Independence period that extends till the 1971 War, the period up to 1995 by which time the corps evolved into a modern fighting force in thought, organisation and equipment, and finally the last twenty year in which one of the most significant aspects has been the corps'

experience in combating the militants. In gathering material for the period that spanned the first part, sufficient published works are available. I also had the opportunity to obtain valuable information from the documents of the India Office Library held in the British Library, and the archives of the British National Army Museum. Entering the post-Independence period, three books by Maj Gen Shaukat Riza, and two by Maj Gen Fazle Mukeem provide an adequate overview of the Army, and some information on the armoured corps. More specific to the corps, I leaned heavily on the first-rate material contained in the autobiographies of three officers: Gen Gul Hassan, Maj Gen Syed Wajahat Hussain, and Brig Zaheer Alam Khan. Detailed work on Punjab Cavalry by Lt Col Yahya Effendi, was also very informative and the Golden Jubilee Issue of the journal *Sabre and Lance* provided comprehensive reference material. It was a commendable effort by Brig Munawar Ahmed Rana, and the Editorial Staff at the School of Armour and Mechanised Warfare. Moving into the period after the 1971 War, apart from some articles, there is little else and I had to rely on my own knowledge and that of my

1. Ressaldar Major Zafar Ali Khan, Sidar Bahador, 3rd Punjaub Cavalry, Mahomedan
2. Ressaldar Lall Singh, 14th Bengal Lancers, Hindoo
3. Ressaldar Major Nad'i Ali Khan, 18th Bengal Lancers, Mahomedan
4. Wordie Major Lena Singh, 2nd Central India Horse, Hindoo
5. Sabadar Ibrahiml Khan, 4th Prince of Wales' Own Light Cavalry, Mahomedan
6. Ressaldar Major Narul Hussun, 6th Prince of Wales' Bengal Cavalry, Mahomedan
7. Ressaldar Major Moozuffer Khan, Bahadoor, 4th Cavalry. Mahomedan
8. Ressaldar Sher Singh, Sirdar Bahadoor, 2nd Punjaub Cavalry, Hindoo
9. Ressaldar Hafiz Muhammad Naway Khan, 15th Bengal 'Cavalry, Mahomedan
10. Ressaldar Major Isri Singh, 19th BengalLancers, Hindoo
11. Subadar Sheik Imdad Ali, Viceroy's Body Guard, Mahomedan
12. Jemadar Kanchan Singh, 2nd Bengal Lancers, Hindoo
13. Ressaldar Muhammad Buksh, 3rd Bombay Cavalry, Mahomedan

INDIAN OFFICERS SUMMONED TO ENGLAND BY THE QUEEN TO REPRESENT HER MAJESTY'S NATIVE INDIAN ARMY IN THE JUBILEE PROCESSION, JUNE 21

The participation of the early breed of Native Cavalry Officers at the Jubilee of Her Majesty Queen Victoria, June 1887. (Look & Learn)

contemporaries as well as material collected from the regiments. The wars of 1965 and 1971 are of course recorded in detail, but there are many more Indian publications available for reference than Pakistani.

Writing history is like detective work connecting together large and small clues to assemble a factual picture, and arrive at a conclusion. In the process of my research, I came to appreciate the value of recording events. No matter how humble or trifling an effort, it is still most appreciated by a historian, and I wish there had been more officers from the corps who had made the effort to pass on their experiences to later generations. Building on the information contained in memoirs, and the Golden Jubilee Issue, it was possible with the support of interviews to construct a coherent picture of how the corps developed. I am extremely grateful to the officers I interviewed, for sharing their memories and thoughts about the corps, most of them printable, but some (much to my regret), not so. Meeting these officers was an enriching experience. I would specifically like to acknowledge those few first generation officers who I had the pleasure to interview including Gen KM Arif, Brig Amir Gulistan Janjua, and Brig Said Azhar. Though many of their contemporaries in the corps have sadly passed away, I was fortunate in being able to contact a number of their offspring whose willingness to share pictures, and anecdotes of their fathers or relatives, has made this history richer.

One of the difficulties I faced in compiling this history was that most of the books written on the Pakistan Army deal with the politico-military dimension, but none with the evolution of the Army's tactical and operational thought which would place that of the armoured corps in context. Where information is available it is fragmented. For example, to assemble details of the famous Exercise TEZGAM held in 1960, I had to extract information from over ten books, many articles as well as interviews. Consequently, while this book focuses on the armoured corps, it will also emerge as a work of value to a reader interested in how the Pakistan Army and one of its predominant arms, the armoured corps, evolved, and the milestones in its development. I must admit that in the process, I have learnt more about the Pakistan Army and the Armoured Corps than I knew in more than 40 years of service. To a great extent I knew the what, but now I know the why and have shared this with the reader.

There are some aspects that require clarification. The British Empire had two armies: the British Army and the British India Army which is a more accurate term than what many authors refer to as the British Indian Army. The book commences with the mechanisation of the Indian Cavalry because the period prior to this is not directly relevant to the evolution of the Pakistan Armoured Corps. However, since the officers commissioned in the 1920s and 1930s provided the senior leadership in the armoured corps after Independence, it was important to include their background and early history of the Indianization of the British India Army. In addition, to understand the classes of soldiers serving in the corps it was necessary to trace their background and the recruiting practices of the British India Army. I have sparingly attached ranks with the names of officers because as they progressed through their service, ranks kept changing. While there were many regiments from the Indian Armoured Corps that participated in the Second World War, I have only covered the operations of those that came to Pakistan. In a work of this nature which deals with the history of many formations, regiments, officers, conflicts, etc. spanning over 95 years, there will be errors that I am prepared to correct.

For this historical account, I had to assemble a great deal of information on the formations and regiments of the corps and I want to acknowledge the assistance provided by Maj Gen Nadir Zeb, Director General Armoured Corps Directorate and his staff for their sterling support. I am also most grateful to Brig Tufail Muhammad, Commandant Armoured Corps Centre for his assistance and valuable advice. However, most of all I am grateful to the current and previous Colonel Commandants of the Armoured Corps, Lt Gen Naveed Mukhtar and Lt Gen Tariq Khan for their unstinted backing.[1]

The generous financial support provided by the Colonel Commandant and by Lt Gen Sadiq Ali made it possible to publish this history. Gen Ahsan Saleem Hyat kindly vetted the draft and provided valuable advice and I am deeply indebted to Lt Gen Israr Ghumman for going through it with a fine tooth comb and giving me over 60 pages of notes, tables, comments, and suggestions. I must also acknowledge the assistance of two noteworthy authors of international repute who always responded to my queries with detailed replies: Ashok Nath, the author of *Izzat. Historical Records and Iconography of Indian Cavalry Regiments 1750–2007*, and Hamid Hussain, the author of countless articles of quality on the British India Army and the Pakistan Army. From his base in the United Kingdom, my son Ameer purchased and dispatched many documents including the citations of officers and soldiers during the Second World War. A special thanks to Sheetal Harris for editing the draft and to my secretary, Rehana Jamal was of great assistance in managing the papers and extracts, and assisting in corrections.

Finally and by no means, the least, I am grateful to my wife Shama for her support and tolerating my long hours on the computer, and to my children for their encouragement. I pray that my grandsons Abdur Rehman, Rafay, Ibrahim, and Faateh appreciate this effort when they are old enough to comprehend the book.

Maj Gen Syed Ali Hamid

1

MECHANIZATION AND THE EARLY YEARS OF THE SECOND WORLD WAR

Any historical account requires a starting point. The genesis of the armoured corps of British India exists in the well-documented history of the British Indian cavalry extending back to the time of the East India Company. However, the appropriate period to commence the history of the Pakistan Armoured Corps would be the eve of the Second World War. The mechanization of the Indian cavalry regiments that began in 1938 propelled them into the modern era of warfare. The manner in which these regiments were organised, equipped, trained, and employed during the Second World War strongly influenced the evolution of the Pakistan Armoured Corps in the first 15 years after Independence. The evolution was also shaped by the experience of the officers who had entered the corps through the process of

Indianisation, and provided the core leadership until the mid-1960s. The transition of the Indian cavalry from horses to vehicles, and to the frontline within a short period of a few years was remarkable. However, the enthusiasm with which the cavalry mechanized could not offset the drawbacks that it initially faced in the quality, quantity, and the assortment of equipment with which it went into combat. The drawbacks were amplified by the many different roles with corresponding organisational structures that were assigned to it, and the absence of any codified or unified doctrine. Consequently, while it performed well against the Italians and the Vichy French, when faced by the German war machine, the results during the early stages of the war, in most cases, were a disaster.

Mechanization of the Indian Cavalry

In 1937, the British India Army had 18 cavalry regiments and though the drums of war had been beating for some time, by 1939 only two had been mechanized – the 13th Lancers and the Scinde Horse. So slow was the process that for three years after orders had been issued to mechanize the first two regiments, there were no more until 1940. Discerning parents like the father of Major General D.K. Palit dissuaded their sons from joining the cavalry because they would find themselves in a backwater in the Army. "There is another Great War brewing, Monty," explained Palit's father, "and when it comes, the Indian Army is bound to be involved. If you are in a horsed cavalry regiment, you will miss the war….My advice is – change to the infantry."[1]

At the advent of the Second World War, Skinner's Horse was still a mounted regiment and when the mobilisation regulations were opened, one of the first instructions was, 'swords will be sharpened'.[2] Mechanization came slowly to the British India Army and its cavalry for a number of reasons; however, lack of realisation on the changing face of war was not one of these. There had been a gradual process of introducing the British India Army and the cavalry to the complexities of modern warfare. Due to close coordination of the educational program with its counterpart at Camberley, the Staff College at Quetta planned, and war-gamed the latest mechanized warfare doctrine.[3] During operations in the Northwest Frontier in the 1930s, aircraft and armoured cars had been employed as part of a combined arms force. In 1935, Eastern Command conducted large-scale manoeuvres near Delhi with a company of tanks of the Royal Tank Corps (RTC) moved from its base in Peshawar and participated for the first time. The aim was to impress upon the members of the Government of India the necessity for introducing tanks into the Army. Unfortunately, during the manoeuvres all the tanks got stuck because they attempted to take a direct but more difficult approach.[4]

As early as 1925 when the British Army started mechanising its remaining cavalry regiments, cavalry officers in India became aware that the days of the horses were numbered. However, there were impediments to shedding the horse. Many officers pointed to Allenby's campaign in Palestine during the First World War as proof that there was a place for horsed regiments in modern warfare. What made matters worse was the indulgence of Indian domestic politics following the First World War that resulted in the reduction in the defence budget, and restrictions imposed on the overseas employment of Indian forces. Coupled to this was the attitude of the British Government and the wisdom in Whitehall that the next war in Europe would be won by a naval blockade and the French. 'If there was no need for the British Army to exert itself, then why the army in India?'[5] In the minds of the policy planners, the threat of the Russian Bear still loomed through the Northwest and the Hitler-Stalin Pact amplified the fear of a joint invasion of India from the Russian Steppes.[6]

General Auchinleck, C-in-C India. (NPG London)

Consequently, the nature of equipment, organisation, and tactics continued to be influenced by operations on the Northwest Frontier.

In 1938, a report by a Modernization Committee under Major General Auchinleck concluded that, 'judged by modern standards, the army in India is relatively immobile and under armed, and unfit to take the field against land and air forces equipped with up-to-date weapons'.[7] The British Government was persuaded to contribute £34 million towards the modernisation of the army in India, but in spite of this, there was a shortage of equipment caused by a slow rate of production in the UK. The army in India was at a low priority obviously to the British Army but also to the Australian, and New Zealand forces. There was also a school of thought that felt that the 'native' soldiers would not be able to grasp either the complexities of the combustion engine or tank combat'.[8] They were grossly wrong on both accounts. 'The Indian cavalry benefitted from the tradition of their recruits coming from the richer peasantry which had avidly taken to education after the First World War. Consequently compared to the infantry, the level of education in the cavalry was higher, and enabled them to mechanize satisfactorily.'[9]

It did not take long for the crews to come to know their vehicles like the palm of their hands. Just two years after the 13th Lancers had mechanized, in an advance into Syria it covered more than 600 km in 20 days in armoured cars that were nearly 20 years old. The Guides Cavalry did even better that same year when it drove 960 km from Damascus to Sidi Barrani in North Africa without losing a vehicle. However, the prize for the longest drive certainly goes to the 19th Lancers when it drove over 3,700 km from Malir to Madras (via Lahore) in 1942.[10] As for combat, the 'native' soldiers fought against what a manual on courses of instruction describes as a 'First Class Enemy'[11] whether it was the Guides and 13th Lancers in North Africa, 6th Lancers in Italy or Probyn's Horse, 11th Cavalry, and 19th Lancers in Burma. Throughout the Burma campaign in which the regiments fought as half squadrons and tank troops, it was 'native' VCOs and Daffadars commanding 'native' tank crews who battled it out with the Japanese. It was not the classical manoeuvre warfare of the African or European theatres, or tank-to-tank engagements but it was deadly combat none-the-less.

The soldiers never lacked enthusiasm in learning the complexities of the internal combustion engine or for that matter, the wireless set, but the shortage of vehicles and equipment was a source of frustration. In spite of these problems, some regiments like the 11th Cavalry rapidly mechanized within one and a half years and departed to a theatre of war.[12] Others did it even faster. The Central India Horse took only 12 months. Regimental zeal outstripped official provision, and many regiments purchased civilian vehicles out of their funds for the purposes of training. In an attempt to 'get a flying start on mechanization', the commanding officer of the 3rd Cavalry used regiment funds to acquire four lorry chassis, and arrangements were made for selected soldiers, and NCOs to work as apprentices in the local garages.[13] In the interests of martial efficiency, some officers even allowed experimentation on their private cars. The focus was on training the Sowars as drivers. Regiments had over 900 all ranks, out of which they trained as many as 350 drivers,

This Crossley was presented to the Tank Museum at Bovington, UK by the Pakistan Armoured Corps in 1952. (Author's Collection)

but the transformation from a Sowar to a driver was not easy.[14] The history of Skinner's Horse records that, 'The first board of officers constituted to assess the capabilities of the men comprised of three majors who were squadron commanders. All three returned ashen-faced after the new drivers were 'through with them' as their driving skills left much to be desired.'[15] According to the History of the Guides 1922-1947, Part II, the Pathans made the best drivers, followed by the Dogras, while the Sikhs who thought themselves the best, were the poorest.[16]

The soldiers took to maintenance as enthusiastically as training. On mechanization the regiment simply transferred the 'daily stables' or looking after the horse to their new mounts; the tanks, armoured cars and trucks.[17] The 'daily stables' was both practical as well as symbolic. In his speech to the Guides Cavalry at their last mounted parade at Quetta, the general officer advised the regiment, "You must be as particular in the care of the armoured and motorised vehicles as I know you are today in the care of your horses. I would recommend that the trumpet call of 'Stables' be kept forever as a reminder of the importance of attending to the wants and needs of your mechanical horses before attending to yourselves."[18] This tradition of summoning troops to the maintenance parade by the bugle sounding the call of 'Stables' continued in the Pakistan Armoured Corps until as late as 1956.[19] Some soldiers were of the opinion that maintaining vehicles was easier than looking after horses. When asked how he liked mechanization, a Sowar remarked, "Sahib. Mein Itwar ko apni tank ko thapki deta hun aur kehta hun 'sit still'. Na us ko pani pene ke lia lejana parta hai, na din mein panch dafa khoraq deni parti hai." (Sahib, I pat my tank on Sunday and say 'sit still'. I have to neither take it to water

nor feed it five times a day).

To assist in the process of mechanization, the Armoured Fighting Vehicle School was established at Ahmednagar in 1938 to train officers, VCOs, and NCOs as instructors for the units being mechanized. The Royal Tank Regiment and various army schools of instructions also provided assistance. The Wireless Centre at Jabalpur imparted wireless training, and the Royal Indian Army Service Corps, trained the drivers. In the twenty-first century, the phrase 'mechanized' conjures images of infantry combat vehicles and main battle tanks. However, for the Indian cavalry, it was far more humble with many regiments being issued and trained on ancient Morris lorries or 15 cwt (¾ ton) trucks and FS6 Radio Sets. 19th Lancers received 'an extraordinary collection of busses' when it moved to join the 31st Armoured Division in Sialkot.[20] More fortunate were the regiments issued with antiquated armoured cars or equally antique Vickers Light Tanks armed with a machinegun. Some 'motor' regiments (another name for motorised infantry) went into the Second World War with only trucks, wheeled armoured carriers, and a sprinkling of Boys anti-tank rifles, with obvious results. In 1941 in Libya, the 3rd Indian Motor Brigade (of which the 11th Cavalry was a part), had the dubious distinction of being one of the first formations of the British India Army to face the Afrika Korps, and was overrun and scattered within hours. In the early stages of the war, the British India Army remained at a lower priority and every setback in North Africa affected the supply of equipment. The first demand by India Command for armoured fighting vehicles was not placed until May 1941 when Stuart Light Tanks and heavier Lee M3A1 were ordered from the US and Valentine tanks from Britain.[21] Consequently, the regiments ended up with an organisation

13th Lancers taking over from 11th Light Tank Company, Royal Tank Corps, at Razmak, 1939. (Author's Collection)

that was less a product of their role, but more the consequence of a shortage of equipment.[22] The eighteen regiments were split into no fewer than five different categories with different war establishments: Frontier armoured regiments, motor cavalry regiments, Indian motor regiments, light reconnaissance/armoured car regiments, and tank regiments.[23]

Until the late 1930s, the focus of operations of the British India Army was the Northwest Frontier Province (NWFP) where a couple of squadrons of Vickers tanks and armoured cars manned by the RTC had been operating since 1921. When the personnel of the RTC were withdrawn from the NWFP in 1939, the Indian cavalry regiments being mechanized replaced them. The 13th Lancers was one of the first of two probably because it was 'well-connected at the Army headquarters in Delhi; either the C-in-C or the Adjutant General or the Quartermaster General were from the regiment'.[24] It was organised as a Frontier Armoured Regiment and issued with the equipment operated earlier by the RTC: one squadron of obsolete Vickers Light Tanks and two of equally obsolete Chevrolet Crossly Armoured Cars. The Vickers Light Tank was a design of the 1920s that the British Imperial General Staff considered well suited to the dual roles of reconnaissance and colonial warfare. The Mk II version that was in service in NWFP weighed 5 tons with a crew consisting of a driver, and a commander who from a small turret also operated the main armament, a .303" water-cooled machinegun. Stationed initially in Peshawar, the regiment was responsible for the Khyber Pass and the road leading to Kohat. However, as fighting spread in Waziristan during the operations against the Faqir of Ipi, its detachments were deployed over a large area.[25] It was during the summer of 1941 when temperatures inside the AFVs, particularly the Crossly Armoured Cars, reached 60° C, that ice and mineral water was authorised to 'native' crews for the first time.[26]

While the 13th Lancers were skirmishing with the tribals in Waziristan, the 11th Cavalry had been motorised, and were heading into the eye of the storm in North Africa. Initially designated as a Frontier armoured regiment, it had organised itself accordingly and for over a year trained around the armoured car. However, in July 1940, it was ordered to convert to a motor regiment and grouped under the 3rd Indian Motor Brigade at Sialkot.[27] The change to a motor regiment necessitated considerable reorganisation.[28] Motor regiment was just another name for lorried infantry and four 15 cwt

(¾ ton) trucks carried each of the three troops in a motor squadron.[29] 'The conversion of some fine cavalry regiments into motor units was, unfortunately very unwise [as they] ......had neither the manpower and bayonet strength to be categorised as motorised infantry, nor the mobility and firepower of a mechanized cavalry formation and therefore lacked flexibility and the potential for shock action'.[30] As Colonel Fowler explained in a regimental newsletter of the 18th Cavalry in 1942, 'Our equipment is a very mixed kettle of fish – and one seems at the moment to be neither fish, fowl nor good red herring'.[31] The problems that the motor regiments faced were not only related to equipment. These were at the lowest priority for the allotment of recruits since the better educated were sent to tank and armoured car regiments.[32] A great deal of training time was spent in long drives over both flat and hilly terrain, but units were handicapped by a shortage of vehicles. Apart from technical training, they also had to train in unfamiliar subjects like foot drill, bayonet practice, and patrolling. Tactical training was however a lot more ad hoc. Initially, there were no wireless sets, and when a senior officer asked a squadron commander in Hodson's Horse how he communicated with his troop leaders, with a presence of mind he replied, 'Thought-reading'!'[33] This poor state of communication plagued the entire British India Army. On the eve of the Second World War the Indian Army's basic hardware of command and control consisted of 'semaphore flags, lamps and heliographs [that] would have been familiar to Lord Roberts as he marched in 1880 from Kabul to Kandahar, and the field telephone equipment dated back to 1918'.[34]

The regiments followed no tested doctrine, with each regiment struggling to evolve its own drills. Tactical Exercise without Troops (TEWTs) were held for training officers in the employment of a motor regiment but everyone was quite hazy about the subject. Mobility was emphasised and the familiar cavalry training suitably adapted to mechanization.[35] Ultimately Lieutenant Colonel Tom Scott, an ex-gunner officer, who had joined the 6th Lancers and later commanded Skinner's Horse on its mechanization, prepared one of the best training notes which became a text book for motor cavalry units operating in Africa.[36] Against this background, the 3rd Indian Motor Brigade was ordered to mobilise in December 1940, and within a month the 11th Cavalry were embarking for Egypt with two squadrons of Punjabi Muslims mixed with some Ranghars, Hindustani Muslims, and Khattak Pathans, and one squadron of a mix of Jat, and Khatri Sikhs.

First Encounter with the Afrika Korps

Following the crushing defeat of the Italians in North Africa in 1940, the Germans deployed a 'blocking force' consisting of elements taken from their 3. Panzer-Division and commanded by General Erwin Rommel to assist their allies in Libya. This is how the 5. leichte Division came into being, in March 1941. At the time, Rommel exercised no control over the Italian forces present in the field: these included the newly-arrived Ariete Armoured Division – the first Italian formation of this kind – and five infantry divisions, which, against all popular misconceptions created by the British propaganda, fought well. Their limitations lay in the equipment, especially the armour, which often relegated them to a supporting role. Indeed, insistent on acclimatising Ariete's troops and providing them with additional training, the Italians did not involve this division in any combat before November 1941.[37]

After shifting troops from North Africa to East Africa and Greece, against the impending threat of the Afrika Korps the British could only muster one British armoured division of three tank regiments, an Australian infantry division and the 3rd Indian Motor Brigade consisting of the 2nd Royal Lancers, 11th Cavalry, and 18th Cavalry. Rushed to Egypt, it arrived in February 1941, and

Gen Auchinleck, C-in-C India visiting a cavalry regiment in the process of mechanisation in 1941. (Author's Collection)

A Vickers Mk IV Tank of the British India Army. (Author's Collection)

after some re-equipping near Cairo, it moved 450 km west to Mersa Matruh in early March. Here it spent a month training for desert warfare and tasks that other motor regiments had been employed on in the recent fighting, such as harbouring, outflanking moves, envelopment, long-range patrolling, and occupation of a firm base. However, it was seriously underequipped for the battle ahead. 11th Cavalry had only light weapons, a pathetic number of four short-range No. 11 wireless sets, and the only anti-tank weapon issued at the scale of one per troop was the Boys anti-tank rifle. It was known as the 'elephant gun' because of its calibre of .55" and a weight of 16kg. Despite being fitted with a recoil slide, a shock absorber and a cushioned butt pad, the jolt from the weapon (along with noise and muzzle blast) was terrific, frequently causing neck strains and bruised shoulders. At 300 meters, it could penetrate only 19mm of armour and was ineffective against even the light Panzer Mk IIs operated by

the Germans. To overcome this drawback, great deeds were expected from soldiers operating this weapon.[38]

Having spent a month at Mersa Matruh, the brigade moved forward to El Adem, an airfield south of Tobruk where it was allotted a large part of the desert to practice in long range patrolling. The object was to make the regiments 'desert minded' and to make their personnel familiar with the terrain over which they could well be operating soon.[39]

Acting on his own – indeed: in disregard of orders he received from Berlin – Rommel ordered what had become known as the 'Afrika Korps' into an advance on Tobruk in late March 1941. After inflicting a decisive defeat on the poorly equipped and ill-prepared 2nd Armoured Division, he dashed in an unexpected direction: instead of following the coastal road to Benghazi, he cut through the desert with two columns advancing via Mechili towards Ghazala and

Indian troops in North Africa with a Boys Anti-Tank Rifle and Molotov Cocktails, Oct 1940. (Author's Collection)

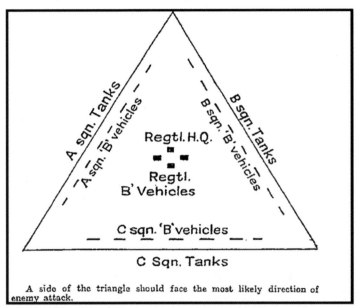
Diagram in a military training pamphlet of a harbour for armoured units in the field, issued in 1941. (Author's collection)

Tobruk. Remnants of the mauled 2nd Armoured Division fell back towards Mechili too, because this was a major communication centre, and a place with fuel and water supplies. Securing the place was the 3rd Indian Motor Brigade.[40]

The War Diary of the 11th Cavalry leaves no doubt that the unit was poorly-informed about the gravity of the situation and importance of its task: 'Regiment reaches EL MECHILI at 1645 hours. Regiment allotted NORTH-EAST and SOUTH-EAST perimeter of harbour.'[41]

Leaving behind the 18th Cavalry to protect El Adem and thus cover Tobruk, the 3rd Motor Brigade gained an Australian anti-aircraft regiment equipped with 40mm Bofors guns while racing to Mechilli. The guns were to be employed in the anti-tank role but like the Boys anti-tank rifles; they were ineffective against medium tanks except at very short ranges and unfortunately, the crews had never fired the weapon. The situation was thus a recipe for disaster. It seems that at some stage the brigade finally formed a defence in a tight box with a perimeter of about four kilometres, but without any anti-tank mines or barbed wire. At the last moment, a squadron of 18th Cavalry that was operating nearby re-joined. Its young second-in-command was Lieutenant Sahabzada Yaqub Khan.

Losing dozens of tanks to mechanical breakdowns or stuck in the sand, the Germans appeared only on the morning of 6 April, when first the positions of the 11th Cavalry, and then the rest of the brigade were shelled: this was a preparatory bombardment for an attack by Italian infantry – which was promptly repulsed and 37 prisoners were taken. A few hours later, the 11th Cavalry increased its bag by capturing a German patrol and its vehicles. Shortly after a German staff officer appeared under a white flag and presented 11th Cavalry the first of three demands to surrender, all of which were rejected. Early that night a column of the 2nd Armoured Division arrived but it must have been a great disappointment to the Motor Brigade: it consisted of the division commander (who had no idea where the rest of his formation was) with his tactical headquarters, one tank and a large number of administrative vehicles. Without the tank support, the capability of the brigade was minimal – small arms, Boys anti-tank rifles, light anti-aircraft guns and one tank, did not amount to much against the German and Italian tanks. By the next morning, the brigade was surrounded and after some more shelling a second demand to surrender was delivered. This was followed by another unsuccessful attack by the Italians, and yet another and a final demand signed this time personally by Rommel 'who was impatient to swat this fly and get his tanks to Tobruk.'[42] The rejection of the third demand triggered an artillery bombardment, for an hour and a half. At sunset '60 German tanks' began mustering to the south of the position, suggesting that the assault would finally come on the morrow. However, at 2130hrs Brigade was informed by the headquarters of the 2nd Armoured Division that orders had been received to withdraw east to El Adem. The breakout before first light the next morning was only partially successful. It was attempted in a box formation with the headquarters and vehicles of 2nd Armoured Division in the centre, and an advance guard provided by 'A' Squadron 18th Cavalry. In a very brave action, the advance guard captured a ridge in its path but was held by a German artillery battery and an infantry company.[43] 11th Cavalry guarded one of the flanks and despite heavy fire, dust, smoke, and confusion, it broke out and continued on to El Adem. However, in the process it lost half its strength. The German assault struck in three waves: fearing mines, the tanks stopped short of overrunning the defences at first. A second attempt to breakout by the remainder of the force was also unsuccessful and the troops finally surrendered. Though the original objective of providing a base for the 2nd Armoured Division failed, this delay of 48 hours achieved by the 3rd Indian Motor Brigade bought valuable time for the 9th Australian Division to occupy Tobruk and prepare its defences. The Official History of the Indian Armed Forces in Second World War records:

But it stands to reason that if the march of events during the fateful days between 4 and 8 April 1941 had nor (sic) interrupted or deflected by the 3rd Indian Motor Brigade, the Axis had a fair chance of reaching Alexandria before Alamein had even been thought of.[44]

For this action, 11th Cavalry was awarded with the battle honour of Mekili, the first of the 12 theatre and battle honours it earned during the Second World War.

Severely mauled, the remnants of the 11th Cavarly re-grouped under the 4th Indian Division. The unit was down to two squadrons: one protected the division headquarters, and the other was placed under the Central India Horse (CIH). Following reorganisation and re-equipment, two months later, in June 1941, the 11th Cavalry – along with the CIH – covered the British withdrawal following the disastrous Operation *Battleaxe*.

The 3rd Indian Motor Brigade at Mechilli. (Map by Tom Cooper, based on *I Serve: The Saga of the Eighteenth Cavalry*)

Its primary position was the escarpment near the coast known as the Halfaya Pass, nick-named the 'Hell Fire Pass' by the British troops: the Indian troops were evicted from there in a division-sized German attack in June, though not without earning themselves two additional battle honours in North Africa.

To the Middle East

While the 11th Cavalry battled the Afrika Korps at Mekili, 13th Lancers were withdrawn from the NWFP and converted to an Indian Armoured Car Regiment. It left for Iraq in April 1941 with a squadron each of Pathans, Ranghars and Sikhs to serve with 10th Indian Division. This deployment was prompted by the emergence of pro-German governments in Iraq and Syria. It went fully equipped with armoured cars having exchanged its Vickers tanks for a third squadron of Crossley Armoured Cars from Scinde Horse. Manned by personal of the RTC, armoured cars had been in service in India since the First World War. Shortly after the war the Indian Government purchased sixteen newly designed Rolls-Royce cars, but they were so expensive that subsequent orders were placed with Crossley Motors in Manchester who made a tough but cheap 50 hp chassis on which was mounted a body built by Vickers. 451 of these 5 ton cars were built, mainly for India. The design was very similar to the Rolls-Royce version and had a number of interesting features. A dome-shaped turret with mountings for four machine-guns, was designed to deflect rifle shots from snipers in ambush positions in the high passes. The crew compartment was lined with asbestos to keep the temperature down, and the entire body could be electrified to keep large crowds at bay. Since pneumatic tires of that era did not survive for long in the Indian climate, these cars were fitted with narrow, solid tires which made them unstable. By 1939, when the RTC in India had handed most of its equipment over to the India Army, the Crossleys were worn out. The bodies were then transferred to commercial Chevrolet truck chassis, with pneumatic tires, at the Chaklala Heavy Repair Depot at Rawalpindi.[45] In this form the armoured cars served with Indian forces in the Middle East (Iraq, Syria, and Persia) in the early years of the Second World War. Communications within the regiment were based on FS6 Radio Sets, which had an effective range of only three kilometres to a maximum of six and a half kilometres in good conditions. All wireless sets of this period operated on valves, and the instructions to the operator were: 'Do not start to speak immediately. You have to switch to send, count till 4 and then speak to allow the valves to warm up'.[46] The signal officer of 17th Poona Horse was of the opinion that: 'The FS6 set was surely one of Hitler's secret weapons and caused more epilepsy and heart attacks than any other single piece of equipment ever invented'.[47] No radio sets were issued below level of the troop leaders so the only communication within the troop was by hand signals.[48]

Sailing from India on 12 April 1941, the leading elements of 10th Indian Division (under Major General Bill Slim, later of Burma fame), made an unopposed landing and occupied the docks and the airfield at Basra. However, the Iraqi Army was making threatening moves, and within a few weeks, the British launched a two-pronged offensive. The 4th Mechanized Cavalry Brigade advanced from Palestine and the 10th Indian Division from Basra supported by 13th Lancers which led the advance beyond the ancient city of Ur. When the forces converged on Baghdad, the Iraqi Government capitulated on 30 May 1941. The troops took up occupation duties and 13th Lancers was split up to support the brigades.[49]

It was Syria's turn next. In June 1941, the British launched a multi-pronged offensive towards Damascus and Aleppo to defeat the forces of the Vichy French consisting of 30,000 troops, 90 tanks, some armoured cars, and a strong air force of 300 aircraft. The aim of the offensive was to prevent Germany from using the territories of Syria and Lebanon as springboards for attacks on Egypt. 13th Lancers supported the advance of the 2nd Brigade (of 10th Division) on the northern most axis along the Euphrates towards Dayr az-Zawr and onto Aleppo. The entire operation took twenty days and involved a number of skirmishes with one main engagement at Dayr az-Zawr. The operation commenced with a squadron of 13th Lancers acting as the vanguard to a Gurkha battalion on the main road while the remaining

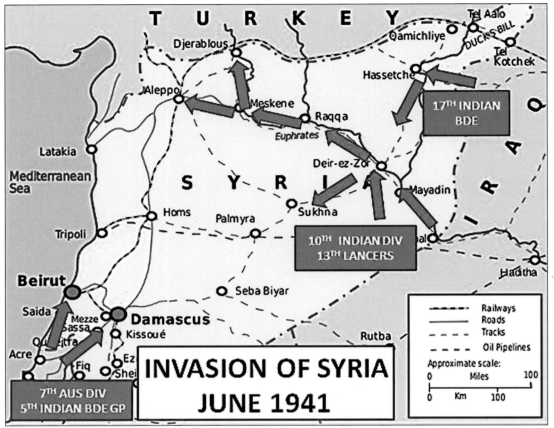

Operations by units of the British India Army during the invasion of Syria in June 1941. (Author's Collection)

regiment was the advance guard of the brigade along a pipeline track to the south. The aim was to outflank and attack Dayr az-Zawr from the west. Commencing its advance on 30 June, within 48 hours the vanguard squadron of 13th Lancers made contact with Dayr-az-Zawr but the main outflanking force was delayed and finally was in position on 3 July. While a battalion launched the main attack, a 'flying column' of 13th Lancers and 4/13th Frontier Force swung round the open flank on a broad front and raced to the town from the northwest. Surprise was complete and 13th Lancers prevented the French from blowing up the suspension bridge over the River Euphrates.[50] By that evening, they had cleared the town and while the POW count was small, they captured a lot of equipment including guns, ammunition, and vehicles. A day later, a squadron of 13th Lancers with an infantry battalion advanced 180km and seized Raqqa, which was halfway to the main objective of Aleppo. The entire regiment supported by infantry then rushed 160km north in an attempt to intercept the French who were withdrawing along the railway to Aleppo. Though the French got away, a squadron of 13th Lancers pursued them another 160km further west and a sharp engagement took place at Djerablous while the French were ferrying across a river. On 11 July 1941, the Vichy French surrendered.

During this entire advance, the main threat to 13th Lancers was from the enemy air, for which the armoured cars were a priority target. With thin armour plating and no anti-aircraft machinegun or any other anti-aircraft defences, the Chevrolet armoured cars were extremely vulnerable to the cannon-firing French aircraft. This long advance of over 600km also put a severe strain on the mechanical state of the armoured cars. Considering that, only two years previously the regiment had been grooming horses, it goes to their credit that they did not allow their new gasoline steeds to fail them. In recognition of their achievements, 13th Lancers was awarded three battle honours, Damascus, Dayr az-Zawr, and Raqqa as well as the campaign honour

of Syria 1941. However, 13th Lancers was soon to do an about turn and head back to Basra for operations in Iran, because of the pro-German leaning of Shah Reza Pehlvi and his government. It was placed under 8th Division, which was tasked to secure the oil installations in south-western Iran and operated alongside a squadron of the Guides, which had arrived from India; and was initially employed for 'show of force' in Iraq.

The Guides had mechanized at Quetta in 1940 as a light armoured reconnaissance regiment for 9th Division which was earmarked for Malaya. To its good luck, since the regiment had not fully converted, it was replaced by 3rd Cavalry which spent the rest of the war as Japanese POWs. Like other regiments, the Guides initially trained drivers on a very mixed collection of old military and civil vehicles, what the history of the Guides referred to as 'any old junk' beginning with old Morris six-wheelers, and then came some lightweight Chevrolets.[51] When their role finally crystallised as that of a light armoured reconnaissance regiment, they were organised into three squadrons each consisting of one armoured car troop of three cars, a lorried infantry troop of four Chevrolet trucks, and two troops equipped with Armoured Carriers Indian Pattern Wheeled MK II. This vehicle was commonly referred to as a 'wheeled carrier' and its armoured hull of 14mm thick plates was mounted on a Ford or GMC CMP truck chassis imported from Canada. The Indian Railways manufactured most of the hulls, and the armament typically consisted of Bren light machine guns (in some variants mounted in a small turret) and Boys anti-tank rifles.

The initial objectives of the 8th Division were relatively limited but important as they covered the oil producing areas of south-western Iran including Abadan, Khurramshahr, and Ahwaz. Actual hostilities in this sector lasted five days. While the Iranian force in the area was significant, it consisted largely of conscript soldiers and most objectives fell easily when subjected to a rapid advance and a rush onto the defences. Both 13th Lancers and the squadron of the Guides were employed in various roles including screening the main body, flank protection, encircling movements as well as assault. In spite of the limitations of equipment, these operations were carried out in the true cavalry spirit. It was only at the fort of Qasr-i-Shaikh that the Iranians put up some resistance but they surrendered after a combined assault by 13th Lancers and a Sikh battalion. An unfortunate incident occurred during this assault as narrated by Z.A. Khan:

The JCOs of the regiment used to tell a story about the action against the Iranians. 'A' Squadron equipped with armoured cars supported an attack by a Sikh battalion on an Iranian position. Before the Sikhs reached the Iranian positions, the Iranians stood up and raised white flags but the Sikhs started bayoneting them. The Senior

Viceroy Commissioned Officer of the squadron ordered the squadron in pushto, on the wireless, to fire on the Sikhs which the squadron did, causing a considerable number of casualties amongst the Sikhs. The squadron commander, Major J.E.A. Moberly was removed from the command of the squadron but after the inquiry the regiment was awarded a battle honour for this action. [52]

After the forming of a new Iranian Government, the British and Indian forces in the region were organised to defend against a possible German advance through the Caucasus into Iran and Iraq. For the next four months, through the winter of 1941-42, the Guides carried out extensive reconnaissance of a possible line of resistance from Mosul across the Kurdish Hills and into Iran. There was a brief moment of excitement when it received orders to move to Egypt in late March 1942, but was diverted to Syria again for a 'show of force' and to reconnaissance the routes. By the end of 1941, a very large portion of the Indian armoured regiments in their various configurations had been deployed in this theatre including the Guides and 13th Lancers, as well as 6th Lancers, which had recently arrived from India. Even 11th Cavalry had moved from Egypt with the 3rd Indian Motor Brigade and deployed in the area of Raqqa along the Euphrates. 6th Lancers had mechanized at Lahore as a light reconnaissance regiment, and was equipped with the Morris Light Reconnaissance Car. It weighed 3.7 tons and had an unusual internal arrangement, with its three-man crew sitting abreast in a multi-sided turret. The driver was in the middle, a crewmember at the right operated a Bren light machine gun, and another with a Boys .55" anti-tank rifle on the left. 6th Lancers was stationed at Mosul as the reconnaissance regiment with 8th Indian Division and 13th Lancers was with 252nd Indian Tank Brigade at Qiriya.

Second Encounter with the Afrika Korps

In November 1941, the British Eighth Army launched Operation Crusader, aiming to lift the siege of Tobruk and eventually driving the Germans and Italians all the way back past Benghazi. Once again acting on his own, Rommel counterattacked in January 1942 and – this time taking Italians with him – forced the Eighth Army back to Ghazala. With this reverse in fortune and the Egyptian Delta under threat, General Auchinleck decided to induct troops from Iraq and Iran. The 3rd Indian Motor Brigade which had already returned in March 1942 was joined by the Guides and 13th Lancers. Along with the other regiments of the brigade, 11th Cavalry was better equipped than when it made its stand at Mechilli, a year earlier. There was a more liberal allotment of radio sets and sixteen 2-Pdr Bofors antitank guns: this 40mm weapon had a rate of fire of 22 rounds per minute but it was only able to penetrate the frontal armour of German tanks at less than 400 metres range – and it lacked high-explosive ammunition.

INVASION OF IRAN AUGUST 1941

Operations by units of the British India Army during the invasion of Iran in August 1941. (Author's Collection)

Assembling an Indian Pattern Wheeled Carrier at an Indian Railways factory. (Author's Collection)

For operations in the desert, the 2-Pdr was mounted on the back of a 15 cwt truck and the combination was known as a 'portée'. Though

A lorry-mounted 2-pounder anti-tank gun of the 4th Indian Division in the Western Desert, April 1941. (Author's Collection)

only intended as a carrying method with the gun being unloaded for firing, for more mobility, crews tended to fire the weapon from the vehicle. Hence, the truck reversed into action so that the gun shield would provide a measure of protection. It also provided a faster disengagement.

The antitank guns were grouped in one squadron and the other two squadrons were organised into one rifle troop in trucks, and three troops in Vickers Universal Carriers. Also known as the Bren Gun Carrier, this vehicle weighed 3.7 tons and had a crew of four. Its main armament was a .303" Bren Machinegun, and it could carry a variety of secondary weapons including the Boys anti-tank rifle.[53] Its Ford V-8 engine gave it a good power to weight ratio and a top speed of 50 km/h. However, it was difficult to control at higher speeds and very easily overturned in rough terrain with fatal results.[54] It was a popular vehicle but designed for a role that it never really fulfilled and was adapted to dozens of others for which it was never entirely suited.[55]

The Gazala Line was a series of 'boxes' each of a brigade strength stretching south from the coast for 50 km with minefields and wire in-between, watched by regular patrols. The southernmost box defended by a Free French Brigade was at Bir Hakim and positioned in depth were two armoured brigades to guard against (what was initially considered as) the unlikely possibility of an outflanking move. However, as evidence mounted that this was what Rommel was preparing to do, at the last minute a decision was taken to insert another box at Point 171 between Bir Hakim and one 25 km further east in depth. This box was to act as a pivot for the brigades of 7th Armoured Division to strike at the Afrika Korps. The 3rd Indian Motor Brigade which had moved west to Mersa Mathru on 12 May and placed under 7th Armoured Division, was now ordered to occupy Point 171. By 1900hrs on 25 May 1942, the brigade moved 320 km west and arrived at the box. It was back in the eye of the storm a year and two months since its previous stand at Mekili which, incidentally, was just 160 km away to the west. Point 171 was a low insignificant feature that lay outside the wired and

mined defences of the Ghazala Line. Notwithstanding, the units started digging in the 36 hours that were available before it was struck by the Afrika Korps, there was not a great deal that the brigade could do.

To put things in perspective, the Free French Brigade, which held out at Bir Hakim for 15 days, had the luxury of three months for digging trenches, setting up machine gun nests as well as spreading a vast amount of land mines. General Koenig commanding this brigade referred to Bir Hakim as: 'A grain of sand (that) curbed the Axis advance.'[56] On the same analogy, Point 171, which was five km southeast of the Bir Hakim Box, was just an atom of sand. 11th Cavalry was defending a frontage of 1,800 metres to the north and northeast, but like the rest of the regiments, it was critically understrength. It had only half the authorised number of anti-tank guns, and parties which had been sent to collect more guns, were expected back but never returned. The carriers were being moved forward on tank transporters and arrived just before the German attack. Thus, the two squadrons had only 70 soldiers each and no communication with the regiment headquarters, because the wireless sets were fitted on the carriers. The brigade's regiment of 25-pdr guns, the 2nd Field Regiment, Indian Artillery arrived only 12 hours before the attack and had a very little time to dig in. What never arrived were two squadrons of tanks that Major General Messervy commanding the 7th Armoured Division had promised.[57] Like Mechilli, Point 171 was also developing into a recipe for disaster and this time there would be no ultimatum to surrender, and no last minute orders to withdraw.

The day the motor brigade arrived, air reconnaissance reported large German columns moving south, which by the evening had swung under Bir Hakim. All through the night, the brigade could hear the rumble of tanks and see flares and Very lights that the Germans were using to guide the tanks and vehicles into harbours. At 2045hrs, the War Diary of 11th Cavalry records information from the brigade headquarters: 'Enemy were advancing in six columns over an area of 30 miles. Flares were seen throughout the night west of the brigade position'.[58] At first light on 27 May, the motor regiments and artillery observation posts (OPs) facing southwards started reporting the presence of large enemy tank and vehicle concentrations 4-6km from their position. The ones further east were already on the move swinging northwards. The brigade commander went forward to confirm and at 0630hrs, he signalled that, 'the whole of the German Afrika Korps was drawn up in front of him as if on a ceremonial parade'.[59] He was not far wrong. The night before, three German Panzer divisions, and the Italian Ariete Armoured Division had bivouacked a few kilometres south of the brigade.

On the morning of 27 May, 3rd Indian Motor Brigade lay in the path of the northern flank of an advance by three Axis armoured divisions as these swung up north. The columns of 15th Panzer Division brushed past to the east before the Indians rapidly dispersed a column of soft-skinned vehicles from the Ariete Division, at 0630hrs. Commander of the 3rd Brigade, Brigadier Filose, nervously reported he was facing 'a whole bloody German armoured division'. Actually, realising there was a 'strong enemy position' in front of them, and convinced they were facing their actual target – the Bir Hacheim box held by the French – the main Italian force deployed quickly, approaching head-on. The 8th Armoured Battalion under Colonel Enrico Maretti on the right, the 9th Armoured Battalion under Colonel Pasqualre on the left, followed by 10th Armoured Battalion under Major Luigi Pinna, the 8th and 12th Bersaglieri Regiments.

The position of the 3rd Indian Motor Rifle Brigade (including the 2nd Field Artillery Regiment), at Ghazala, on 27 May 1942. (Map by Tom Cooper)

Wrongly identified as 'Germans', the first two Italian battalions – who thought they would be attacking 'Congolese' troops – drove straight through the hurriedly constructed Indian positions, before leaving the mopping up to the 10th Armoured Battalion and resuming their advance northwards. A short delay in the ferocious action allowed Filose and few of his troops to escape: by 0710hrs, the 3rd Indian Motor Brigade lost 453 killed and 670 captured: amongst the latter was Captain Sahabzada Yaqub Khan from 18th Cavalry, while captured officers of the 11th Cavalry included el-Effendi and Ashraf Jan.[60]

In turn, the Indians claimed the destruction of '50 tanks' (indeed, some of the related reports cited as many as 80). Amid all the confusion and fire, an anti-tank troop of 11th Cavalry on 'portées' conducted a parade ground withdrawal; stopping to fire and then withdrawing to the next position, until it was destroyed.[61] 'But among other deeds of bravery there was a sowar of PAVO who jumped onto a tank, trying to wrench open the hatch and get at the men inside.'[62] The Free French were observing this unequal contest with awe, and admiration. Only two days earlier, the 'Anglo-Hindu Brigade' (this is what the French called the 3rd Indian Motor Brigade), had arrived in their vicinity and they fully comprehended and realised the sacrifice that it was undergoing.[63] When 'B' Squadron, 18th Cavalry, was overrun, its two officers remained near a 2-pdr gun pretending to be dead. They engaged the enemy whenever possible and knocked out three tanks. Both received the MC.[64]

Equally courageous was the performance of No. 1 Anti-Tank Troop of Gardener's Horse commanded by Daffadar Ghulam Rabbani. Isolated from the regiment and in spite of losing two forward guns, he kept the rear two engaging the Italians at extremely short range. In front of his troop were 10 knocked out tanks. He was awarded an IDSM for the fine leadership he displayed.[65] Lance Daffadar Mehboob Ali Khan, operating one of the forward 2-pdrs, made a stand-unto-death and was awarded an IOM.[66]

The War Diary of 11th Cavalry contains the following terse entries of the day's battle on 27 May: [67]

0600 Hrs: Second Lieutenant J.F.W. Howes arrives with carriers. Carriers drove onto the Regiment's position, and dismounted their guns and returned to where the soft vehicles were positioned.

0800 Hrs: Message received from Brigade that position was surrounded by tanks.

0815 Hrs: Light artillery bombardment commenced.

0845 Hrs: GERMAN & ITALIAN Tanks have broken through South face of the Box arrived on our position and overran it.

0900 Hrs: Resistance having ceased, Tanks rolled onto BIR HACHIEM. Enemy left small force of tanks and armoured cars to deal with any further resistance.

0945 Hrs: Enemy infantry arrived on position and took those remaining there, prisoners.

This not very descriptive account conceals the bravery, and determination with which 11th Cavalry and the rest of the brigade challenged the might of the Ariete. 'The battlefield was a mass of wreckage, enemy tanks knocked out and on fire, anti-tank guns overrun and crippled, and soft-skinned vehicles ablaze and disabled. Panzers crawled all over the position.'[68]

Ariete admitted 30 killed, 6 missing and 40 wounded in this short but sharp encounter. A British report from the next day cited the finding of 26 M14 tanks found abandoned on the field, of which 23 were completely burned out.[69] Actually, it seems that most of Italian losses were caused by the 25-pdr guns of the 2nd Field Regiment: in the battle for the first time, this unit engaged the tanks over open sights.[70]

Churchill also praised its action in the House of Commons. It was an accolade well deserved. The motor brigade was a mobile force and neither organised for nor provided with the resources for fighting a

Daffadar Ghulam Rabbani, IDSM, 2nd Royal Lancers. (Author's Collection)

battle of position. While it held over one of divisions of the Afrika Korps for two crucial hours, more significant were the losses caused to Rommel's armour. For this action, 11th Cavalry was awarded with the Battle Honour of Bir Hakim, the third it had earned in North Africa. The remnants of 3rd Motor Brigade reformed at Buq Buq, and were employed in a screening role as the Eighth Army withdrew towards Al Alamein.[71]

While the Battle of Ghazala was at its peak, on 27 May 1942 an advance squadron of 13th Lancers joined the 5th Indian Division south of Tobruk. It participated in the division's attacks in an area that came to be called as the 'Cauldron' where Rommel was trapped for six to seven days. Within a week, the rest of the regiment arrived. It was placed under the command of 7th Armoured Division (the famous Desert Rats), and carried out reconnaissance during the bitter tank battles. 13th Lancers was now equipped with Humber Armoured Cars, which were far superior to the Chevrolet Crossley that they had been using in Iraq. The Humber was one of the most widely produced British armoured cars of the Second World War. The earlier versions were armed with a 15mm Besa machinegun, but the Mk IV had an American 37mm high velocity gun; the same that was mounted on the Stuart tank. Well-armed, with a good power-to-weight ratio, a top speed of 72 km/h and a range of 400 km, it was well suited for reconnaissance as well as convoy escort.

Withdrawal to el Alamein

As the Eighth Army started to withdraw from the Ghazala Line, 13th Lancers, as well as all the regiments of the motor brigade, were deployed in the rear guard to provide information on the Afrika Korps. With the wide open spaces in the desert, reconnaissance was indispensable, and these regiments did an excellent job. Consequently German reconnaissance was hard pressed in penetrating the screens thrown up by these regiments. The Germans acknowledged the aggressive employment of reconnaissance units by the British in North Africa: 'The British carry out dashing (reconnaissance) patrols by means of wheeled AFV's and on foot. They also appear from the desert to make thrusts deep into our rear lines, launching shock troops or attacking our rear columns with fast wheeled armoured fighting vehicles.'[72] It was an exacting and dangerous task demanding guts, and initiative, and the history of the Poona Horse acknowledges that 13th Lancers

'had done extremely well in the Western Desert'.[73] In fact out of all the Indian motor regiments operating against Rommel, after the Central India Horse, it was the next most highly decorated.[74] A flavour of the dangers and value of battlefield reconnaissance conducted by 13th Lancers is mirrored in three of its citations for battlefield awards.[75]

Risaldar Muhammad Rafiq Khan. 13th Lancers. Awarded Indian Distinguished Service Medal.[76]

On 15 June 1942, this troop leader contacted and reported an enemy column 6 miles south of El Adem and was heavily fired on by Field and A/T guns. He succeeded in getting on to a flank and keeping the enemy under observation. As our own forces were known to be in the area, there was some doubt as to whether the column was friend or foe. Twice Risaldar Muhammad Rafiq Khan was told to verify his previous report. On both occasions, he went forward with disregard to his personal safety and under intensive fire to within a few hundred yards of the enemy and his accurate and confirmed report must have been of the utmost value to the higher command.[77]

Dafadar Muhammad Bashir. 13th Lancers. Awarded Indian Distinguished Service Medal.

This NCO was in command of a troop on 16 June 1942 when the Germans advanced on El Adem. On the previous night, he had acted as a listening post and remained very close to the enemy so that at first light he was able to submit valuable and timely information regarding their movements. In spite of heavy shelling and being in danger of being cut off from the escarpment running west from the El Adem box, he stayed within a thousand yards of the enemy, sending back valuable information. On 12 June 1942 when surrounded by the enemy in the morning mist on the Trigh Capuzzo between El Adem and Sidi Razegh he fought his way out to safety and again supplied information of the first importance. [78]

Risaldar Prag Singh. 13th Lancers. Awarded Military Cross.

On night 17/18 Jun 1942 Risaldar Prag Singh commanded the Rear Guard at El Adem. This officer displayed great coolness and courage of the highest order. When the Main Body had encountered the enemy and were heavily engaged he got his Armoured Cars into action under trying conditions and rendered great assistance. Later in the morning when surrounded by enemy he disengaged himself, fought his way through the enemy, and got his charge home intact. On 16, 17 June 1942 this officer handled his troops with great skill. He maintained constant touch with the enemy and was responsible for invaluable information. The energy, devotion to duty, coolness, and calmness displayed by this officer signal him out as a magnificent leader worthy of immediate recognition.

Not everyone was that brave. An officer who was commissioned into 13th Lancers during the early 1950s and served with some of the JCOs and NCOs who had fought against the Germans recollected:

There was a Daffadar from Swabi-Mardan area who to avoid going into battle in the North African desert, had cut his armoured car's battery lead. When the order to move was given, his armoured car did not start, it was examined and the cut lead was detected. He was punished to sit outside on the tank turret whenever the squadron went into action. He did this and survived. [79]

The Battle Honours awarded to 13th Lancers during the Battle of Gazala and the subsequent withdrawal included: Gazala, Bir Hacheim,

El Adem, Sidi Rezegh 1942, Gambut, and Tobruk 1942. In this withdrawal, elements of the Guides also operated with 13th Lancers. Comprised of a squadron each of Jats, Sikhs, and Pathans, the Guides had moved from Iran for the defence of the Egyptian Delta. Around the same day that 11th Cavalry had its second fateful encounter with the Germans at Point 171, the Guides moved forward in support of 10th Indian Motor Brigade. This brigade had been raised in Egypt in March 1942 with Indian units, for service with the 10th British Armoured Division.[80] It was now holding a defensive position in depth to stop the Germans if they broke through at Alamein. The squadrons of the Guides were not as well equipped as 13th Lancers, and had a mix of Indian Pattern Wheeled Carriers Mk

An Indian Pattern Wheeled Carrier of the Guides in the North African Desert. (Author's Collection)

IIs, and Marmon-Herrington Armoured Cars. This reconnaissance vehicle was manufactured in South Africa as well as in India and was used by Commonwealth troops. It was a 6.4 ton, 4x4 vehicle fitted with a Ford V8 engine and was underpowered due to the weight of the armour thus making it slow and cumbersome. It had a crew of three and the Mk III version in service with the Guides armed with the Boys anti-tank rifle, a coaxial Bren machine gun in a turret, and one or two additional machine guns for anti-aircraft defense.[81] The rifle troops were mounted in American Chevrolet trucks, which were excellent vehicles: fast, robust, and reliable.[82]

The squadrons of the Guides fanned out into the desert encountering large columns of the rear services of the Eighth Army retreating back to Alamein in what was referred to as the 'Ghazala Gallop'. Soon the Guides pushed further ahead, and on 18 June 1942 came under a mobile force being built up on a much-depleted British 1st Armoured Division. This force operated ahead of the Matruh Line with 13th Lancers along the coast, and the Guides watching the open desert flank. Only four days later as the Germans broke through gaps in the armoured division and with the coastal road blocked, both regiments withdrew along the desert route, and slipped back to the

General Auchinleck, C-in-C India, inspecting a motor regiment in Iraq. (Author's Collection)

Alamein Line. However, 'B' Squadron of the Guides remained forward and operated with various forces ultimately being placed under a mixed Anglo-French force known as the Long Range Desert Force. It was 320 km south of the coast operating on a flank deep in the desert on the edge of the Great Sand Sea.

Having fallen back, the Guides (without 'B' Squadron) were now again ordered to go forward with the 22nd British Armoured Brigade, and conduct reconnaissance for 40km south of Matruh. The 22nd Armoured Brigade was protecting the open desert flank and the Guides Cavalry covered a front of 110 km. They were probed by German patrols, and on 27 June, there was a major engagement between the Germans and the armoured brigade. Finally, the brigade, with the Guides covering their withdrawal, was ordered to fall back to the Alamein Line and on the way was bombed, and strafed by German aircraft. Meanwhile, the Long Range Desert Force, along with 'B' Squadron of the Guides, kept withdrawing along the desert flank but through sand dunes that put a severe strain on the vehicles. To show what problems the armoured cars encountered, the diarist of the Guides, records the following transmissions:

First Message: "Hello Colo, Sano calling, Hamara left wala armoured car ke half-shaft tut gya." (My left armoured car's half-shaft is broken).

Second Message: "Hello Colo, etc. Hamara right wala armoured car ke short propeller shaft tut gya." (My right armoured car's short propeller shaft is broken).

Third Message: "Hello Colo, etc. Hamara apna armoured car rhet men fass gya." (My own armoured car is stuck in the sand). [83]

The force was in a dilemma when ordered to move back to Alamein because it did not have enough fuel. The French elements of the Long Range Desert Force were inclined to march north and submit to the Germans, but Randall Plunkett was not prepared to surrender his squadron of the Guides.[84] From the Oasis of Siwa, he decided to negotiate the treacherous terrain of the Qattara Depression.[85] After an adventurous trek of 400 difficult kilometres, he arrived behind the Alamein position at Abu Mena much to the consternation of Auchinleck's Staff.[86] The British right flank at Alamein rested on the sea, its left, 64km south on the hitherto 'impassable 99 quicksand's of the Qattara Depression'. Plunkett's feat was given a MOST SECRET label, to prevent Rommel becoming aware of it, and was never replicated by any other troops, British or German.[87]

2
ROME TO RANGOON

The year 1943 marked a watershed in the Allies' war against Germany and Italy. The Afrika Korps was decisively beaten in North Africa, and Sicily had been captured, thus opening the back door for Allied Forces to make their first landing on mainland Europe. It also marked a watershed for the Indian Armoured Corps. Based on an assessment of the performance of the regiments, and a visit by the Commander Royal Armoured Corps, the Indian Armoured Corps underwent a major overhaul across the entire spectrum of training, organisation, and logistic support. On the European front, three regiments well trained and equipped for the role of reconnaissance, were to land in Italy to battle 'a first class army'.[1] On the Burma front, there was an increasing acceptance by the sceptics that large tanks could be used against the Japanese. The credit for this change in mind-set was in no small measure attributed to Major General Frank Messervy during his tenure as Major General Armoured Fighting Vehicles in India. It was around this period that units of the Indian Armoured Corps were issued Shermans, and started serious training for jungle warfare. Little did General Messervy know that a year later what a crucial role two squadrons of tanks would play while he was commanding the 7th Indian Division in the Battle of the Admin Boxes; the first significant defeat of the Japanese in Burma. What he also did not know was the decisive role of tanks in the battles of Mandalay and Meiktila that would result in the defeat of the Japanese in Burma and the capture of Rangoon.

Reorganisation of the Indian Armoured Corps
During 1942 and into 1943, there was a heavy deployment of regiments of the Indian Armoured Corps in North Africa and the Middle East. At the apex of the German push to the Nile Delta, there were eight Indian motor and reconnaissance regiments in North

Africa but as the situation stabilised at Alamein, all of them were recalled to west Asia to guard against the emerging German threat. In June 1942, the German Army had launched its strategic summer offensive in Southern Russia aimed at capturing the oilfields of Baku. By July, Rostov had fallen, and the Germans had reached the northern foothills of the Caucasus. It seemed as if they would penetrate into Iran by October, and pose a direct threat to British interests in the Middle East particularly the oilfields. Anticipating this threat, the headquarters of the 31st Indian Armoured Division had moved from India to Kermanshah, and both 11th Cavalry and 13th Lancers came under its command. Meanwhile, the Guides Cavalry joined the 5th Indian Division in Iraq, and 6th Lancers continued to be the corps reconnaissance regiment. In addition to the eight regiments of the IAC that had arrived from North Africa, four more came under a new command called the Persia and Iraq Command (PAIFORCE) with its headquarters in Baghdad. Initially the troops available to PAIFORCE including the two infantry divisions, were deployed in the Iranian highlands covering the approach between the Turkish border and the Caspian Sea, but as the Germans became embroiled in Stalingrad and the threat diminished, they were pulled back to winter in a less severe climate. The formations and units spent time in extensive training, and some of the regiments were finally issued tanks. In the spring of 1943, the threat had further abated, and PAIFORCE slowly dissolved except for the troops that were left to ensure that 'Aid to Russia' was expeditiously transited northwards through Iran.

On the home front too, there was very little commitment of regiments of the IAC against the Japanese and it provided a breathing space for it to implement, and benefit from some important and far-reaching changes. These changes occurred due to a visit by Major General Giffard Martel, the commander of the Royal Armoured Corps of the British Army to India in the autumn of 1942.[2] He toured all the armoured regiments and training establishments and submitted a detailed report to General Wavell, C-in-C, India.[3] The focus of the report and its recommendations were largely based on the measures that had been already implemented in the Royal Armoured Corps and revolved around personnel, training, organisation, and logistic support. The British India Army did not wait for his report to be formally submitted and 'action was taken with commendable speed on each main point as it arose during….. [his] visit'. Martel did not think that the recruits he saw at the Armoured Training School at Lucknow were suitable for the corps, and to attract better soldiers, their salary was almost doubled from Rs.18 to Rs.33 per month.[4] Concurrently the corps started weeding out the undesirable and inducting a higher class of soldiers. On the training of recruits, his opinion was that, 'What was clearly required was one basic training Centre; the most mechanically minded recruits would be sent to a tank training Centre, and the less skilled to another Centre for Armoured cars and scout cars etc. In this way, the Indian recruit would specialise and be able to concentrate on one type of machine'. Based on this proposal, the basic training of all the recruits was centralised at Lucknow while the training centre at Ferozepur trained those earmarked for armoured car regiments, and the one at Babina for the tank regiments. A break was placed on the loss of trained personnel by reducing the number of armoured formations, and the motor regiments were brought back into the fold of the IAC. In Martel's opinion, 'Some of these are old regular units and contain excellent men……The I.A.C. with its high rate of pay must be kept for work requiring mechanical knowledge and education, and not be used as infantry'. Actually, until December 1941, a very large number of personnel of the Armoured Corps were employed on semi-infantry roles. Apart from the motor regiments whose entire strength of 467 performed the role of motorised infantry, the reconnaissance regiments of the Indian infantry divisions employed 228 in the dismounted role. This was reduced to 132 by eliminating the rifle troop in the squadron.[5] Each squadron now had one armoured car troop of four armoured cars, and two carrier troops with 16 carriers.[6]

Two proposals of Martel that were also accepted by the British India Army had a far-reaching impact on the efficiency of the IAC. The first was related to the maintenance and repair of equipment. Unlike the British Army, in India there was no corps of Electrical and Mechanical Engineers (EME), and the IAC was heavily dependent on the Indian Ordnance Corps. In Martel's opinion, the Ordnance Corps was very weak, and the issue of tanks and spares as well as the servicing and repairing of AFVs was in a state of chaos. On Martel's recommendation, the British India Army immediately established the Corps of EME, which became responsible for the repair, and recovery of tanks, and vehicles at every stage as well as their recovery on the battlefield.[7] The role of the Ordnance was only limited to storekeeping of stocks, vehicles and weapons, and the repairs of textiles and leather. Considerable steps had already been taken to train Indians in the repair of AFVs at the base workshops, but British NCOs were brought in to give them a lead. In addition, steps were taken to create a pool of well-trained technicians within the Armoured Corps who became key men in units for repairing and maintaining equipment.[8] The second proposal was to expand the Directorate for Armoured Fighting Vehicles. Just recently, the British India Army had established general staff directorates to deal with various arms and branches of the army, but only a brigadier with a small staff looked after affairs of the Armoured Corps. On Martel's recommendation, the post of Director Armoured Fighting Vehicles was upgraded to a major general. The director was supported by a staff of 12 officers

Lieutenant-General Giffard Martel, Royal Armoured Corps, British Army. (NPG, London)

who were responsible for the establishment, organisation, technical training, equipment, and the general wellbeing of the corps. Major General Charles Gairdner was appointed as Major General Armoured Fighting Vehicles, but his initial tenure was brief and he was replaced by Major General Frank Messervy, who had returned from North Africa and was raising an armoured division in India.[9] In his new assignment, he successfully convinced the sceptics that the operations by tanks was feasible in Burma. This would have far-reaching effects on the IAC. It may also have been Messervy, who got the IAC to wear the black beret. When the Indian Cavalry had mechanized, it had to change its combat dress from breaches, puttees, and riding boots to shirts, khaki shorts, and ankle boots.[10] However, it continued to wear the turban except in the desert where side caps were adopted. It was only in 1943 that it adopted the black beret.[11]

The Italian Campaign

When the threat of a German offensive into the Middle East diminished, some of the formations with PAIFORCE, including 8th Indian Division, were moved to Lebanon in 1943 to prepare for the invasion of Italy. 6th Lancers was to see extensive combat as the reconnaissance regiment with 8th Indian Division. Within a month of conquering Sicily, a combined Allied landing was made in the south of Italy in August/September 1943. In the initial stages of his command of the Eight Army in North Africa, General Montgomery did not have a high opinion of Indian troops: during the Alamein offensive, the 4th Indian Division was relegated to garrison duties and clearing of the battlefield, in spite of being one of the most battle-hardened formations in North Africa.[12] However, its exemplary performance during the advance on Tripoli forced Montgomery to change his mind. Consequently, when the Eighth Army landed in Italy apart from an assortment of British, Polish, South African, and Commonwealth formations, it also had three Indian divisions: the 4th, 8th and 10th.

The role of the Eighth Army was to advance up the right side of the peninsula along the Adriatic coast towards the Gustav Line. 6th

Sikh and PM crews of the 6th Lancers in Italy. (Author's Collection)

Lancers was the reconnaissance regiment with the 8th Indian Division, and one of the three Indian Armoured regiments that participated in the Italian campaign. It had one squadron each of Jats, Punjabi Muslims, and Sikhs, and each squadron was organized into five troops. Three were equipped with four Bren Gun Carriers each; the fourth with 3-inch mortars again in carriers, and the fifth was a rifle troop.[13] However, within a year as more equipment became available, the Bren Gun Carriers were initially replaced by Humber, and later by US Staghound Armoured Cars. The Italian Campaign lasted from September 1943 until April 1945, and for most of this time, 8th Indian Division with 6th Lancers in support, was in the frontline. It operated first along the Adriatic coast, and then up the centre of Italy west of the Apennine Mountains until it broke out into the plains of Umbria, crossed the High Apennines, stormed across the River Po, and reined in short of the prize of capturing Venice. It would be beyond the scope of this account to record the entire operations of 6th Lancers over one and a half years of intense conflict, but described in the subsequent pages are the type of tasks and engagements that the regiment faced which provide a flavour of its operations.

The Germans had a formidable line of defence called the Winter Line, which was the collective name for the main Gustav Line, and two connected lines on the west of the Apennine Mountains: the Bernhardt Line, and the Hitler Line. The Winter Line lay south of Rome across the narrowest and the most mountainous part of the Italian Peninsula with the citadel of Monte Cassino as the lynchpin covering the central highway to Rome. It took the Allies five months and four major assaults (the final one being launched by 20 divisions) to break through this line. Once the Winter Line was penetrated, the Germans established a number of lines north of Rome, the main being the Gothic Line. In the initial stage of the Italian Campaign, 8th Division encountered a series of rivers on the Adriatic side, with steep escarpments cutting across the line of advance. On these river-crossing operations, 6th Lancers was generally involved in flank protection, and held strongpoints in a dismounted role. However, reconnaissance regiments operate best

in a fluid battle where they can penetrate through the gaps, provide valuable information to the advancing forces, and upset rear guard actions. Thus it was only when the Germans were withdrawing to the next river line, that 6th Lancers played its traditional role. Shortly before the operations commenced, a welcome change occurred, and each squadron was issued with a troop of Humber IV Armoured Cars replacing the Bren Gun Carriers. There were concerns that the NCO would not be able to operate the 37mm gun on which they were untrained. However, this worry was unfounded as one of the squadrons was using the new guns against the enemy fewer than twenty-four hours after receiving the armoured cars.[14]

When 8th Division broke out from the River Sangro, the Germans had prepared numerous bridges and culverts for demolition. The armoured cars of 6th Lancers raced along the roads to surprise rear guard groups and demolition parties. If resistance stiffened, tanks and infantry were close on call. Operations were often a combination of mobile and dismounted actions where stealth, speed of response, and surprise were the critical ingredients for success. During the breakout from the River Sangro, after the town of Lanciano had been captured, 'B' Squadron, which was operating on the division's main line of advance towards Frisa was fired upon at a demolished bridge. It found a diversion, and drove into the village where a German observation post was captured. However, four German machineguns located in another village 1,500 meters away engaged the squadron. The leading troop leader sent a dismounted patrol with an NCO and seven sowars to outflank the enemy. The patrol stealthily closed up and after hand-to-hand fighting, captured one machinegun, and destroyed three. The carriers then raced for the village to link up, and captured twenty-five POWs.[15]

All this was dangerous work particularly in the first year of the campaign when the German troops encountered were well-trained, and very aggressive. During an advance towards the Gustav Line, 6th Lancers operating as the left flank guard to the division, penetrated deep into enemy territory supported by anti-tank guns, and mobile infantry. Observation posts were shot up, prisoners snatched, and communication interrupted. However, the Germans were quick to respond. When a detachment of 6th Lancers rushed the village of Castello and seized prisoners, they were charged by motor-cycle troops armed with machine-guns. The alacrity with which the enemy struck back on such occasions was characteristic of the perfect training, and exuberant morale of the German troops who confronted the Eighth Army.[16] Wherever the German defences hardened, and each feature was bitterly contested, the reconnaissance regiments ended up performing other tasks, which were equally essential and no less dangerous. At the opening stages of the fourth battle of Cassino, when 8th Division was assaulting across the River Gari, amidst the din of battle, a different noise tinkled through the fog; the faint clank of metal on metal. The Germans presumed that a bridge was under construction on the River Liri and poured artillery fire onto the suspected crossing site. Actually it was troops of 6th Lancers who were banging bits of angle iron, and road rail together to deceive the Germans and it worked. The Germans then switched the fire to the dummy posts and fake emplacements which the Lancers had built. Throughout the early hours of the main attack, a number of German guns, which might have done damage elsewhere, continued to shell empty ground.[17]

At the initial stages of the breakout from Monte Cassino it was still tough work. 6th Lancers was supporting an infantry brigade group that had struck across country with a view to harassing the flank of one of the main lines of retreat. On approaching Veroli, about 10 miles west of the River Liri, they encountered an enemy rear guard several hundred strong. In an attempt to encircle Veroli from the north, 6th Lancers lost three armoured cars in an ambush by anti-tank guns. The crews took cover, and as the Germans advanced towards them, they called for support. Immediately two infantry companies rushed forward, and repulsed the attack barely 50 meters from the squadron headquarters.[18] Once Rome fell and the Umbrian countryside unrolled, with its gentle contours and heavy cultivation, the advance screens of 6th Lancers gave the retreating Germans no rest. 8th Division advanced with three brigades in parallel and a squadron covering each axis. Persistent operations often scattered German rearguards, their missions unfulfilled. The tasks of German demolition teams in particular were badly disrupted; mines were often hurriedly sown, and ammunition and supply dumps left unexploded. However, the casualties to 6th Lancers kept mounting particularly as the Allies closed up to the Gothic Line and the long retreat by the Germans finally drew to an end in June 1944. 'C' Squadron was leading the advance of an infantry brigade towards Bastia when on the outskirts of the town they ran into trouble. The bridge was blown, and an anti-tank gun knocked out two of its armoured cars and destroyed a jeep. A rifle troop, which dismounted to deal with the gun, was also pinned down and its troop leader killed. Meanwhile, 'A' Squadron made contact with the Germans on the Chiascio River and lost an armoured car. Shortly afterwards, the squadron lost four Universal Carriers resulting in the death of a VCO, and two Sowars. Finally, 'B' Squadron, which worked down a lateral road to make contact with a British armoured division at Torgiano, lost four armoured cars to anti-tank guns. These were heavy casualties for a regiment, which in a space of 36 hours lost seven armoured cars, four carriers, and a jeep.[19]

It took the Allies all of the autumn, and winter of 1944 to break through the Gothic Line. In some places, fighting was as intense as the earlier battles along the Gustav Line and at Monte Cassino. The sector of 8th Division was part of the High Apennines Mountains and 6th Lancers was held in reserve. The Allies were strong in tanks, but short on the infantry and to defend sectors, reconnaissance units like 6th Lancers as well as British tank regiments often operated dismounted. 6th Lancers also performed admirably well in this role. Major General Dudley Russell 'Pasha' (who commanded 8th Indian Division all through the Italian Campaign),[20] gave 6th Lancers what the regiment considered to be a back-handed compliment by calling them 'the best foot soldiers in his division.'[21] Though the Allies managed to overcome the Gothic Line, severe winter set in, and the breakout into the valley of the River Po had to be postponed until the spring of 1945. By now, 6th Lancers was equipped with American M8 armoured cars that the British named as Greyhound. Not all the Humbers were replaced, and the regiment operated with a mix of the two. The Greyhound was faster than the Humber, better protected with more firepower. While it

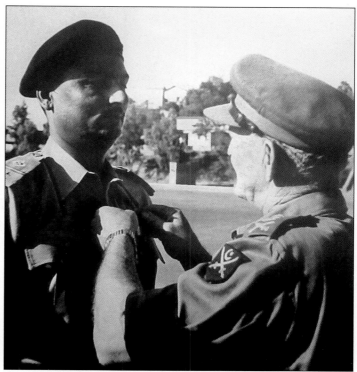

RM Fazal Dad of the 6th Lancers being presented his MC by General Gracy, C-in-C Pakistan Army. (Author's Collection)

had the same 37mm gun, it stowed over eighty rounds of ammunition and carried two Point 30 Browning machineguns. Since the engine ran very quietly, the M8 could maintain an element of surprise, a significant factor to its role of reconnaissance. Its major drawbacks were a limited cross-country capability that largely confined it to roads, and a meagre 3mm of floor armour, which made it particularly vulnerable to mines.[22]

The spring offensive into the valley of the River Po was launched in April 1945, and in 48 hours, the battle hardened 8th Division crossed two rivers, the Senio and Santerno; no mean feat. 6th Lancers was now commanded by the indomitable, Lieutenant Colonel Francis Ingall and back to its classical role, patrolling ahead and on the flanks of the advancing brigades.[23] The next major operation was the successful crossing of the River Po on a two-brigade front, and 6th Lancers was ferried across on rafts. "It was a dizzy experience," recollects one of the squadron commanders. "Driving the heavy cars on to the raft was a juggling act in itself and the navigation on the rafts would have given a Hooghly River pilot apoplexy."[24] It then raced ahead to secure bridges on the Rianco Canal and the leading troop of 'C' Squadron commanded by Jemadar Fazal Dad arrived just in time to disperse the Germans, and extinguish the flames on a wooden bridge which had been set on fire. For the next eight hours, Fazal Dad held the bridge until troops started crossing over.[25] 'The officer's prompt appreciation, coolness, and leadership under fire was a fine example to his men' and for this action he was awarded a Military Cross. 8th Division was now all set to advance, and secure the prize of Venice. 6th Lancers "…crossed the Adige at 0905 hours and were off; the three squadrons up to three miles apart as we sped northwards. On every side there was confusion: enemy units firing on one another and the dreaded 88s spinning on their mountings, firing armour-piercing and high-explosive shells in every direction, vainly trying to hit our speeding cars.[26] It was exhilarating. In the occasional lull in the firing one could hear the powerful V8 engines of the cars screaming as at times they hit 60 or 70 miles an hour. It was just like three foxes chasing chickens in a hen run."[27] However, the regiment halted on direct orders of the

Humber armoured cars of Skinner's Horse advancing through the rolling Umbrian countryside north of Rome, in 1944. (Author's Collection)

instructors from the US Army. The Stuart was one of the first tanks to be supplied by the US to Commonwealth forces. It was a light tank armed with a 37mm gun and because it was far superior in mobility to any tank possessed by the British, it was nicknamed 'Honey' by the British Royal Tank Regiments fighting in North Africa.[30] While at Quetta, Probyn's was not only issued a squadron of Stuarts, but also two squadrons of US M3A1 Lee tanks, and in 1942 it came under the 255th Indian Tank Brigade and moved to Secunderabad for training in jungle warfare. However, it was not until 1944 after having been re-equipped with Shermans that it finally entered the combat theatre at Imphal to take part in the counter-offensive by the Fourteenth Army to recapture Burma.

There was a gradual shift in thinking about the employment of tanks in Burma accelerated by the tour of India in 1942 by Major General Martel, the commander of the Royal Armoured Corps. After carrying out a major overhaul of the IAC, he also visited the formations in Burma, and recommended that armour could operate through the valleys.[31] There were sceptics, which included the Director of Military Training at GHQ. On a visit to the 254th Indian Tank Brigade, which was being formed for operations in Burma, he told the officers that they should arrange a transfer to the infantry if they expect to see any fighting during the war.[32] His views may have been based on the pitiful use of eight Valentine tanks in 'penny-packets', during the First Arakan Campaign in the winter of 1942-43. Without proper training in jungle warfare, or coordination with the infantry, all the tanks were lost to no avail.[33] After the end of the monsoons in 1943, Brigadier Scoones who was commanding the 254th Indian Tank Brigade visited his brother who was commanding IV Indian Corps in the Imphal Plains. Based on a very positive assessment by Brigadier Scoones on the employment of tanks in the valley, the commander of the IV Indian Corps asked for the allotment of the 254th Indian Tank Brigade. The same year, the Fourteenth Army was formed under General Slim who supported the idea of using tanks in jungle warfare but was determined that they should be used properly. Consequently, considerable experimentation and training in combined arms operations and tactics was undertaken, and it was not until 1944 that tanks of the IAC started operating in Burma in a sizable number.

One of the first regiments to arrive was 11th Cavalry, which had been recalled from the Middle East. The regiment was given the role of a light armoured regiment, issued Daimler and Humber armoured cars, and after having rested and reorganized at Rawalpindi, it was ready to take the field again. Fortunately, it was destined for a reversal of fortune 'after its consistent run of bad luck in the Western Desert'.[34] By the end of the war, it would be the only regiment of the IAC that had fought against the Italians, Germans and the Japanese. It arrived in the Burma theatre in April 1944, well before the counter offensive

corps commander who insisted that the *autostrada* be cleared for the New Zealand armoured division to take Venice. It seemed that even though the Commonwealth troops fought alongside through a bitterly contested campaign, the British India Army remained at a disadvantage.

A few days after the capture of Venice, the German forces in Italy surrendered unconditionally. After a long slog, 6th Lancers now looked towards home with the satisfaction of having fought well, and in the process earning eight battle honours and the theatre honour for the Italian campaign. 50 years later, an armoured regiment from the sub-continent would again set foot in Europe but this time as part of a UN Peacekeeping Mission.

The Burma Campaign

As early as 1942, the British had employed tanks in Burma against the invading Japanese. Since the Indian Armoured Corps was poorly equipped, 7th Armoured Brigade (the original Desert Rats), was rushed 7,400 km by sea from North Africa, and performed sterling service throughout the long retreat to the Chindwin. The brigade was equipped with two regiments of Stuarts, which were hampered by a near-complete lack of high explosive ammunition and the fact that the thirsty tanks required aviation fuel.[28] On the opposing side, the Japanese also used two tank regiments and several independent squadrons. In spite of the excellent operations by the Desert Rats in covering the withdrawal of the Burma Corps, commanders in Burma (and the staff at Delhi) perceived no sizeable role for armour in jungle terrain.[29] However, the lessons gained in the use of tanks in Burma were not entirely discarded. In 1942, Probyn's Horse had been equipped with tanks and commenced training for jungle warfare. It had mechanized in 1940 as a light armoured regiment at Risalpur, and then moved to Sialkot to join the 1st Indian Armoured Brigade. A year later, it had its first feel of tanks when it moved to Quetta. Three Stuarts were issued for training and came with a complement of a few

by the Fourteenth Army, and participated in two operations that changed the course of the war – the Battle of Kohima, and the Relief of Imphal. To forestall the counter offensive, the Japanese had launched a desperate attack across the Indo-Burmese border to capture the Allied bases of Kohima, Imphal, and Chittagong. Without the benefit of training in jungle warfare, 11th Cavalry had been rushed to join elements of the 50th Indian Tank Brigade at the railhead at Dimapur, and a detachment managed to reach Imphal before the road was cut on 6 April 1944. At the sieges of both Kohima and Imphal, the Allies relied entirely on resupply from the air by the British and American aircraft flying from India until the road from Dimapur was cleared. It was therefore critical that the line of communication was opened up as soon as possible and XXXIII Corps was tasked to relieve Kohima and link up with Imphal. The Battle of Kohima lasted for 13 intense days from 6 to 18 April, and it took the best part of XXXIII Corps to affect the relief. 11th Cavalry was operating as the corps reconnaissance regiment, and was initially entrusted with patrolling the road from Dimapur to Kohima. However, after the relief of Kohima from 6 June onwards, it operated with 2nd British Division and the Grant tanks of 149 RAC Regiment to advance 100 km, and link up with the troops from Imphal. This operation took 16 days and the actual linkup was made by the armoured cars of the 11th Cavalry with a Stuart troop of the 7th Light Cavalry at Mile 109.[35] For its role during this operation, the regiment was awarded with the battle honour of Kohima.

The Arakan Offensive

Through the monsoons and late into 1944, the Allies pursued the Japanese and pushed them back across the Chindwin River. The Japanese fought hard but they were not the major enemy; it was sickness and disease. In July 1944, an infantry brigade of the 5th Indian Division lost only 9 killed and 85 wounded in fighting, but 507 to sickness and disease. The Allies were now poised for a major offensive to retake Burma. While the main effort was to be launched through central Burma, a subsidiary effort by XV Corps was planned west of the Arakan along the coast to capture Akyab, and the Mayu Peninsula. The initial purpose was to secure airfields for supporting the main offensive and ultimately culminate in an enveloping manoeuvre by an air and sea landing south of Rangoon. The 50th Indian Tank Brigade raised in Poona at the end of 1944 was allocated to XV Corps. Apart from a motor battalion, the brigade had three tank regiments one of which was 19th Lancers, the last regiment to be mechanized. In 1941, it converted to a reconnaissance regiment and joined the 31st Indian Armoured Division in Sialkot. In 1942, it moved to Malir, and was equipped with Humber Armoured Cars. However, when only the headquarters of the Armoured division moved to Iraq, 19th Lancers was sent to Madras in 1943 on coast-watching duties against an anticipated Japanese landing. It moved by road 3,700 km from Malir to Madras because no rail transport was available. There was also no tarmac road between Karachi and Bahawalpur, and the regiment drove on desert tracks. It completed the move in 27 days (from 17 April to 13 May), including stops, with a daily run of 140 kilometres.[36]

In 1944, 19th Lancers joined the 50th Indian Tank Brigade near Poona, and converted to a tank regiment with Shermans. The Medium Tank M4, known as the Sherman, was the primary tank used by the US during the Second World War and thousands were also distributed to the Allies, including the British Commonwealth, and the Soviet Union.[37] The Sherman was one of the most produced tanks of the war (only out-manufactured by the Soviet T-34), and had many versions. 19th Lancers was equipped with the M4A2, which carried a 75mm gun and was powered by a General Motor diesel engine, which reduced the risk of gasoline fires. Against German tanks, the Sherman had certain disadvantages, but in Burma, this had little relevance. What was more important were the ninety rounds of main gun ammunition it carried with a wide variety including armour piercing, high explosive with variable fuses, and phosphorus. Consequently, it was well suited for the nature of engagements conducted during operations in the jungle. The tank was simple to operate, robust, and well supplied with spares. It was operated by a crew of five, which greatly helped in numerous out-of-combat tasks like repair, maintenance, replenishment of fuel, and stowage of ammunition for the main gun, and the three machineguns.[38]

The 50th Indian Tank Brigade joined XV Corps in Arakan during November 1944. 19th Lancers had a squadron each of Jats, Sikhs, and Punjabi Muslims (Tiwanas and Awans from Shahpur District). 25th

Sherman Mk.III tanks of the 19th Lancers advancing during the Arkan Campaign, in 1945. (Author's Collection)

Sherman of 'B' Squadron, 19th Lancers, getting into position to shell the Japanese in the Arakan hills, January 1945. (Author's Collection)

Repairing a Sherman at the 5th Indian Division's tank workshop near Taungtha, in March 1945. (Author's Collection)

Second Arakan Offensive, the tanks had perfected a system of close support in which the Sherman used its highly accurate 75mm main gun in slow, methodical shoots firing super-quick HE shells to strip vegetation, and remove camouflage, solid AP rounds to loosen up packed soil, and then delayed HE shells to blast apart bunkers at close range. If not all the slits were exposed, a white phosphorus smoke shell was fired through one of them. To avoid endangering the infantry as it covered the last 20 meters, the tanks would switch to firing accurate solid AP shot and machineguns to suppress the surviving Japanese defences.[39]

The advance down to and the capture of Akyab was relatively quick as the Japanese were withdrawing but it still took a month because of the difficult terrain, and resistance. Ahead of Akyab the fighting became more intense, as the South African Division advanced inland and

Indian Infantry Division and an East African Division were given a squadron each, while the third was retained in reserve under the corps. The main tasks for the squadrons were to destroy Japanese bunkers and outflank strongly held positions. During the earlier

the 25th and 26th Divisions along with a commando brigade carried out seaborne landings to intercept the Japanese. So effective were tanks, that when faced with a shortage of landing craft for the landing on the Meybon Peninsula, half a squadron of 19th Lancers was taken to support the attack instead of artillery. The tanks landed with great difficulty and the first one off the landing craft sank into mud, 400 meters from the beach. Once the rest were put ashore on a more suitable beach, they were employed both for direct and indirect fire controlled by a Forward Tank Officer. The crews performed amazing but dangerous feats. In an effort to clear a hill one tank managed to climb up and destroyed six bunkers from as close as 40 meters. But the gradient was so steep that the tank finally toppled over backwards, and tumbled down.[40]

A decisive engagement in which 19th Lancers participated was the landing at Kangaw, to block the only route available to the Japanese to withdraw their guns and vehicles. In fact, the Battle of Kangaw that lasted for 22 days was described by the commander of XV Corps as the most decisive battle of the whole Arakan campaign. Because of the sea-borne landing, the Japanese defences were caught facing the wrong way, but they quickly rallied, and counter-attacked to capture a hill located between the beach and Kangaw village. The Allied forces consisting of a commando brigade, an infantry brigade and tanks of the 19th Lancers fought a desperate battle. In a suicidal attack, a Japanese engineer party armed with explosive charges at the end of bamboo poles, penetrated up to a troop of tanks. They set fire to one, killing the crew, and damaged the track of another. The tanks fought back and with the help of the infantry killed the Japanese.[41]

After this battle, the Japanese abandoned their heavy equipment, and in small groups fled east across the Arakan. Two divisions pursued the Japanese, and captured the passes that linked up with the Irrawaddy Valley. The bulk of the tank brigade withdrew to India but 19th Lancers stayed on. In a subsidiary operation to clear the track towards Tamandu by an infantry brigade, the tanks supported each battalion as they leapfrogged forward. In one engagement, they fought a duel with two 25-pdr guns captured by the Japanese and fired over 460 rounds before the guns could be silenced. In recognition of its commendable role during the Arakan campaign, 19th Lancers was awarded the battle honours of Buthidaung, Mayu Valley, Myebon, Kangaw, Ru-Ywa, Dalet, and Tamandu.

Counter-offensive by the Fourteenth Army

Crucial to the Allied offensive to drive the Japanese out of Burma were the operations of the Fourteenth Army commencing at the end of 1944 with two Indian corps – the IV and XXXIII. General Slim aimed to fight a decisive battle in the Shwebo, and Ye-U Plains west of the Irrawaddy by utilising the overwhelming superiority of two armoured brigades. IV Corps operating on the left had under its command 255th Indian Tank Brigade with Probyn's Horse (comprising of a squadron each of Sikhs, Dogras and Punjabi Muslims), Deccan Horse, a regiment of the Royal Armoured Corps, and a motor battalion. XXXIII Corps had 254th Indian Tank Brigade with 7th Light Cavalry equipped with Stuarts, and two British Armoured regiments with heavier Lee and Grant tanks. 11th Cavalry was the reconnaissance regiment with XXXIII Corps and a squadron detached to IV Corps. One of the squadrons of the 11th Cavalry operating with XXXIII Corps was commanded by Hissam el Effendi who after escaping from a POW camp in Italy had re-joined to fight with the regiment. By the end of December 1944, Fourteenth Army had three bridgeheads across the Chindwin but it became apparent that the Japanese had no intentions to comply with the plan of the Fourteenth Army. They withdrew their four divisions, which were in the process of re-equipping and deployed them to defend the line of the River Irrawaddy.

'Bill' Slim commanding the Fourteenth Army decided to execute a strategic shift, combined with a turning move. While the divisions already across the Chindwin were placed under XXXIII Corps, IV Corps with the 7th and 17th Indian Divisions, and the 255th Indian Tank Brigade sidestepped west. It then moved south over 600 km along the Chindwin, to outflank the Japanese. The commander of IV Corps who executed this strategic shift was none other than Lieutenant General Frank Messervy, the man who as the Director of Armoured Fighting Vehicles at Delhi had strongly advocated the employment of armour in Burma, and oversaw its training for jungle warfare. It took over one and a half months to execute this change in plan, and position the forces at Nyaungu for crossing the Irrawaddy. Though a tank transporter company was available, the mountainous track was in such an appalling condition that the tanks had to cover more than half the distance on tracks. Sprockets broke and had to be changed or re-welded, bogies and idler wheels had to be replaced, and spares flown in. The EME workshops and the light aid detachments of the tank regiments were the unsung heroes of this backbreaking but successful move. They worked day and night, to keep vehicles running in spite of the suffocating dust, which clogged air-filters and carburettors, blanketed radiators, and penetrated every bearing.[42]

General Slim had always been a proponent of tanks as the principal strike weapon in land warfare. However, he was almost obsessive in his concern for their reliability, and inspected 255th Indian Tank Brigade shortly before the jump-off towards Meiktila. He quizzed the brigade major about the Shermans and was irritated by the bland replies he received. "The most important thing is reliability," he snapped. "Mechanical failure could make them a liability. How reliable are those Shermans?" he asked. "Very, sir," replied the unflappable brigade major. "Given sufficient fuel, some essential spares, and some time at night to do maintenance on them." Slim seemed unconvinced and growled, "You had better be right."[43] The brigade major was right. The Sherman had its weaknesses, but was generally a very reliable tank; however, it required a very high standard of maintenance to keep it serviceable. Maintaining a tank during continuous operations was tough since the only time that the crews had was at night labouring in the fighting and engine compartment as well as refuelling and replenishing the ammunition. It was noisy work to which the infantry objected. A training pamphlet observed that: 'Cases have been known where higher commanders objected to the mechanized units doing maintenance at night because the noise kept other troops awake.'[44]

The design of the operation was for IV Corps to capture the logistic base of the Japanese Army at Meiktila, which would isolate five Japanese divisions to the north. IV Corps would then act as the anvil for the hammer of XXXIII Corps that would cross the Irrawaddy in the area of Mandalay. In the words of Gen Slim, "As XXXIII Corps proceeded so vigorously to clear the Shwebo plain and establish its divisions along the Irrawaddy, Messervy's IV Corps was on its long march to Pakokku to deliver what we hoped would be the decisive stroke at Meiktila."[45] [46] An elaborate deception plan had been executed by XXXIII Corps to cover the move of IV Corps, and 11th Cavalry played an important role in this plan. IV Corps employed the 7th Indian Division with a tank regiment to establish the bridgehead on 13 February 1945, and the squadron of the 11th Cavalry attached to IV Corps provided a protective screen to the bridgehead. The Japanese considered this crossing a feint and did not react seriously. The stage was now set for a decisive action by the 255th Indian Tank Brigade in which Meiktila was the 'Schwerpunkt'. The tank brigade was operating with two brigades of the 17th Division, which had been converted into lorried infantry to keep up with the tanks. For the thrust to Meiktila the entire force, including the divisional artillery moved self-contained from harbour to harbour, and was supplied from the air until a secure line of communication could be established. The Allied air supremacy played a critical role not only in keeping the force supplied but also in

A Diamond T tank transporter carrying a Grant ARV makes its way along the road to Tamu in January 1945. (Author's Collection)

ground support. Taking a leaf out of the air operations conducted to support forces in other theatres, fighter-bombers flew 'cab rank' over the advancing columns always-ready on-call to engage targets.[47] The first clash that Probyn's Horse had with the Japanese in any strength was at Oyin (22 km from the bridgehead) where in the words of a tank commander, "It was just plain murder". The tanks, along with a Rajput battalion, killed 200 Japanese.

The advance towards Taungtha northwest of Meiktila was conducted on two axis with the tank brigade (led by Probyn's Horse), moving on a subsidiary axes to outflank the Japanese. The force converged at Taungtha by 24 February where it was replenished by a supply drop. By 26 February, it was 25km short of Meiktila, and a column was detached to capture an airfield to the northeast, which the engineers rapidly repaired. A day later reinforcements were being flown in. On 27 February, Probyn's Horse advanced down the main road to Meiktila outflanking roadblocks, and shooting up the Japanese as they withdrew. That night they harboured 7km from Meiktila, and could hear the Japanese blowing up their dumps. The next day the advance guard of the 255th Tank Brigade moved rapidly towards Meiktila and

…was soon at the main airfield which was taken at the gallop. 'As far as I could make out' recollects Fred Joyner, second-in-command of a squadron of the 11th Cavalry, 'it was everyone for himself. It was a sight I shall never forget, with everyone joining in, nothing fancy, just a straight line from A to B and get there as quick as you can. Everything joined in, tanks, armoured cars, jeeps, trucks, straight across country against fairly heavy opposition, but it was successful – maybe it was the surprise element.[48]

The capture of this second airfield enabled an infantry brigade to be flown in as well as fuel to replenish the tanks.

The Japanese never appreciated the scale at which their opponents would employ tanks and consequently ignored the development of antitank weapons. Even their antitank mines like the Type-93 had insufficient explosive to damage a tank and the charge had to be boosted with additional dynamite.[49] Improvised explosive devices in the hands of suicide bombers were dangerous, but with mixed results against

alert crews. As a squadron of Probyn's Horse advanced through a burning village, a Japanese threw himself under the squadron commander's tank, and detonated an explosive, killing the driver, and disabling the tank. Another climbed onto a tank of a troop manoeuvring from a flank but was shot by a tank following behind. Almost instantly, a third rushed under it with a box of explosives but the Sherman rapidly reversed and shot the attacker. It was not over. The last attacker managed to climb up the front but luckily, his charge exploded prematurely.[50] On the very same day of the advance, a troop leader had all his periscopes shot-up by a sniper, and a tank commander was shot through the head.[51] To protect the Shermans, an infantry squad was detailed with each tank, and so close was the cooperation that they became a part of the crew.

Meiktila was a major communication centre with a garrison of 5,000 troops. Most were from the Japanese administrative echelons but there was also a regular infantry battalion. It took four days for 17th Division, and the tank brigade to isolate and capture Meiktila. The tanks were used for close support of the infantry as the brigades converged onto the town from different directions. Two actions in which Probyn's Horse participated, illustrate the nature of the fighting and the determination of the defender. On 1 March, a squadron of Deccan Horse closed up to an objective and for an hour, every bunker that could be spotted was engaged without any response. Next, 'B' Squadron Probyn's Horse arrived carrying a company of infantry, which was to take over the objective, and relieve the tanks. As the dismounted infantry approached the objective, the whole feature burst into life with machine guns, and small arms fire from well-concealed bunkers. Both the tank squadrons replied with every weapon they carried but it took a good 10 minutes before things quieted down. A day later on 2 March, 'A' Squadron Probyn's Horse, was tasked to clear a village and its surrounding area with an infantry battalion. The squadron deployed in the forming-up place but while waiting for an air strike, the infantry was pinned down. Regardless, the squadron advanced through thick scrub but the left troop was separated from its infantry, and attacked by tank hunting parties. One tank was disabled but four Japanese were killed. The remaining two tanks continued to advance, systematically destroying bunkers. In the open ground beyond the scrub many more Japanese were killed. The infantry was still held up, and two more tank troops advanced ahead and reached the village. The village was constructed of stones, and the Japanese survivors had holed-up in a strongly built house, which was subjected to heavy fire by the squadron. As a result large bodies of Japanese were forced to withdraw into the open, and a tank troop 'had a fine Ahmednagar shoot at 2,000 yards range'.[52] [53] [54]

The Japanese fought hard to defend Meiktila and after losing it, fought desperately to retake the town. They launched over a division from three directions with violent but uncoordinated attacks. The 17th Indian Division along with the tank brigade conducted an offensive-defence to deny the Japanese firm bases from which to launch attacks. For the next 26 days, nearly every day, tank and infantry columns sallied out to sweep areas, clear villages, and destroy roadblocks. On 5 March, a column comprising of 'B' Squadron Probyn's Horse, two infantry companies, and an artillery battery, which was sent out of the perimeter to destroy a roadblock, fought a typical action. The tanks approached the block from the rear; and were fired at by a 75mm and a 37mm gun, both of which were destroyed. Riaz ul Karim who was commanding a tank troop in 'B' Squadron probed further to the left, but lost a tank to another 75mm gun. Finally this block, and another reported by the reconnaissance a couple of miles further on, were both cleared and the column returned with four captured guns.[55] For his courage, coolness and initiative during this action, Riaz ul Karim was awarded a MC.

Infantry watching Sherman tanks of Probyn's Horse advancing towards Meiktila in March 1945. (Author's Collection)

One of the principal efforts of the Japanese was to disrupt the supplies and reinforcements being regularly ferried into the airfield at Meiktila. Consequently, the tank brigade had to conduct a number of sweeps to clear the area in and around the airfield. On 14 March, two squadrons of Probyn's Horse carried out a very successful sweep to destroy Japanese guns, which had taken up positions within range of the airfield. The next day, a squadron along with an infantry battalion swept the perimeter of the airfield clear of Japanese, thus enabling the resumption of flights. A third sweep on 17 March, by a large force of an infantry brigade supported by two squadrons of Probyn's Horse enlarged the perimeter of security, and pushed the Japanese further back. It took three days of hard fighting to complete the task, during which they destroyed four anti-tank and two 105mm guns, and killed 264 Japanese.

By the end of March 1945, the 7th Indian Division advancing with a tank regiment from the bridgehead at Irrawaddy had linked up with the defenders of Meiktila, and the Japanese lifted the siege. It was a culmination of three months of operations from the move down south to the bridgehead, the crossing of the Irrawaddy, the advance to Meiktila, and its successful defence, which broke the back of the Japanese. The Japanese had fought as hard as they could; and in the process destroyed 50 tanks and inflicted 300 casualties, but in the same period, they had suffered 2,500 casualties and lost 50 big guns, which were irreplaceable.[56] For its performance in this operation, Probyn's Horse was awarded with the first two battle honours it earned during the Second World War – Capture of Meiktila, and Defence of Meiktila. The Battle of Meiktila was a great success for General Slim, and his Fourteenth Army but it was also a defining moment for the Indian Armoured Corps. No one could have been more pleased than the corps commander, Lieutenant General Messervy who had been a leading proponent of the use of tanks in Burma. In a letter congratulating the commander of 255th Indian Tank Brigade, Brigadier C. E. Pert on the award of the DSO, he wrote: "You and your two regiments of the Indian Armoured Corps have had the chance at last of showing the world what the I. A. C. can do."[57] This sentiment was also expressed by General Slim in a similar letter of congratulations to Brigadier Pert in which he stated: "You have helped to put the Indian Armoured Corps on the map."[58] The IAC had come of age.

The final phase of the operation was the pursuit of the Japanese Army, and a race to get to Rangoon before the Japanese could organize any form of a serious delay and equally important, before the start of the monsoons. The main effort to capture Rangoon was by IV Corps with the regiments of the 255th Tank Brigade forming the advance guards, and following close on the heels of the reconnaissance regiments. However to successfully execute this drive, the two tank brigades needed a large number of replacement engines, no fewer than 101 Grant, 47 Stuart, and 68 Sherman engines. There was a serious issue regarding the unsatisfactory reconditioning of tank engines in base workshops in India and it required a major effort, not only to improve the performance of the base workshops but also to transport these engines in time to the frontline by rail, air, and sea. No one was more concerned than General Slim:

With daily demands on our armour, opportunities for the extra maintenance so badly needed were not easy to find. I visited the tank, and armoured car units to thank them for their magnificent efforts in the past battle and to impress on them how much I should rely on them for the next. I told them that, when I gave the word for the dash on Rangoon, every tank they had, must be a starter, and that every tank that crossed the start line must pass the post in Rangoon. After that they could push them into the sea if they wanted! But they had to get to Rangoon![59]

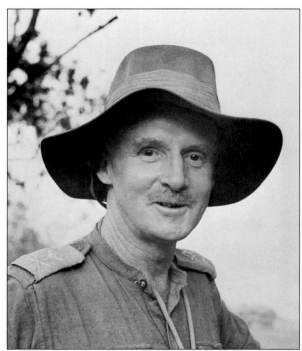

Lieutenant-General Frank Messervy, commander of the IV Corps in Burma. (Author's Collection)

A Sherman of Probyn's Horse carrying infantry for close protection. (Author's Collection)

The armoured troops did not disappoint Slim. When the advance commenced, IV Corps covered 480km in three weeks (averaging 23km a day) and the credit for this mainly goes to the tanks shooting their way through villages, storming or bypassing roadblocks, intercepting the retreating Japanese, fighting off suicide attacks, and along with the infantry assaulting positions that the Japanese chose to defend. Once the advance guard had passed, the Japanese sometimes infiltrated back, and blocked the main body following behind. One of the major engagements took place at Paybwe during which Probyn's Horse was part of a column that ultimately outflanked the town, cut the main road to Rangoon, and advanced onto the rear of the Japanese defences. During this operation, the regiment had the rare opportunity to destroy five Japanese tanks of the 14th Tank Regiment, the only armoured force that the Japanese had committed to Burma.[60] The Japanese regiment was initially employed in the offensive on Imphal/Kohima, and by the end of it had been reduced to only four tanks. It was rebuilt near Mandalay, and re-entered the fray at Meiktila with the new Type 97-Kai Shinhoto Chi-Ha. In March 1945, Shermans of the 255th Indian Tank Brigade wiped out its last tanks on the Mandalay Road. The last desperate stand made by the Japanese was at Pegu, and it took a combined operation of two days by the 17th Division and 255th Tank Brigade to capture the town.

The monsoon was setting in, and with only 80km to Rangoon, a mobile force, which included a squadron of Probyn's Horse, was instructed to go 'hell for leather'. Following it was the 17th Indian Division 'which had carried out such a gallant withdrawal from Burma three years earlier, and only the previous year, had fought so magnificently in the defence of Imphal. 17th Indian Division had an old score to settle, and if it was humanly possible, it was going to be settled. But the obstacles to be overcome were serious'.[61] The route was heavily booby-trapped and mined. In a section of 6.5km, 7,000 mines were lifted. Finally, on 6 May the advance guard linked up with a squadron of 19th Lancers advancing north from Rangoon. In the course of this advance to Rangoon, Probyn's Horse earned no less than five more battle honours and two theatre honours – Pegu 1945, and Burma 1942-45. Having sat out most of the Second World War in

India, Probyn's Horse ultimately had the opportunity to prove itself in the hard fought Burma Campaign.

While IV Corps dashed toward Rangoon on the main axis, XXXIII Corps advanced to its west along the Irrawaddy. For most of this operation, the 11th Cavalry operated under the command of the 20th Indian Division commanded by Major General D. D. Gracey who would later command the Pakistan Army. As a motor regiment, it had met its share of disasters earlier in the war, but was now on the winning side, and the feeling must have been exhilarating. 'A' Squadron, 7th Cavalry with its Stuart tanks operated with the armoured cars of the 11th Cavalry and as always the reconnaissance led the advance, exposing the enemy by drawing its fire, and then the follow-up tanks, and infantry cleared the opposition. The senior commanders recognised the danger involved in such operations. Endorsing the citation of a Kaim Khani risaldar of 16th Light Cavalry for a MC, the corps commander Lieutenant General Frank Messervy wrote: 'The work of Armd Cs [armoured cars] in these operation has been an extremely difficult, and dangerous task, exposed as they had been to close range fire from guns in ambush. I can think of few duties requiring more courage than the leading car of an Armd Car Patrol in this condition.'[62] Lance Daffadar Muhamamd Hayat of 11th Cavalry was awarded a MM for displaying 'outstanding leadership and gallantry when his troop was ambushed within [a] village. Bayoneting a suicide Jap who was attacking his vehicle with a picric acid bomb, he rallied his section under heavy mortar and rifle fire and beat off the initial Jap attack'. For its full range of operations from 1944-45 in support of the two corps fighting in Burma, 11th Cavalry was awarded with no less than seven battle honours including Relief of Kohima, Monywa 1945, Mandalay, Myinmu Bridgehead, Capture of Meiktila, the Irrawaddy, and Rangoon Road as well as the theater honour of Burma 1942-45.

Actually, the race by Fourteenth Army to capture the prize of Rangoon was partially driven in its final stages by General Slim's desire

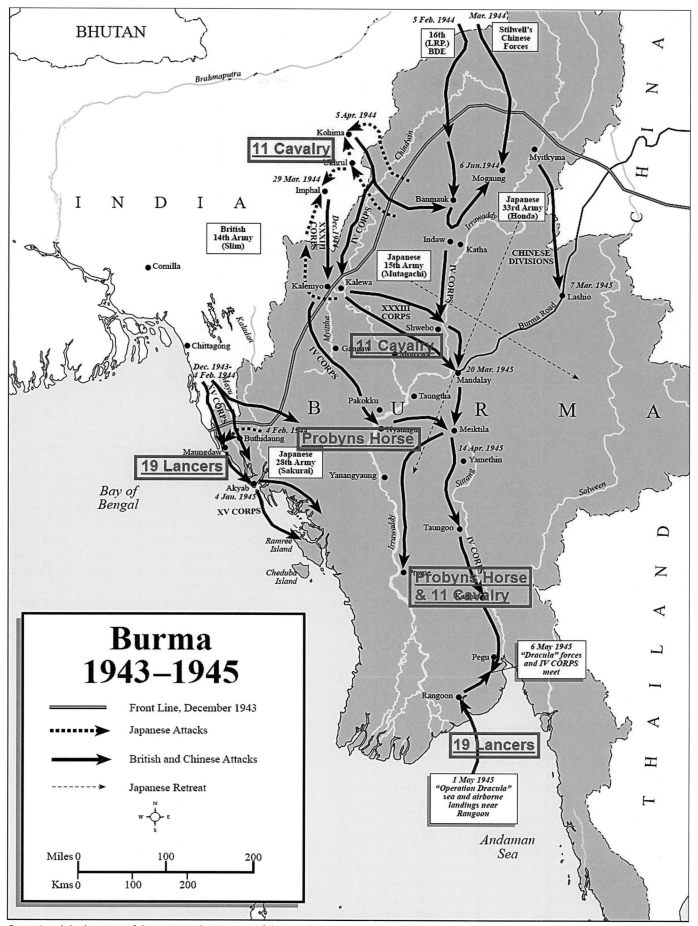

Operational deployment of the armoured regiments of the British India Army during the Burma Campaign that were subsequently allotted to Pakistan. (Author's Collection)

Soldiers of the 17th Indian Division inspect a Japanese 75mm anti-rank gun. (Author's Collection)

big change to the *sowars* of the GGBG, who were selected more for their height and looks than physical strength.[69] In July 1945, the new division moved from Rawalpindi and Secunderabad to Bilaspur, and new camps were built in the jungle to train for an airborne landing in Malaya. Troops completed the parachute course, and 'had over 30 jumps to their credit, including 7 night jumps'.[70] However, there were no real opportunities for unit parachute jumps, and the air landing troops (whose role was to go into combat via gliders); were hampered by the lack of gliders. The division participated in only Operation DRACULA, the capture of Rangoon. The landing was a near disaster as the Japanese had invitingly cleared several areas (which were selected as dropping zones), but spiked them with sharpened bamboo staves less than two feet apart. The Gurkha battalion, which was the first to jump, suffered over 70 percent casualties, and the assault was called off. A troop of the reconnaissance squadron with Captain Jehanzeb from the Guides, which was to jump after the first wave, flew all the way to the drop zone, and was turned back when the Gurkhas fired off red flares 'a sign of the plan going awry'. There were no further airborne operations and at the end of the war, the division redeployed to Karachi (Malir) in November 1945 and its designation was changed to 2nd Indian Airborne Division. The move was a big relief, as the troops did not like Bilaspur due to its heat and humidity. Soon after, the GGBG was relieved from the division, and reverted to its former role and designation.[71] However, it continued to wear the maroon beret and turban that was initially only worn after qualifying as paratroopers.[72]

to beat a seaborne landing south of the city. This landing was planned in apprehension of the monsoons setting in before the Fourteenth Army reached Rangoon.[63] At the end of the Arakan operations, 26th Indian Division and 19th Lancers were extensively trained and equipped for amphibious operations. As the Fourteenth Army raced for Rangoon, this force landed up the mouth of the Rangoon River on 2 May.[64] When they entered the city next day, they found that it had already been abandoned by the Japanese. None-the-less for participating in this operation 19th Lancers earned an additional battle honour of Rangoon Road, and the theatre honour of Burma 1942-45. The above account primarily covers the operations of the 255th Indian Tank Brigade of which, Probyn's Horse was a part. However, the 254th Indian Tank Brigade participated far longer in the Burma campaign in the defence of Imphal/Kohima, and the counteroffensive in which it fought in the central plains of Burma as well as the drive to capture Rangoon. In recognition for the immense contribution made by this brigade in defeating the Japanese, General Slim obtained permission from India Command for the 254th Indian Tank Brigade to wear the Fourteenth Army insignia as its formation sign. It was this brigade with its post-war designation of the 3rd Armoured Brigade that Pakistan inherited at Independence.[65]

This account would be incomplete without a mention of the Governor-General's Bodyguard (GGBG), the senior most regiment of the armoured corps. It was the only regular cavalry unit of the 'old' Bengal Army to have survived the revolt of 1857.[66] In 1944, it was mechanized by converting it into a reconnaissance squadron though it retained a ceremonial mounted squadron. In April 1944, the 44th Indian Airborne Division was activated, and took over the number, headquarters, and the service units from the recently disbanded 44th Indian Armoured Division. The GGBG was designated as the 44th Indian Airborne Division Reconnaissance Squadron.[67] The squadron was 'given extremely hard and exhaustive training on the waterless terrain of Campbellpur District in the Punjab, marching 40 miles in 18 hours while carrying a 42 lb. pack every week, and practicing para-drop jumping in Chaklala'.[68] It must have come as a

3
THE OFFICER CORPS PRE-INDEPENDENCE

The officer corps that the Pakistan Army inherited at Independence was the product of debate and action that spanned nearly 150 years. There was a momentum for reform in the cadre of Native Officers created by Lord Curzon. However, it took the catastrophe of the First World War, and the rise in influence of the Indian political leaders for an institutionalised approach in creating a corps of commissioned Indian officers. The progress remained slow and had it not been for another world war, the Indianisation of the officers would have been incomplete until 1967. At the beginning of the Second World War, only three Indian cavalry regiments had Indian officers. Even when the entire army became open to Indian officers, many of the senior regiments accepted only three to four at a time. A small cadre of pre-war officers commissioned from Sandhurst and Dehradun transferred to the Pakistan Armoured Corps at Independence along with a larger number of Emergency Commissioned Officers (ECOs). However, above the level of a tank troop their combat experience was very limited, since only a few were entrusted with the command of a squadron during the Second World War.

The Early Years

Concerned about the soldiers' lack of initiative within of the Presidency Armies, prominent British administrators argued for 'employment of natives that could stimulate the ambition of a better class of them'. What they were alluding to was creating an officer class. The debate persisted until the turn of the century with concerns whether this would actually increase efficiency and the fear that Indian officers may lead another mutiny. There were also apprehensions about British officers ending up subordinate to the Indians. A proposal on a few native regiments officered entirely by Indians, was stalled by opposition from Lord Roberts.[1] For the British officer, it was sufficient to have an intermediate cadre performing a link with the Indian soldier. This link was the Indian Officers (IOs) who were subordinate to the British officers and had authority only over Indian troops.

A special form of King's Commission was instituted in 1902 to create an Indian officer corps, qualified through the Viceroy's Corps later known as the Imperial Cadet Corps (ICC). The cadets were young men from the princely and noble families selected solely from the five Chiefs Colleges.[2] The scheme was discarded because enthusiasm for joining the corps dropped rapidly.[3] The British also granted honorary commissions to members of prominent families, and those who rendered exemplary service to the Crown. Amongst the Muslims was Sher Muhammad Khan (18/19th Lancers) and Muhammad Ayub Khan (22/25th Cavalry). Malik Umar Hayat Khan of the Tiwana clan was granted an honorary commission and attached to 18th Tiwana Lancers. He had a distinguished military career serving in the Somaliland War of 1902–1904, in the Tibet Expedition of 1903–1904, in France in the First World War, and then in the Third Afghan War. He was ultimately granted the honorary rank of major general.[4] Malik Khizar Hayat Tiwana, who joined his father Umar Hayat on active service, was commissioned into the 17th Cavalry in 1918.

The process of 'Indianisation' had been introduced within the civil government, but within the Army it was the First World War and pressure by the Indian politicians, which initiated a gradual process for replacing British officers by Indians. There was great disquiet amongst the British who believed that only entrants from proper stock

The Honourable Major-General Malik Umar Hayat Khan Tiwana, 18th KGO Lancers. (Author's Collection)

and educated through a public school system could provide the right kind of officer.[5] The process began in 1918 after the publication of the celebrated Montagu-Chelmsford Report. Seven Indians from the ICC scheme who had served during the First World War were made King's Commissioned Indian Officers (KCIOs). In addition, a number of IOs who had distinguished themselves during the war were also granted the King's Commission. One of them was Sardar Sir Hisamuddin Khan (affectionately known as Sir. H.D.), a famous IO from the Indian Cavalry who rose to the rank of an honorary brigadier. The rank of IOs was changed to Viceroy Commissioned Officers (VCOs).[6]

Concurrently, an annual entry to Sandhurst of 10 Indian cadets was granted for the duration of the war. Their selection was restricted to leading families of martial races and of high social standing.[7] The third step was establishing a Temporary School for Indian Cadets (TSIC) at the Daly College in Indore in 1918, with the aim of training Indians for an officer's commission and those who qualified were referred to as the Indore Commission. The majority were from the landed aristocracy, and those with a long-standing family history of military service.

Muhammad Akbar Khan (PA-1), 11th/12th Cavalry and RIASC. (Author's Collection)

Muhammad Ali Jinnah, Member from Bombay Central Legislative Assembly, 1926. (Author's Collection)

Faiz Muhammad, first Indian officer commissioned into 16th Light Cavalry. (Author's Collection)

Thirty-three were granted a temporary commission in 1919 including Abdur Rahim Khan (Guides) and Muhammad Ali Khan Hoti (9/10th Cavalry), both from the Swabi area of Khyber-Pukhtunkhwa (KPK). Malik Gulsher Khan Noon and Malik Mohammed Munir Khan Tiwana joined 18/19th Lancers and Muhammad Akbar Khan, who had served in the ranks and was commissioned into 11/12th Cavalry. He ultimately transferred to the Royal Indian Army Service Corps (RIASC), and commanded an animal transport company with Force K6 in France during the early stages of the Second World War.[8] At Independence he was a major general and the most senior officer in the Pakistan Army.

The Sandhurst Commissioned Indian Officer

From the large number of applicants for entry into Sandhurst, only five were accepted for the Spring Course of 1919. Syed Iskander Ali Mirza, a great grandson of Nawab Nazim Feradun Jah, the last Nawab of Bengal was the only one to qualify from the first batch of five. After commissioning, Indian officers were to spend a probationary year with a British battalion. However since Mirza would be on an equal basis with his British counterparts in the battalion and commanding British troops, it caused uproar. After a debate of six months, Mirza was able to join a British battalion and was subsequently accepted by 17th Poona Horse. However after four years he transferred to the IPS.[9]

From the early days of Indianisation, there were racial, cultural, and political tensions between the British and Indian officers. Some tensions were the result of Indian officers receiving less pay but a greater source was discrimination. Justifying why he commuted the sentences of three officers of the Indian National Army after the Second World War, Field Marshal Auchinleck reminded British officers that:

> They forget, if they ever knew, the great bitterness bred in the minds of many Indian officers in the early days of 'Indianisation' by the discrimination, often very real, exercised against them, and the discourteous, contemptuous treatment meted out to them by many British officers who should have known better.[10][11]

One of the more visible forms was not allowing Indian officers membership of the club; but it was in the mess which had an exclusively British environment that where they were made aware that their race was inferior. Consequently, in the early days of Indianisation, many Indian officers spent as little time in the mess as possible.

There was no clear policy on Indianisation, and it was a slow and laborious process. The results of the early cadets sent to Sandhurst was not promising and it was decided to establish feeder institutions like the Prince of Wales Royal Indian Military College (RIMC). The first formal step towards Indianisation was taken on the recommendations of the Shea Committee, and an 'Eight Unit Scheme of Indianisation'

Iftikhar Khan as a captain in 7th Light Cavalry. (Author's Collection)

Shahid Hamid in the Full Dress Order of 3rd Cavalry. Notable is his uniform including a khaki kurta, gold sword belt and cross belt with pouch. (Author's Collection)

was announced in 1923.[12] Indian officers could only be posted to six infantry battalions and two cavalry regiments – 7th and 16th Light Cavalry. 3rd Cavalry was Indianised nine years later. These were the least attractive regiments for British officers to serve in for a variety of reasons and with no royal patronage carried an unofficial title of 'Nobody's Own'.[13] One of the principal exponents for more rapid Indianisation was Muhammad Ali Jinnah who vehemently criticised the government for failing to fulfil its recent promises. On his recommendation, the government appointed an Indian Sandhurst Committee and Jinnah was appointed as the chairman of a sub-committee that toured England, France, Canada and the USA to study at first hand their military training institutions and the system of education for admission to military colleges.

Sahibzada Faiz Muhammad Khan was one of the first Indian officers accepted by 16th Light Cavalry in 1923.[14] He was nominated for Sandhurst by his uncle Nawab Ahmed Ali Khan of Maleer Kotla. Like Iskander Mirza, he transferred to the IPS and served in the Frontier Province. The trickle of officers into the Indian cavalry continued with two sons of Sir HD amongst the first batch from RIMC commissioned

from Sandhurst. Ahmed Jan was commissioned in 1927 and joined 7th Light Cavalry while Khalid Jan was commissioned a year later into 16th Light Cavalry.[15] He joined Khairuddin Muhammad (K.M.) Idris, commissioned earlier in 1925, who was from the aristocracy of

A group of five Muslim cadets at Sandhurst, July 1920. Sitting, from left to right: Nawab Sarwar Ali Khan, Sahibzada Iskander Ali Mirza (Poona Horse), and Idris Yousaf Ali (20th Lancers). Standing, left to right: Sardar Muhammad Nawaz Khan, Sahibzada Faiz Muhammad Khan (16th Light Cavalry, PA-2)

Hyderabad State. Raja Hyder Zaman Khan from the Ghakkar clan passed out in 1928 and was commissioned into 7th Light Cavalry but he transferred to the reserve list in 1930.

The results of Indian officers commissioned from Sandhurst gradually improved with around 50 percent graduating, but in 1927 there were only 44 Indians serving within an officer corps of 3,600. In 1929, a commission was granted to Mohammad Yusuf, an Afridi Pathan and the son of Khan Bahadur Sharbat Khan, a member of the Baluchistan Political Service. Yusuf was accepted by 7th Light Cavalry and was an extremely capable and keen horseman, and the first Indian to be awarded a distinction by the Army Equitation School at Saugor.[16] Seven months later, Muhammad Iftikhar Khan a Minhas Rajput from Chakwal, was also accepted by the regiment.[17] His father, Khan Bahadur Risaldar Major Raja Fazal Dad Khan was a man of means who owned large tracts of land.[18] 7th Light Cavalry was the most expensive of the Indianised cavalry regiments and attracted scions of the princely families like 'Bhayya' of Cooch Bihar, and Dinkie Rajwade of Gwalior. When D.K. Palit applied for a posting to the cavalry from IMA, he was warned by his father against 7th Light Cavalry because 'the officers were a high living lot with fat allowances from home'.[19] Two more Muslim officers were commissioned into the cavalry in 1932/1933; 'Tommy' Masud Khan[20] was posted to the 7th Light Cavalry and Nawab Agha Khan (N.A.K.) Raza also known as 'Windy' Raza was posted to the 3rd Cavalry.[21] It was a tradition in the British Army, and replicated in the Army in India to use nicknames to address officers within the regiment both on and off parade.

It was not a smooth sailing for some of the Indian officers who joined the cavalry. Nawabzada Sher Ali Khan, the son of Nawab Ibrahim Ali Khan and Syed Shahid Hamid were from one of the last batches of Indians commissioned from Sandhurst in 1933/1934. They both ultimately left the cavalry for different reasons. Shahid Hamid was not comfortable serving in 3rd Cavalry, which according to him was 'an unhappy regiment' in which the regimental bond was not strong. The British officers were unhappy about their regiment being Indianised and resented the presence of the natives. After five years Shahid he requested a transfer and was attached to the RIASC. Unlike Shahid Hamid, Sher Ali's remembers his initial tenure of six years with 7th Light Cavalry as the happiest years of his career. In the middle of 1943, he was posted back from staff to command a squadron in 7th Light Cavalry in Burma. However, the history of the 7th Light Cavalry records that its Indian officers were posted out at short notice during the Imphal Campaign due to 'the INA episode and unjustified British fears about tank crews deserting to the Japanese with their AFVs'. The officers included Sher Ali as well as Muhammad Yusuf, another of the Indian squadron commanders.

IMA Dehradun and the Indian Commissioned Officers

The Indian Military Academy (IMA) was inaugurated in the autumn of 1932 and a new class of officers known as the Indian Commissioned Officers (ICOs) was introduced to the Army. The ICOs entered only three arms – cavalry, infantry, and engineers. No ICOs were permitted to serve in the artillery regiments and there was no direct entry into the Supply or Ordnance Corps. The corps' of Signals and Electrical and Mechanical Engineers had not yet been born.[22] The alumni of the first batch to pass out of Dehradun in December 1934, are known as the Pioneers, and amongst them was Haji Iftikhar Ahmad who had studied at RIMC, and was commissioned into the 3rd Cavalry.[23] In spite of initial prejudice against the ICOs, the IMA scheme was a great success. In 1938, a government committee reviewing the performance of the IMA cadets over the past six years was of the opinion that 'the young officers from the Indian Military Academy were considered

… to be better trained than the average product of Sandhurst. Their tactical training was thorough, and of a very high order'.[24]

The batches commissioned from IMA comprised of only 45 cadets, and entrants to the cavalry were selected from the top few. Since aspirants for the cavalry had to be 'men of means', a review of the Muslim officers entering the cavalry reads like a 'who's who' of the prominent Muslim (and possibly well-to-do) families in British India. Amongst the early ones who followed Haji Iftikhar into the cavalry were Mirza Masood Ali (Hesky) Baig, and his younger brother Mirza Sikander (Sikku) Ali Baig who were the grandsons of Sir Afsarul Mulk, C-in-C Hyderabad Army. Hesky was an outstanding cadet, who was awarded the Sword of Honour and was commissioned into the 7th Light Cavalry. His brother Sikku, was also awarded the gold medal for academics and commissioned into 16th Light Cavalry. He joined Muhammad Afzal Khan who was one of the younger brothers of Iftikhar Khan and was followed by Sardar Shaukat Hayat Khan, the eldest son of Sir Sikandar Hayat Khan, the famous statesman from the Punjab.

On the advent of the Second World War, all units of the Indian Army (less the Ghurkha Brigade) threw open their doors to Indian officers. In August 1940, Sardar Hissam Mahmud el Effendi, a recipient of the Sword of Honour was the first ICO to be accepted by, 'a very elitist and exclusive group of officers for which 11th Cavalry was well known in the Indian Army'.[25] He was of Afghan ancestry, and a grandson of Sardar Ayub Khan who defeated the British at the Battle of Maiwand during the Second Afghan War.[26] [27] Sahabzada Yaqub Khan a Rohilla Pathan who was the son of Sahabzada Sir Abdus Samad Khan Bahadur, a statesman and diplomat, joined the 18th Cavalry which was mobilising for North Africa. Three officers were commissioned into the cavalry from the last regular courses before IMA changed over to the large-scale 'manufacture' of Emergency Commissioned Officers (ECOs). Muhammad Asghar Khan, was commissioned into the 18th Cavalry, Nawabzada Abdul Ghafoor Khan a Yusufzai Pathan from the landed family of Hoti Mardan was commissioned into the 6th Lancers, and Sidi Muhammad Mustapha Khan from the princely lineage of the Hyderabad State, was commissioned into Probyn's Horse.

The Second World War and the Indian Emergency Commissioned Officers

In October 1939, the strength of the Indian armed forces was around 352,000. A year and a half later, a major programme of expansion was initiated and by the end of 1941, the size of the army had nearly tripled to 900,000. To meet the increased demand for officers, a large number of British Emergency Commissioned Officers were inducted. However, there was a severe shortage of Indian officers. Through the first 16 regular courses that passed out of IMA, by May 1941 only 524 officers had been commissioned for the entire Indian Army. When 17th Poona Horse sailed for Iraq in November 1941, it had 17 British officers, but not a single Indian. 18th Cavalry was no better off when it arrived in North Africa with Sahabzada Yaqub as the only Indian officer.[28] [29] Only the Indianised regiments had a sizable number but when hostilities commenced, their officers were spread more evenly within the other cavalry regiments.

To meet the unprecedented demand for officers, the army started a short service scheme with courses of six-month duration run at IMA and three Officers Training Schools (OTS). After completing 16 weeks of basic military training the cadets transferred to the Armoured Corps OTS (ACOTS) for eight weeks of special arm training and were then commissioned as Indian Emergency Commissioned Officers (IECO).[30] Over 3,000 Indians were commissioned and enabled the army to meet the unprecedented demand. Hazur Ahmed Khan was

Sardar Shaukat Hayat, 16th Light Cavalry and Skinner's Horse. (Author's Collection)

Officers of the CIH in Greece in 1945. From left to right: Gussy Hyder, Maharaja of Jaipur and Zorawar Singh, who commanded CIH during the Kashmir Operations, 1947-1948. (Author's Collection)

Raja Ghulam Murteza, 19th Lancers. (Author's Collection)

Khan Bahadur Sardar Moghal Baz Khan, the Guides. Father of Jahanzeb Khan. (Author's Collection)

a Rajput from the small princely state of Pataudi and joined Skinner's Horse. In 1944, his regiment joined 10th Indian Division in Italy and within a few months, while leading a rifle troop Hazur earned a MC. In 1941, Raja Ghazi ud din 'Gussy' Hyder, a Lehri Ghakkar, followed his father Honorary Captain Raja Ali Hyder into Central India Horse (CIH). He was one of the only three Indian officers with the regiment and served with it through the entire campaign in North Africa and Italy.[31] A number of IECOs from the North West Frontier Province (NWFP) were also commissioned into the cavalry. Jehanzeb Khan, an Afridi whose father was the famous Risaldar Moghal Baz Khan of the Guides, was fortunate that the war broke down barriers of entry and he could join a regiment in which his family had served since its raising in 1846. Muhammad Umar Khan was commissioned into 2nd Lancers where two generations before him had served his father Risaldar Major Akhtar Munir and his grandfather Risaldar Major, Khan Bahadur Sher Baz.

The high demand for Indian officers during the Second World War also opened the door for a more rapid induction from the ranks. Previously soldiers selected for IMA attended a preparatory course at the Kitchener College but were now sent directly to one of the OTSs after an interview. Another avenue for commission into the Indian Army was through a Boys Scheme that enrolled young lads of 15 to 16 years for entry into the ranks with the better ones aspiring for a commission. Pir Abdullah Shah, a Pathan from Kohat, who joined a Boys Regiment of the Indian Armoured Corps in Lucknow in 1943, and was commissioned into Scinde Horse in which his father Risaldar Altaf Hussain Shah had served.

A number of Muslim officers fought with the 7th Light Cavalry including Nawab Khawaja Hassan Askari who was the son of Nawab Habibullah Bahadur, the Nawab of Dacca. He was commissioned in 1942, and fought in the Battle of Imphal/Kohima in 1944 during which he was seriously injured. Hesky Baig also fought with the 7th Light Cavalry in the counteroffensive by the Fourteenth Army in Burma during which Sahibzada Sidi Mustapha and Riazul Karim

Hashim Ali Khan, 16th Light Cavalry. (Author's Collection)

TO INDIAN SOLDIERS!

All Indians in our Greater East Asia Co-prosperity Sphere are now combined and marching for India's freedom. Inspite of British oppression, the independence movement is progressing in all parts of India. They are fighting for the establishment of India for Indians. Now you are at the point of choosing slavery or freedom for India.

Don't be a tool in the hands of the English. Kill English officers and come to our side. We heartily welcome you as a comrade of Asia.

A Japanese propaganda leaflet urging Indians to fight for India's freedom. (Author's Collection)

were in combat with Probyn's Horse at Meiktila and onwards till Rangoon. Riazul Karim distinguished himself during the intense battle at Meiktila and as a temporary captain, was awarded with the Military Cross. A number of Muslim officers also fought with 16th Light Cavalry, which arrived in Burma from Quetta with much fanfare created by its Co, Lieutenant Colonel J.N. Caudhuri (who ultimately became Chief of Army Staff of the Indian Army). He ensured that the progress of the move of the regiment to Burma regularly appeared in the newspapers.[32] The senior most Muslim officer was N.A.K. Raza who had luckily been away from the 3rd Cavalry when it sailed to Singapore, and surrendered to the Japanese. Amongst the others were Nawab Abdul Ghafoor Khan Hoti from the landed family of Mardan and Hasham Ali Khan a Kaim Khani who was commissioned in 1943.

There was a sprinkling of Christian officers in the armoured corps during the Second World War who opted for Pakistan. Mervyn Cardoza was commissioned in 1944 into 13th Lancers, and Anthony (Tony) Albert Lumb commanded a troop in the Royal Deccan Horse during the Battle of Meiktila. S.R.C. Daniels fought with the 11th Cavalry ahead of Meiktila in the advance to Rangoon.

In the early stages of the Second World War, it was not unusual to find Indian officers commanding squadrons in the three regiments that had been Indianised. In 1940, except for the commanding officer all the other 18 officers in 7th Light Cavalry were Indian.[33] 3rd Cavalry had nine Indian officers out of 23 when it embarked for Malaya in December 1941 with Indian captains commanding two of its squadrons. However, with the rapid expansion and the raising of

wartime formations, most of the KCIOs and ICOs were posted on staff or training establishments where their seniority and experience was greatly needed.[34] Consequently, during the war only a small percentage of Indian officers had an opportunity of commanding sabre squadrons. In spite of the fact that a large number of officers were inducted into the corps, the numbers on active operations actually decreased. Whether it was policy, prejudice or caution, the paucity of Indian squadron commanders resulted in a woeful lack of battle experience in the armoured regiments of both India and Pakistan at the time of Independence.[35]

The end of the War brought about large-scale demobilisation and appointments of squadron commanders and adjutants hitherto held mostly by British officers, opened up to Indians. It also created opportunities for Indians to command units. While there were a number of Indians who commanded infantry battalions during the Second World War (Sher Ali was one of them), J.N. Chauduri was the only Indian to command an armoured regiment. However soon after the war, Iftikhar Khan was also given command of 7th Light Cavalry in Japan where it was part of the Allied Occupation Force.[36] K.M. Idris commanded 3rd Cavalry at Rawalpindi and Mohammad Yusuf commanded 18th Cavalry when it was part of the Punjab Boundary Force (PBF). The history of the 18th Cavalry records that Yusuf was 'extremely popular amongst all ranks and it was unfortunate that Partition deprived the regiment of his services.'[37]

4

TWILIGHT YEARS AND THE GREAT DIVIDE

At the end of the Second World War, some regiments of the IAC performed similar occupation duties as the Indian Cavalry had done in the Middle East at the end of the First World War.[1] It included some bitter fighting against the Indonesian Nationalists which the Indian troops – particularly the Muslims – resented. However, the bulk of the

armoured regiments returned from the combat theatres to three main garrisons in India – Secunderabad, Ahmednagar, and Risalpur. Except for the regiments on active duty in the Northwest Frontier Province, the post-war IAC was supposed to be an all track force equipped with war surplus left by the Americans in India.[2] Unfortunately, the large-scale demobilisation of officers and soldiers after the war was a setback to the combat efficiency of the corps after independence. The task of dividing the army was accomplished in less than three months, and made possible with the spirit of camaraderie and goodwill that existed amongst all ranks.[3] In the turbulent times that followed Independence, it is admirable how the regiments and the relatively inexperienced officers of the fledging Pakistan Armoured Corps simultaneously dealt with a multitude of crises and tasks, and yet in a few years moulded the corps into a credible force.

A Sherman of the 13th Lancers during the street fighting in Surabaya, November 1945. (Author's Collection)

The Closing Stages of the Second World War

As the Second World War wound down, most of the armoured regiments were not only spread from Italy to Burma, but some went even further. The 13th Lancers, which had moved back from the Middle East in June 1945 (while the war in the Far East was still in progress), was assigned to participate in Operation ZIPPER, an amphibious landing on the Malayan coast behind Japanese lines. With the Japanese surrender in August, only the regimental headquarters with one squadron landed in the Straits of Malacca as part of the occupation force.[4] The landing was a disaster due to the muddy sub-soil just below the sand on the landing beach. Innumerable gullies criss-crossed the beach and a shallow sand bar ran parallel to it. As a result, over 300 submerged heavy vehicles were spread up to a mile offshore as well as many stranded landing craft. At a speech by Lord Mountbatten in Singapore announcing the landing, Sher Ali heard General Slim murmur, 'They are all bloody well sinking in the mud on those bloody muddy beaches'. One of the officers in the landing was Zia ul Haq who was saved from drowning by a VCO.[5]

The next operation was even further east and was a lot more dangerous. There was an urgent requirement to despatch troops to take charge of the Dutch East Indies (Indonesia), and repatriate thousands of mostly Dutch civilians interned by the Japanese. Indonesians, declaring Independence from the Dutch, complicated the situation and mobs were on the rampage. A brigade, which initially landed at Surabaya, lost the brigade commander, 17 officers, and 374 men within a space of three days. A semblance of order had to be re-instated through a full-scale military operation, and two Indian divisions were despatched to Indonesia supported by 11th Cavalry and 13th Lancers. 11th Cavalry had moved to Secunderabad after the capture of Rangoon, but then re-shipped to Malaya. The regiment was scattered from Taiping to Malacca when it was ordered, at zero minutes' notice to proceed to Java.[6] Both regiments were equipped with relatively unused surplus US equipment: 11th Cavalry with the latest variant of Stuart tanks and 13th Lancers with Shermans.[7]

The 11th Cavalry landed with the leading elements of 5th Indian Division at three sites along the coast of Java. Since the Indonesians opposing them were armed with Japanese weapons, the situation was highly charged and dangerous. The worst of the fighting was in Surabaya where 'B' Squadron was involved in street fighting, and clearing

Stuart light tanks of the 11th Cavalry during an internal security operation in Surabaya, November 1945. (Author's Collection)

Aftermath of the disastrous seaborne landing in Malaya, in which General Zia ul-Haq nearly drowned. (Courtesy britishempire.co.uk)

roadblocks. In the initial days of battle, the squadron destroyed or captured an assortment of armoured vehicles used by the Indonesians including a Japanese tank.[8] The squadrons rescued and transported 6,000 Dutch internees to the coast through blood-thirsty mobs who killed and mutilated every Dutch, British or Indian falling into their hands. Ironically, Japanese soldiers were not disarmed and assisted in the escort and evacuation.[9] 'A' Squadron had a particularly difficult task of clearing one roadblock after another, on the way into the interior as well as the way out. As the resistance in Surabaya intensified, 'C' Squadron also moved into the city, and finally 13th Lancers with their Shermans arrived in November 1945. The city was ultimately cleared (in what was subsequently referred to as the Battle of Surabaya), through a systematic operation by an infantry brigade, and tanks of 11th Cavalry and 13th Lancers. Despite fanatical resistance, half of the city was secured in three days, and the fighting was over in three weeks. While these battle-hardened regiments performed extremely well, the Indian troops questioned their commanding officers about their purpose of being in Indonesia.[10] Some Indian officers told their British commanders that, 'We have nothing in common with the Dutch. We have everything in common with the Indonesians. Further the Dutch call us niggers'.[11] Zia ul Haq who had accompanied 13th Lancers to Indonesia, told the VCOs that as Muslims they should not fight the Indonesians who were their brothers. This was reported and the same afternoon the officer was returned to India on an adverse report.[12] By February 1946, the situation had largely stabilised in the Dutch East Indies, and 11th Cavalry returned to India in May (having handed over all its equipment to the Dutch forces), followed by 13th Lancers in August. Both the regiments joined the 1st Armoured Division in Secunderabad.

The Post-War Indian Armoured Corps

The post-war IAC was organized into an armoured division with an armoured and lorried brigade, and two independent armoured brigades. Ten tank regiments formed part of these formations while seven were retained as light regiments.[13] (The 3rd Cavalry was not

included in this total because following the war it was re-raised as an airborne reconnaissance regiment.) The 13th Lancers joined the 1st Armoured Brigade (under the 1st Armoured Division) at Secunderabad and 11th Cavalry became the reconnaissance regiment of the division. With so much surplus war material available, 11th Cavalry was also equipped with Sherman IIIs. Probyn's Horse had moved back to Meiktila in November 1945 after the fall of Rangoon with orders to remain in Burma for two years as part of the occupation force. However, in January 1946, it returned to India and joined the 1st Armoured Brigade at Secunderabad.[14] The Guides had returned from Persia in November 1943, converted into an armoured car regiment, and was based at Kohat with its squadrons deployed in Waziristan. It remained in the Frontier for two years though it was very keen to get to the fighting in Burma. Finally, in 1945, it handed its vehicles to 6th Lancers and moved to Jhansi with the role of the reconnaissance regiment with 8th Indian Division. The division was earmarked for operations against the Japanese in Malaysia (if the war had not ended), and the Guides were ecstatic with the equipment issued.[15] However, with the war suddenly over, the Guides moved to the 2nd Indian Armoured Brigade at Ahmednagar, and was unfortunate to be issued with Churchill tanks. Even before the war ended, the Churchill was obsolete, but the British had transferred three regiments of this tank to the Indian Armoured Corps.[16]

The 3rd Independent Armoured Brigade, with the honours bestowed on it by Slim's Fourteenth Army, was stationed in Risalpur, and 19th Lancers along with its Shermans that had fought in the Arakan, and then landed by ship for the capture of Rangoon, joined the brigade, but a squadron was sent on Frontier duties to Mir Ali. Of the regiments that subsequently came to the share of Pakistan, 6th Lancers was the only one which did not join an armoured formation. On its return from Italy it relieved the Guides at Kohat, and took over their Humber armoured cars as well as the role of policing the Frontier.

With the reorganization of the combat formations and units, the training establishments also underwent a change. Back in 1937, cavalry regiments were organized into three administrative groups, with one regiment in each group permanently allocated the role of a training depot. These three (unlucky) regiments, which became the training depot, were 12th Cavalry at Ferozepur, 15th Lancers at Jhansi, and 20th Lancers at Lucknow.[17] While there is no documented reason for selecting these three, like the regiments earmarked for Indianization (3rd, 7th Light and 16th Light Cavalry), the ones converted to training regiments had no royal title or patronage, and therefore the least influence. At the outset of the war, these regiments were absorbed into three Armoured Corps Training Centres, which only provided basic training of recruits. The training for the 'trades' of gunner, radio operator, and drivers were conducted by the regiments. Obviously once the regiments went overseas, they could not continue with trade training, and trained manpower was 'milked' from the regiments still in India. This system could not last – the casualties placed an increasing demand and ultimately there were more regiments overseas than in India. After the visit of Major General Martel in 1942, the basic training of all the recruits was concentrated at Lucknow. The centre at Ferozepur provided trade training for those earmarked for armoured car regiments, and the one at Babina for the tank regiments. At the end of the war, the school at Ferozepur closed down and trade training for all types of AFVs was centralised at Babina.[18] From when the Indian cavalry commenced mechanization, the training of officers and VCO/NCO instructors had been organized at the Armoured Fighting Vehicle School, which had existed at Ahmednagar since 1938. With certain modifications and expansion, this school continued until after the war when it was re-designated as the Armoured Corps School.

Since it had mechanized seven years ago, the Indian cavalry had transformed into an experienced force that had fought from Rome to Rangoon. Sadly, neither Pakistan nor India inherited the battle-hardened organization that symbolised the corps at the closing stages of the Second World War. There

Daimler armoured cars of the Guides at the Hartley Lines in Kohat, 1950. (Author's Collection)

The mess silver being returned to 19th Lancers in 1952. (Author's Collection)

were a number of factors responsible for a degeneration of the corps. For a start, during the war, the leadership in the corps (down to nearly all the squadron commanders) was British, and when they chose to depart, it created a serious vacuum. With the demobilisation of the British emergency commissioned officers, this vacuum extended even down to the level of the troop leaders. 'Therefore the efficiency of units dropped considerably as British officers left on premature retirement, and Muslim officers' interest in the Indian Army visibly decreased with the prospect of forming their own service in Pakistan.'[19] To address the deficiency in officers, the British granted a short service commission to selected VCOs. However, the deserving cases had already been commissioned during the war, and those who subsequently became officers did not do particularly well. Most were too old for service in

an armoured regiment, and limited in their capabilities.[20] Wartime establishment was considerably larger and when the British India Army reverted to peacetime establishments, the rank and file was also seriously affected. Many experienced soldiers retired and the remaining were provided the option of signing up for a year at a time. Some good soldiers opted for release rather than serve on in a state of uncertainty. As the large number of establishments (headquarters, static units, etc.) folded up at the end of the war, VCOs and NCOs reverted to the regiments displacing those with temporary wartime promotions. Instead of being demoted, the combat experienced VCOs and NCOs chose to retire.[21] The IAC was steadily losing its cutting edge.

If there was a problem with its leadership and manpower, the

Vehicles of the 3rd Armoured Brigade during an exercise near Peshawar, 1946. (Author's Collection)

The Q Command's ACV Juliet, along with the vehicles of the headquarters of the 3rd Armoured Brigade during an inspection at Risalpur, 1946. (Author's Collection)

armoured corps also had a problem with equipment. Though now much better equipped than it had ever been during the war, a lot of the equipment was war surplus from combat theatres, and had undergone extensive wear and tear. 19th Lancers, which joined 3rd Independent Armoured Brigade at Risalpur before Independence brought with it the same Shermans that it had fought with in Burma. The tanks that Poona Horse handed over to 13th Lancers at Risalpur had also seen extensive service in Burma with the Dragoon Guards, and even Poona Horse had to put in some heavy and careful maintenance to get them in a fit state.[22] However, Z.A. Khan who joined 13th Lancers in 1951 levelled a serious allegation against Poona Horse and states: '...the tanks and vehicles were found to have been sabotaged by the Poona Horse by putting sugar in the petrol tanks and destroying all the

batteries before leaving for India. The tanks were overhauled, but were never reliable again'.[23] So severe was the damage that for nearly two years 13th Lancers could field only one squadron until new tanks were found for them.[24] 19th Lancers, which was based in Peshawar, had a similar complaint. The Sikh squadron before departing sabotaged the equipment by also mixing sugar in the petrol tanks of AFVs and the other vehicles.[25] When the Guides Cavalry took over the Daimler Armoured Cars from Skinner's Horse in Dera Ismail Khan, they found to their dismay that 'Skinners had played extremely dirty by sabotaging all the armoured cars and vehicles. They left these in terrible unserviceable condition, lying all over Waziristan'.[26] A severe shortage of spares made things worse. The crews had to move the batteries from one armoured car to the next to start them, and telephone cables were used as a substitute for fan belts.[27]

At the time of Independence, the Indians believed that the British had been partial to Pakistan by allotting it regiments that were both wealthier and with more combat service. The reason they cited for this partiality was that Pakistan had inducted a large number of British officers to serve in its army after Independence.[28] While it is not possible to carry out a comparative assessment across the divide of which regiments were wealthier, with their large estates Skinner's and Probyn's Horse were both well off, but then they landed up on the opposite sides of the 'divide'.[29] In 1946, Probyn's Horse had Rs. 150,000 in a private fund and received Rs. 31,000 annually from its farm at Probynabad. Probyn's Horse also had a large collection of silver which in 1946 was valued at Rs.65,000 for insurance.[30] Certainly 13th Lancers was one of the wealthiest with a trust fund held by the Imperial Bank of India consisting of the princely sum of Rs. 750,000. 13th Lancer's newsletter of December 1947 provides details of a plan to manage/distribute the trust fund after Independence that would have resulted in the regiment receiving a pittance. It actually received 55 percent of the income which ceased after the 1965 War with India'.[31] While there is no information available on the funds held with 19th Lancers, the regiment did have a substantial Sterling account in the UK which was used to purchase items of uniform like peak caps and 'wangee' canes from Bernard Weatherill, Tailors and Outfitters in London.[32][33]

19th Lancers also had a large collection of silver, but based on a vote dominated by British officers at a mess meeting in Peshawar, the regiment's silver was taken to the UK.[34] However, a wily mess daffadar, after informing the Pakistani officers of the regiment, concealed some of the silver before the bulk was transported.[35] The transfer of the silver was brought to the notice of the C-in-C, General Gracey by Wajahat Hussain, his ADC from 19th Lancers.

The retired Major-General Sir Frederick Gwatkin (ex-18th Tiwana Lancers) presented the silver to the regiment at a parade held for the occasion.[36] Not all the silver was returned, and three of the

A Humber armoured car of the 6th Lancers (element of the 9 (F) Division) as seen during the Republic Day Parade at Peshawar, in 1949. (Author's Collection)

5th Battalion of the Frontier Force Rifles (10th Frontier Force Battalion) in 15cwt 4x2 trucks: they were the 'lorried infantry' under the command of the 3rd Armoured Brigade in 1949, and based in Nowshera. (Author's Collection)

largest pieces remain in possession of the Cavalry and Guards Club in London, the Royal Military Academy at Sandhurst and the Staff College at Camberley.[37]

If a comparison of theatre and battle honours forms the basis for the assertion that the six regiments allotted to Pakistan had more combat experience, there is admittedly a huge difference. These six regiments had 60 theatre and battle honours compared to 46 of the 12 Indian regiments. However, many regiments allotted to India were no less combat-hardened. 7th and 16th Light Cavalry, 8th Cavalry and Deccan Horse participated in the Burma Campaign; Skinner's Horse, and CIH fought against Italians in East Africa and then battled their way up the Italian Peninsula. Both 2nd Lancers and 18th Cavalry did

Table 1: Pre-Independence Composition of Squadrons in Armoured Regiments allotted to Pakistan

Regiments	Kamim Khanis	Pathans	Punjabi Muslims	Sikhs	Hindu Dogras	Hindu Jats
13th Lancers	1	1		1		
The Guides		1		1	1	
11th Cavalry	1		1	1		
Probyn's Horse			1	1	1	
6th Lancers			1	1		1
19th Lancers			1	1		1
Total 18 squadrons	**2**	**2**	**4**	**6**	**2**	**2**

exceptionally well during the two encounters that the 3rd Indian Motor Brigade had with the Afrika Korps. Only three regiments, Hodson's Horse, Scinde Horse, and Poona Horse remained relatively inactive in the Middle East, but then so did two of the six regiments allotted to Pakistan. 3rd Cavalry was re-raised after the Second World War and could therefore fall in the same category as those regiments which had no battle experience. The Guides and 13th Lancers did not take part in any major operation except for a short spell in North Africa during the Battle of Ghazala and withdrawal to El-Alamein, and what (in the larger perspective of the Second World War), amounted to some skirmishes in Iraq, Syria and Persia. In the post-Independence scenario, the real issue was less to do with battle honours; and how many of the regiments on both sides had combat experience, but more to do with the nature of this experience and the type of equipment with which they fought. During the Second World War, only six Indian regiments fought with medium tanks and that too during the Burma Campaign where armour was employed mostly in support of the infantry in half-squadrons and tank troops. Nearly all the other regiments at the conclusion of the war were either reconnaissance regiments (with armoured cars) or light tank regiments (with Stuart tanks), which were also employed in a quasi-reconnaissance role. The regiments had operated in four different theatres – Italy, North Africa, West Asia, and Burma. There was a marked contrast in the characteristics of each theatre, where through trial and error forces developed their own doctrine; and what was relevant to the operations in Italy was irrelevant to Burma. Thus in the post-war phase, from the perspective of doctrine and training, there was probably a great deal of variation and irrelevance which continued after Independence.

The Great Divide and the March to Freedom

After the visit of the Cabinet Mission to India in 1946, there was a general realisation by British and Indian officers that a system which had lasted for almost a century, was going to change altogether. British officers in the armoured regiments felt that they had to organize one last celebration (before they finally relinquished control) which took the form of a reunion or a regimental day celebrated by some on a grander scale than usual.[38] The celebrations for Gauche Wood Day[39] by 19th Lancers at Peshawar lasted non-stop for 24 hours commencing with a function for ex-servicemen, a dinner and dance at the Peshawar Club for over a thousand guests, and that ended with a champagne breakfast the next morning. The Peshawar Valley Hunt, a mounted parade, a beer party, and a late lunch followed this.[40] The cause of so lavish a celebration may well have been the fact that the Post-war Reorganization Committee for the Indian Army had recommended a reduction in strength of the cavalry regiments, and as the junior-most regiment, 19th Lancers faced disbandment.[41 42] The

Guides Cavalry at Ahmednagar had the occasion to celebrate a more auspicious occasion – their centenary. The festivities lasted for four days, but unlike those of 19th Lancers, they were less lavish because the regiment was shifting to Kohat, and centred more on the troops and the pensioners.[43 44]

When Lord Mountbatten announced the date for the 'partition' of the sub-continent, the C-in-C, Field Marshal Sir Claude Auchinleck, and his staff produced the plan for the division of the army based on a ratio of two to one. The British officers looked at this 'partition' with great sadness, and termed it as the Great Divide.[45] A committee under Major General Irwin had the delicate task of allotting the regiments.[46] There were 19 Muslim squadrons in the 18 regiments of the armoured corps, but only eight Muslim squadrons in the six regiments earmarked for Pakistan. Consequently, 10 non-Muslim squadrons from Pakistani regiments and 11 Muslim squadrons from Indian regiments had to be transferred.[47]

The Irwin Committee applied a simple principle to the task of selecting the regiments; the ethno-religious preponderance within each regiment would determine its allocation to either India or Pakistan, in accordance with the communal majorities of each country.[48] However, there were complications to applying this simple principle. Thus, only two regiments allotted to Pakistan had two Muslim squadrons each – 11th Cavalry and 13th Lancers. The remaining – namely Probyn's Horse, 6th Lancers, the Guides, and 19th Lancers – had just one. Therefore, the allocation of regiments was probably based on a combination of other factors. It would have been inappropriate to allot regiments to Pakistan whose names were associated with India e.g. Deccan Horse, Poona Horse and Central India Horse. The presence of 6th and 19th Lancers within the boundaries of the new nation may have been a consideration, as also the association of 19th Lancers with the older 18th Tiwana Lancers and the Guides association of over ninety years with the Northwest Frontier Province.[49] It seems that there was some struggle to get the Guides to this side of the border, but the fact that it had already been decided to transfer the Guides Infantry to Pakistan may have further swung the decision in its favour. It was expected that Scinde Horse with two Muslim squadrons would be allotted to Pakistan. According to Brigadier Amir Gulistan Janjua, Randolph Plunkett met Field Marshal Auchinleck and had the decision reversed. Just as the decision to allot Skinner's Horse to India was influenced by its large estate and regimental assets that were located in Hansi in India, similarly it is likely that Probyn's Horse was allotted to Pakistan because of its large farm at Probynabad. Lieutenant Colonel Probyn had established this farm near Okara on 1,200 acres of land.[50] It enjoyed a long excellence in mounts, and reared 2,000 horses, which were sold to the army.[51]

Based upon the agreed distribution of assets between Pakistan and India, detailed lists were prepared in each training establishment by a board comprising of British, Hindu, Sikh, and Muslim officers under the chair of a British officer. It took approximately two months to distribute the training equipment including tanks, and armoured cars as well as the small arms, mess stores, and other equipment and clothing. Pir Abdullah Shah was with the Armoured Corps Training School at Ahmednagar. Under his responsibility, a contingent of over 900 Muslim troops, and their families moved by train from Ahmednagar to embark at Bombay. When the initial trains carrying military personnel and their families were attacked in Punjab, a sea route to Pakistan was adopted under Operation SEA CROSS. Before the train left for Bombay, Indian troops carried out a thorough search for extra weapons that the Pakistani contingent was erroneously reported to be taking. Pir had been authorised to take an official fund of Rs. 10,000 to Pakistan and showed great presence of mind. He placed Captain Qutub ud Din of 13th Lancers under close arrest, and hid the money in his 'small pack'. The Indians wanted to search the officer, but Pir refused because the officer was involved in a serious crime, and no one was allowed to get close to him.[52] This contingent had an uneventful journey to Karachi by sea, but the ones who had gone by train were not so fortunate.

The cantonment at Babina close to Jhansi was a major collection and staging point for personnel and equipment of the armoured corps heading for Pakistan.[53] The Recruits Training Wing was also located at Babina, and commanded by Anthony 'Tony' Albert Lumb, a Christian officer from Deccan Horse, who had opted for Pakistan. He was one of the 400 'Gallians' from Lawrence College, Ghora Gali, who were commissioned into the forces during the Second World War. The training wing had a number of Muslim officers who too had opted for Pakistan including Qamar uz Zaman, Shahzada Alam, and Sahibzada Aitizad ud Din. It took these officers 15 days to divide the equipment and stores of the Wing and load them onto trains. Shahzada Alam was commanding the first train, which was stopped at Delhi for a search. The Pakistani officers refused and warned the Indians that they would fight until the last man and bullet, and destroy the railway station if the Indians attempted to search the train.[54] The general headquarters at Delhi was informed, a British colonel was sent to diffuse the highly charged situation, and the train was allowed to proceed to Pakistan. En route, an attack at a railway station between Rohtak and Hissar was beaten off. An Indian brigadier arrived to control the situation, and the train continued its journey towards Pakistan.[55] Others encountered even worse. Captain Muhammad Aslam Khan was commanding the Ranghar squadron of Scinde Horse that was transferring to 13th Lancers. After the departure of the Guides, this squadron was the only Muslim fighting force left in Ahmednagar, and Aslam along with the Muslim officers of Hodson's Horse, made a secret contingency plan to protect the lives of the families of the Muslims against any threat. Finally, on 10 September 1947, he moved his squadron along with other contingents in a troop train via Delhi to Risalpur. During the journey that took seven days, he witnessed some soul breaking sights, and when the train stopped at Delhi, the platforms were covered with pools of blood of slain Muslims.[56]

After despatching a number of Military Specials loaded with personnel and their families, equipment and stores, Tony Lumb commanded the last train to leave. When the train made an unscheduled stop at Amritsar, the heart of rioting in the Punjab, Tony and another officer got down onto the dark platform to stretch their legs, and saw several Sikhs approaching. As they passed by the other officer whispered, "They're turning." Expecting trouble, they too turned, but instead of trouble, a shout of joy from the Sikhs greeted them. They were officers from Deccan Horse and threw their arms

Major Abhey Singh, 18th Cavalry and Poona Horse. (Author's Collection)

Francis Ingall, commander of the 6th Lancers. (Author's Collection)

round Tony. They thought that he had come to re-join the regiment, which was stationed in Amritsar at the time. Tony had a hard job convincing them that he had opted for Pakistan.[57] Most of the trains that carried military personnel to Pakistan also had a number of carriages loaded with refugees. It was a huge responsibility for the officers in charge of the trains. Some of them had as little as two years of service – like Zia ul-Haq who was in charge of one of the last trains of military personnel and refugees that left Babina for Pakistan.

The Kaim Khani squadron from Poona Horse, which ultimately joined 19th Lancers probably had the most difficult and longest journey to Pakistan. At Independence, Poona Horse was stationed in Risalpur as part of 3rd Independent Armoured Brigade. Even though the Kaim Khanis had opted for India, the harrowing scenes witnessed during the move of Poona Horse from Risalpur to Jhansi, and the widespread communal riots that had engulfed both India and Pakistan, made them apprehensive about their future. Their fears were exacerbated by the fact that most Muslim squadrons had opted for Pakistan. Many of them came to Jhansi to be accommodated en route and on its arrival at Jhansi, Poona Horse organized a Collecting and Despatching Point. At one time it was looking after four of these squadrons.[58] The officers of Poona Horse – and particularly their squadron commander Major Abhey Singh – tried their best to reassure the Kaim Khanis that they and their families would be safe in India but the squadron decided to migrate to Pakistan.[59] Loyal to his squadron until the last, Abhey Singh accompanied it until Amritsar where he bade farewell with tears in his eyes.[60] Muhammad Bashir Khan also accompanied the squadron from Poona and became its squadron commander in 19th Lancers. Every effort was made to get them, and other Kaim Khanis well re-settled across the border, and amongst those who helped was Iskander Mirza, the Defence Secretary who had commanded the Kaim Khani squadron 26 years earlier when he was serving in Poona Horse. Their re-settlement in fairly good areas in Hyderabad, Sind was also largely due to the interest taken by General Frank Messervy, the first C-in-C of the Pakistan Army[61] as well as Major General Millis Jefferies, the Engineer-in-Chief.

There were acts of comradeship from both sides. 3rd Cavalry, which was stationed at Rawalpindi was ordered to leave behind their personal weapons, and ammunition. This order was given by GHQ Pakistan Army in retaliation to similar actions being taken by the Indians. K.M. Idris, the CO of 3rd Cavalry, and Aulia Khan the Risaldar Major, both of whom had opted for Pakistan, realised the dangerous implications of this order, and refused to disarm the squadrons. This was just as well as the train was attacked as soon as it left Rawalpindi and subsequently in its journey through Pakistan, but the regiment got through unscratched.[62] The Sikh squadron of 19th Lancers moved from Peshawar to join Skinner's Horse in India. Their security was a matter of great concern to the regiment, and the operation to get the squadron to safety was carried out with such secrecy that not even the police knew of it.[63] The Punjabi Muslim squadron escorted the Sikh squadron through the Frontier Province, which was seething with hatred for the Sikhs.[64] 6th Lancers did no less with their Sikhs and Jat squadrons transferring to India, 'with one troop of armoured cars under Risaldar Mohammad Yusuf escorting their train all the way from Kohat to Rawalpindi where they were met by their former CO, Lieutenant Colonel Francis Ingall at the railway station'.[65]

Undivided India was a large country and at independence most of the regiments allotted to Pakistan (and the squadrons they were receiving) were spread far and wide. Apart from 6th and 19th Lancers, along with their Muslim squadrons, all the other regiments were located in areas falling to India. Three of the regiments allotted to Pakistan, Probyn's Horse, 11th Cavalry, and 13th Lancers were stationed at Secunderabad under the 1st Armoured Division. Secunderabad was a large military cantonment near Hyderabad Deccan established by the British in 1806, and 2,500 km from the border at Lahore. Having shed its Dogra and Sikh squadrons, Probyn's Horse entrained at Secunderabad in August 1947, and the journey to Lahore took over seven long days. Its Punjabi Muslim squadron from Royal Deccan Horse moved from Ahmednagar under the control of Gustasib Beg. Its Kaim Khani squadron, which transferred from 18th Cavalry, was already located at Risalpur. Probyn's Horse was designated to join the 3rd Independent Armoured Brigade, but was temporarily based in Lahore to assist in maintaining law and order. Its first Pakistani commanding officers were Haji Iftikhar Ahmed followed by the internationally famous polo player M.M.A. 'Hesky' Baig. Brilliant as

he was, Hesky had qualified from the Command and Staff College at Camberley and was at this stage one of the most promising officers in command of a regiment.

11th Cavalry moved to Pakistan with its two Muslim squadrons consisting of a mix of Punjabi Muslims, Pathans, Hindustani Muslims and Ranghars. Its Sikh squadron was replaced by Punjabi Muslims from 3rd Cavalry, and it received personnel from Skinner's Horse, 8th Cavalry, and Deccan Horse. While travelling up-country to Pakistan, the troops were exposed to revolting scenes of communal carnage. At a railway siding in Amritsar, a Sikh mob made a deliberate show for the benefit of the Muslim troops, who watched helplessly as captive Muslim women were violated and butchered.[66] The regiment detrained at Rawalpindi where it came under command of 7th Division and 'Tommy' Masud Khan was appointed as its CO. 13th Lancers also moved from Secunderabad in August 1947 bringing only their personal weapons, regimental stores, and fortunately the entire mess silver. There were only four Indian officers in the regiment and all opted for Pakistan. Cardoza brought the advance party to Risalpur on 20 August 1947, and the main body accompanied by S.H.A. Bokhari and Ishaq, arrived four days later. A large contingent of Punjabi Muslims from Skinner's Horse was brought to the 13th Lancers by Hazur Ahmed Khan, MC, but the officer was subsequently posted to the 19th Lancers. The Ranghar squadron transferring from Scinde Horse did not initially opt for Pakistan as some 50 of its members wanted to remain in India. Two VCOs of the squadron requested Captain Muhammad Aslam Khan, who had recently transferred to the Guides to return to the squadron. Instead of moving with the Guides, Aslam cycled to Scinde Horse, and requested its CO to give him back the command of the squadron.[67] He then persuaded the entire squadron to move to Pakistan, and brought it to 13th Lancers. Shortly after 13th Lancers arrived at Risalpur, a convoy with an officer and an escort were sent to the areas of Rohtak, Hissar, and Gurgaon to evacuate the families of the Ranghars. For the next three years, the regiment had British commanding officers until I.U. 'Bob' Babar took over in 1950 as the first Pakistani commanding officer.

The Guides was part of the 2nd Independent Armoured Brigade at Ahmednagar along with Scinde Horse, and Hodson's Horse. Thus, it was fortunate to collect the Pathan squadron from Scinde Horse, and the Punjabi Muslim squadron from Hodson's Horse, and move en bloc. The journey of 2,300 km to Dera Ismail Khan[68] took 16 traumatic and tragic days, but the regiment arrived unscathed. Less fortunate was an advance party under Major Reid that had departed earlier to take over the lines at Dera Ismail Khan. It was never heard of again. One account states that they were attacked by a Hindu mob somewhere south of Delhi, and when their ammunition ran out, they fought on with their bayonets. Naturally, the British officer fought alongside the men but eventually they were overwhelmed.[69] Its first Pakistani commanding officer was N.A.K. 'Windy' Raza who had been commissioned in January 1932. After a year's customary attachment with a British regiment he had joined 3rd Cavalry in 1933 but was amongst those fortunate in not embarking with the regiment when it sailed for Singapore, and into captivity. While the tanks were being loaded on the ship for Singapore, his hand was crushed under a tank cupola. Windy Raza commanded the Guides for a year and handed over the regiment to Sidi Muhammad Mustapha Khan. 'Musti' as he was fondly known, 'was a fine gentleman, great fun to be with, and very social and lively'.[70] He was very fair and good-looking, and known by the nickname Prince of Wales. His charming wife Mumtaz 'Mumti' was the daughter of Sir Shahnawaz Bhutto, and a stepsister of Zulfiqar Ali Bhutto who would become the Prime Minster of Pakistan after the 1971 War.

The raising the flag of Pakistan on Independence Day in Razmak, 14 August 1947. (NAM)

19th Lancers was one of the two regiments already based within the borders of Pakistan. It was under command the 3rd Independent Armoured Brigade, but located at Peshawar. It absorbed a Punjabi Muslim squadron from Central India Horse, and Muhammad Bashir Khan brought the Kaimkhani squadron from Poona Horse. The Kaim Khani squadron from Poona Horse initially joined Probyn's Horse and later moved to the 19th Lancers. This was the same squadron that Abhey Singh had bid a tearful farewell to at Amritsar. In 1950, its first Pakistani commanding officer, Muhammad Asghar Khan took over from his British predecessor, and commanded the regiment for four years. 6th Lancers was located close to Peshawar at Kohat. It had returned from Italy in May 1945; and stationed in Ferozepur but four months later; it relieved the Guides at Kohat. It exchanged its Jat squadron with the Punjabi Muslim squadron of 7th Light Cavalry. The squadron moved to Jhansi, which was an assembly point for the squadrons of other regiments, and moved to Pakistan under Lieutenant Rahmat Ali Khan.[71] Its other Punjabi Muslim squadron from 8th Cavalry moved from Ahmednagar to Kohat. All three squadrons of 13th Lancers consisted of PMs and the commanding officer Lieutenant Colonel Chauvel drew up one list of the entire rank and file, and reconstituted the three squadrons. It was a wise move since it 'scoured out old prejudices and ensured a fresh Pakistani spirit in the regiment'.[72] In early 1948, the regiment arrived in Sialkot after assisting the army in its withdrawal from Waziristan. Sardar Hissam Mahmud el Effendi, originally from 11th Cavalry, took over as the first Pakistani commanding officer, and was with the regiment for the next two years.

Finally, there was the Viceroy's Bodyguard, stationed in Delhi at the time of Independence with Thakur Govind Singh as the Commandant

and Sahabzada Yaqub as his Adjutant.[73] After his repatriation from the POW Camp and a stint as an ADC, Sahibzada had returned to 18th Cavalry, his parent regiment that was based at Risalpur, but was posted to the Bodyguard soon after.[74] The Viceroy's senior ADC, Lieutenant Commander Peter Howes, oversaw the division of assets. The Viceroy had two carriages; gold and silver, and Yaqub and Govind agreed to a gentleman's deal of tossing a coin for the gold carriage. Peter tossed the coin and Govind won the gold carriage. The Bodyguard had an equal number of Sikhs, and Muslims (both Punjabi and Hindustani Muslims) and in November 1947, the Muslim contingent, with the carriage, horses and all, moved to Karachi by ship via Bombay. However, a small dismounted detachment was despatched earlier to Karachi to take part in the ceremonies related to the transfer of power. Befittingly, Sahabzada Yaqub was appointed as its first commandant, but he left within the year on promotion to serve under Syed Shahid Hamid in the fledging Directorate of Inter-Services Intelligence. Abbas Khan Durrani from the Guides replaced Sahabzada Yaqub, and his adjutant was Khawaja Hassan Askari 'Arthur' who had re-joined the armoured corps after Independence.[75]

Coping with the Consequences

Like the rest of the Pakistan Army, the Armoured Corps struggled to deal with multifarious tasks during the first six months after Independence. It included assisting the army to disengage from Waziristan, evacuating refugees, flood relief, and the crisis in Kashmir. The remarkable manner in which the armoured regiments performed was recognised, and appreciated by the Quaid when he addressed the 3rd Independent Armoured Brigade during his visit to Risalpur in 1948.

The PFF Mess at Kohat, as seen in 1908. (Emmy Eustace Collection)

The withdrawal of forces from Waziristan was the first major operation of the Pakistan Army in which the Armoured Corps participated. Based on the policy of Forward Defence against the perceived Russian threat, the British had garrisoned regular military forces in the tribal areas of the NWFP. The presence of these troops always provoked tension with the local tribesmen and in spite of the fact that the subcontinent was gaining its freedom, for the tribesmen it was business as usual. On the evening of 14 August 1947, as officers in the mess at Razmak celebrated the birth of Pakistan, 'the tribesmen joined in with a little more sniping'.[76] In 1944, a British committee under Lieutenant General Sir Francis Tucker had recommended implementing the Curzon Plan.[77] The newly formed Pakistani government decided to act on the recommendations of the Tucker Committee, and ordered a withdrawal from Waziristan, which was appropriately codenamed Operation CURZON. It was no peacetime move of troops since it amounted to a general withdrawal through hostile territory. The withdrawal was executed under the control of 9th (Frontier) Division whose area of responsibility extended from Dera Ismail Khan to Peshawar. Stationed in the Sam Brown Barracks in Dera Ismail Khan; the Guides had already operated in this area for two years and were deployed forward to Wana. Also taking part in this operation were squadrons of 6th and 19th Lancers equipped with Stuart tanks. The squadron of 19th Lancers was based at Mir Ali with a troop each at Razmak and Damdil, and the squadron of 6th Lancers was at Bannu.

Operation CURZON began on 6 December 1947 and was completed successfully by the end of the month. The major withdrawal, conducted like a pre-war Frontier operation, was from Razmak. It was a large military base in the heart of South Waziristan and known as 'Little London' because of its weather and beautiful landscape. There were Road Opening Days five times a week when pickets were occupied and armoured cars, and light tanks escorted the convoys.[78] It was a delicate operation since most of the units inside both the Agencies of North and South Waziristan were non-Muslim and transferring to the Indian Army.[79] A large contingent of troops flew across to India in a fleet of Dakotas from Miran Shah on 10 October 1947. Much to its credit, the nascent Pakistan Army completed the operation without mishap. The Tribals could not resist the occasional sniping, but sometimes there was a lot more. On joining 19th Lancers, Said Azhar recollects that he was despatched by the commanding officer to Mir Ali 'to gain first hand field experience. True to the commandant's desire and prediction, Mir Ali Camp received a huge volley of machine gun fire rattling over the tinned roof barracks on the very first night of my arrival, as if to induct a young subaltern into active service through this battle inoculation'.[80] Once Operation CURZON was completed, the Guides relocated to Kohat under the operational command of the old Kohat Brigade, now re-designated as 101st Infantry Brigade and commanded by Shahid Hamid, a 3rd Cavalry officer. Kohat Cantonment was a nice, well laid out garrison town – a clean and pleasant station with wonderful gardens, and good accommodation for the regiment in Hartley Lines. The lines were named after Major General A. F. Hartley, ex-Probyn's Horse, who commanded a division during the 1938 Waziristan operations. They were considered as one of the best lines for a mechanized cavalry unit in the whole of the sub-continent.[81] To the delight of the Guides Cavalry, 'the Guides Infantry, 3/12th Frontier Force Battalion, intrinsic twin infantry part of the Corps of Guides, also rejoined the Risala at Kohat after operational duties in Kashmir. They promptly joined our [the Guides] Mess again, becoming the Corps Mess, after separation in 1926, completing the historical Corps of Guides by adding their silver and artefacts to the excellent Mess's glamour, prestige and get-up'.[82]

While the Guides and the squadrons of the 6th and 19th Lancers were busy in extricating troops from Waziristan, all the other regiments remained occupied in escorting refugees into or out of Pakistan. The squadrons of the 19th Lancers radiated out from their base in Peshawar, for Internal Security Duties in Nowshera, Risalpur, and Mardan and assisted in the evacuation of non-Muslim refugees. The regiment also participated in Operation SNOW LINE in which it transported 6,000 tons of stores from Balakot up the Kaghan Valley to the Babusar Pass. The purpose of this operation was to assist the forces liberating the Northern Areas from the yoke of the Maharaja of Kashmir. On the return trips, the vehicles carried non-Muslims out of the valley to safer locations. Alongside 19th Lancers, 13th Lancers was also involved with the movement of refugees, and a squadron was escorting trains of non-Muslims from Nowshera to Attock. The task of evacuation was complicated by unusually heavy rains in the first week of September, which flooded refugee camps and cut major road arteries.

One of the most difficult tasks related to the period of Independence was assigned to the Punjab Boundary Force (PBF) organized in

July 1947. It had an ad hoc organization of seven under-strength infantry brigades, 18th Cavalry commanded by Mohammad Yusuf, and an additional squadron from CIH. The PBF was responsible for maintaining law and order in the troubled districts of Central Punjab stretching from Sialkot to Montgomery (now Okara), and Lyallpur (now Faisalabad) to Ludhiana. Though the intended role was peacekeeping, in the carnage that erupted, it ended up trying to ensure the safe transfer of population. One of the junior-most officers serving with the PBF was Syed Wajahat Hussain who had obtained a regular commission from IMA in May that year, and joined CIH at Ahmednagar. Within months, he was appointed the second-in-command of an independent squadron (of Dogras, Hindu, and Jat tank crews) detailed with the PBF. Wajahat moved the train with 14 Stuart tanks, and 30 men to Lahore while the squadron commander brought the rest by road. At nearly every stop past Delhi, he was confronted with menacing crowds of Sikhs who were heavily armed. His concern was as much for the safety of his small party of tank crews as also for over a hundred soldiers of a field ambulance in a bogey attached to his train. Whenever the train stopped, 'all tanks with one crew member were manned ready for action, with

Indian troops arriving at Srinagar airfield in 1947. (Author's Collection)

Armoured Cars of 11th Cavalry securing Bagsar Fort in Azad Kashmir. (Author's Collection)

extra guards on the sides, and guards placed in the engine and the rear.'[83] He successfully fended off the threats to his train, but like other officers, Wajahat saw some harrowing sights. While still in the process of detraining at Lahore, he was ordered to reload the tanks and take them back to Jullundur where the situation was very bad. On arriving at Jullundur, the squadron went straight into action, rescuing Muslim families that mainly comprised of Jullundur Pathans.

A week later, the squadron 'thundered into Ludhiana' and entered a city that looked deserted with, 'the streets littered with dead bodies, looted belongings and burnt down houses'. For the next two months the squadron was 'acting as a fire brigade', despatched at short notice in various directions, rescuing Muslims, and escorting them to the border as they escaped on foot, bullock carts, trucks or trains. One of the most difficult situations that Wajahat had to deal with was evacuating refugees from the boundaries of the State of Kapurthala. In one incident a train full of refugees being escorted by his tank troop was threatened by 'hundreds of well-armed horsemen followed by thousands of Sikhs, forming up to attack'. The tanks responded the

only way that tanks know how to. "We moved towards them in battle formation," recollects Wajahat.

I ordered all the tanks to fire with their main 37mm guns and machineguns. Picking their main leader, a saffron-robed Nahang [a Sikh militant priest] in glittering armour on a white charger, my tank fired, followed by the hell let loose by the rest, causing a complete pandemonium amidst the attackers. Horsemen were tossed over, their horses collapsed, while the charging cavalry overran the following footmen and were in full retreat without collecting casualties. This powerful and timely knock eliminated any further threats.[84]

The PBF was disbanded on 1 September 1947, because apart from other reasons, its troops were finding it extremely difficult to act impartially in protecting the refugees. 18th Cavalry, which was spread between Lahore, Amritsar, and Jullundur, handed over its equipment and protection duties to Probyn's Horse. The regiment took over the responsibility for the section between Jalandhar and the Wagah border. While Wajahat's squadron of Central India Horse continued to escort refugees from outlying areas to the Grand Trunk Road, and shepherded convoys between Ludhiana and Jalandhar,[85] working on the Beas-Attari and the Moga-Ferozepur-Ganda Singhwala routes, Probyn's Horse escorted the astonishing number of 2,400,000 refugees without a single loss. [86] In his book *The Story of the Pakistan Army*, Major General Fazl Muqeem states that Probyn's Horse was one of the units whose role deserved special mention.

The First Kashmir War

The 11th Cavalry arrived at Rawalpindi from Secundrabad and while it was taking over the lines and equipment from the 3rd Cavalry at Ojhiri Camp, it was simultaneously escorting convoys and trains of non-Muslim evacuees. One squadron under the command of Akhtar Islam did some excellent work within the Mianwali District. Another squadron was entrusted with the task of escorting refugees from Abbottabad, Gujar Khan, and other parts of Rawalpindi District. However, a greater challenge for 11th Cavalry came in the last week of August 1947, when its commanding officer Masud Khan, and the second-in-command Muhammad Nawaz Khan (known in the corps as 'Naboo'), were summoned to GHQ, and ordered to support the operations in Kashmir.[87] Initially, 11th Cavalry was tasked to procure, store, and supply arms, ammunition, and explosives for the Azad Forces. The term Azad Forces was used for the armed local civilians (some of them ex-servicemen) and the Tribal Lashkars who had come from the Northwest Province. Subsequently 11th Cavalry had to establish and supervise various Wing Headquarters manned by ex-officers who had served in the INA. 11th Cavalry was also instructed to be prepared to participate in the operations at an appropriate moment. The regiment initially deployed observation teams on the road leading from Muzaffarabad to Srinagar to report on the progress of the Lashkars, and subsequently covered their withdrawal in the Uri Sector.

Jeeps and armoured cars of the 7th Light Cavalry in action in terrain similar to where they were ambushed by 11th Cavalry. (Author's Collection)

Two captured armoured cars of the 7th Light Cavalry as put on display at the 11th Cavalry's base at Nowshera, photographed during a rare snowfall in the winter of 1963. (Author's Collection)

Colonel Tommy Masud and Nawaz complimented each other in dash, courage and daring, and while Masud was deeply involved in the management of logistics of the fledging Azad Forces and Lashkars, Nawaz was at the forefront of the fighting that developed in the Southern Sector where 11th Cavalry carried out offensive operations.[88] The only operation in which the regiment used armoured cars was in the capture of Bhimber. For the subsequent operation against Mirpur, the regiment was permitted to only employ the rifle troops reinforced with machineguns and mortars. While the capture of Bhimber and Mirpur were politically and geographically significant, the greatest military success for 11th Cavalry was an ambush that Nawaz conducted on the road leading from Naushera to Kotli. Assisted by a 1,000 strong Lashkar and a battalion of Azad forces, 11th Cavalry carried out a very successful ambush on a convoy travelling on the road leading from Naushera to Kotli. Apart from capturing a large number of trucks and stores, the regiment also captured armoured cars of 7th Light Cavalry which were escorting the convoy. Only two and a half years since they had been fighting alongside in the drive to retake Rangoon, 11th Cavalry and 7th Light Cavalry were now engaging each other as enemies.

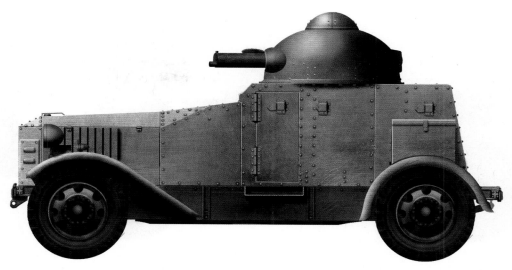

The Crossley Armoured Car combined a tough and cheap 50 hp engine, 5 ton chassis built by Crossley Motors with a body by Vickers. It had a large hemispherical turret with four machine-gun mounts and the crew area was lined with asbestos to keep the temperature down. The entire body could be electrified to keep large crowds at bay and the cars were originally fitted with narrow, solid tires which made them unstable. 451 were built between 1923 and 1925 mainly for internal security duties and Frontier operations in India. When the Royal Tank Corps handed them over to the Indian cavalry that was being mechanized in 1939, the Crossley chassis were worn out and the bodies were transferred to Chevrolet truck chassis with pneumatic tiers. They served in the Middle East (Iraq, Syria and Persia) in the early years of the war and were then gifted to the Iranian Government. (Artwork by David Bocquelet)

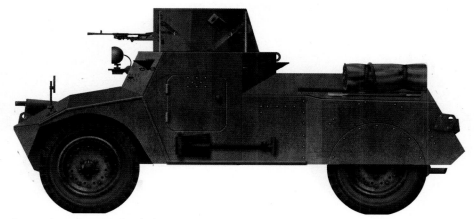

Morris Light Reconnaissance Car was issued to an Indian light reconnaissance regiment while it was serving in Iraq in 1941. The vehicle weighed 3.7 tons and was powered by a 72 hp Morris 4-cylinder petrol engine. It had an unusual internal arrangement, with the three-man crew sitting side by side by side with the driver in the middle, a crewman manning a small multi-sided turret mounting a Bren machinegun on the right, and another with a Boys Anti-tank rifle on the left. (Artwork by David Bocquelet)

The Universal Carrier, also known as the Bren Gun Carrier was the most produced armoured fighting vehicle in history. It was powered by a Ford V-8 petrol engine that generated 85hp at 3,500 rpm and had a top speed of 48 k/ph. Initially issued to motor cavalry regiments in North Africa as troop carriers during the Battle of Ghazala (1942), the Vickers Carriers had a more useful role with the Indian reconnaissance regiments during the Italian Campaign. In the early years of the Pakistan Army it was used as a mortar carrier and for the basic training of tank crews. (Artwork by David Bocquelet)

Prior to the Battle of Ghazala, in 1942, 16 Bofors-made 2Pdr (40mm) anti-tank guns were issued to each regiment of the 3rd Indian Motor Brigade. This weapon had a high rate of fire (22 rounds per minute) but could only destroy a German tank from 400 meters range. It was mounted on the back of a Chevrolet truck (or other type) and the combination was called a 'portèe'. Although only intended as a transport method for the gun, and the latter supposed to be unloaded for firing, for greater mobility, their crews preferred to deploy them while mounted, with the vehicle standing in a reversed position. (Artwork by David Bocquelet)

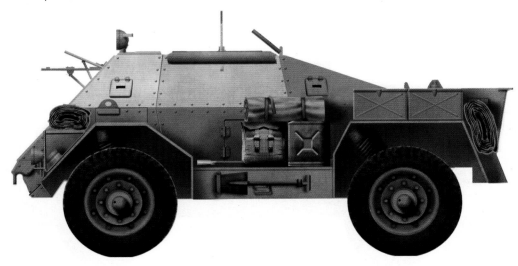

The Indian Pattern Wheeled Carrier Mk. III which served with some of the Indian reconnaissance regiments in North Africa and the Middle East in the early years of the Second World War was lightly armed with a Bren machinegun and a Boys Anti-tank Rifle. The hull was manufactured in railway factories in India and mounted on a Ford GMC or CMP truck. (Artwork by David Bocquelet)

The Marmon Harrington Mk. III Armoured Car which was manufactured in South Africa as well as in India, was one of the early issues to the Indian reconnaissance regiments in North Africa. With a Ford V-8 engine pushing a weight of 6.4 tons it was underpowered. It had a crew of three and the two-man turret had a Boys Anti-tank rifle and a coaxial Bren machinegun. Two additional machineguns were mounted on the turret roof for air defence. The Marmon Harringtons were replaced by the far superior Humber Armoured Cars. (Artwork by David Bocquelet)

The Humber Mk. IV was one of the most widely produced British armoured cars during the Second World War. Armed with the American 37 mm high velocity gun, and with a good power-to-weight ratio, a top speed of 72 kph and a range of 400 km, it was well suited for reconnaissance. They performed admirably with the Indian reconnaissance regiments in North Africa and in Italy and after Independence were grouped with Stuart Tanks in the Light Armoured Regiments of the Pakistan Armoured Corps. (Artwork by David Bocquelet)

The Daimler Dingo scout car was a 4x4 armoured vehicle that entered service with British and Commonwealth forces in 1940. Despite its small size, it was considered one of the best British armoured fighting vehicles of the Second World War. Weighing 3 tonnes, it was well protected for its size, with 30mm armour to the front, and 12mm on the sides. Main armament consisted of a .303" Bren gun or a .55" Boys anti-rank rifle. The Dingo was powered by a 55hp, 2.5 litre, 6-cylinder Daimler petrol engine. (Artwork by David Bocquelet)

The AEC (Dorchester) 4x4 Armoured Command Vehicle (ACV) was based on AEC Matador chassis. It weighed 12 tons with 10-12 mm of armour and was powered by an AEC-187 6-cylinder diesel engine generating 95 hp. This robust vehicle was used for the first time in the North African Campaign. Big and comfortable, it was nicknamed Dorchester by the troops, after the luxury hotel in London. Two of these ACVs, nicknamed Romeo and Juliet, were brought to Risalpur from Burma by the 254th Indian Tank Brigade at the end of the war and remained in service with the Pakistan Army until 1963. (Artwork by David Bocquelet)

Designed for reconnaissance and colonial warfare, the 5 ton Mk. IV version of the Vickers Light Tank that was in service on the Frontier in the inter-war years had a two man crew and a .303" machinegun mounted in a turret. In 1939 they were transferred by the Royal Tank Corps to the regiments of the Indian Cavalry that were being mechanized but were not employed overseas. (Artwork by David Bocquelet)

The Daimler armoured car was the 'big brother' of the Dingo: it had a hull made of welded steel that was closely related to the Dingo, entirely welded but for a few bolted elements, and received a (cramped) turret for two atop of it, with the 2Pdr gun – the standard British anti-tank gun of the time. The turret roof had a large hatch opening to the rear. Due to additional weight, it had a more powerful petrol engine with 95hps. Daimler armoured cars were phased out of the Pakistan Armoured Corps when it became an all-track force in 1953. (Artwork by David Bocquelet)

M3A1 Stuart Light Tank served with the Indian reconnaissance regiments during the counteroffensive in Burma. After Independence it was employed by the Pakistan Armoured Corps in the light armoured regiments as well as the reconnaissance troops of the armoured regiments. It had a large magazine of 103 rounds for its 37mm gun but the ammunition had serious limitations in penetrative power and explosive content. A significant weakness was the two man turret, however the crews liked its maximum speed of 58 kph and mechanical reliability. The tank weighed 15 tons and was powered by an air-cooled Twin Cadillac radial engine generating 220 hp at 3,400 rpm. (Artwork by David Bocquelet)

Sherman Mk.III was the British nomenclature for the US variant of the M4 that was powered by the Grey Marine 6046 Diesel Engine. The Grey Marine consisted of a twin pack of engines that generated 375 hp at 2100 rpm and gave the tank a better road performance than the Chrysler Multibank. Its 75mm gun had its origins in a French field gun of the First World War with a very effective high explosive round and well suited for operations in Burma. However, parallel developments were not carried out on an AP round. Its M61A1 APC round with a muzzle velocity of 620 m/s could penetrate 94 mm of armour but only at ranges under 500 meters. (Artwork by David Bocquelet)

The Sherman Mk.V was powered by the US A57 Chrysler Multibank petrol engine which had a novel design of coupling five banks of engines each of five cylinders to a common crankcase. The result was 25 cylinders generating 370 hp at 2400 rpm. It had the same 75mm gun and Wireless Set No. 19 as the Mk.III. The RCA Victor WS No. 19 was a very successful HF set installed on US vehicles supplied to Commonwealth and Soviet forces. When serving in the Pakistan Armoured Corps, the turret marking consisted of a letter designating the sabre squadrons (A, B and C), followed by a number for each tank in the squadron. (Artwork by David Bocquelet)

Pakistan purchased 352 Sherman M4A4E1/76mm Medium Tanks through the US Lend-Lease Program in 1953. Its 52-calibre 76mm M1 Gun had better types of ammunition, including HVAP with a core penetrator of tungsten, which doubled the penetration power compared to the 75mm gun by penetrating 90mm of armour at 1,000 metres.. The M4A4 was powered by the Continental R-975 9 Cylinder Radial, which was superior in performance to the engines fitted in the Sherman IIIs and Vs. It was an air-cooled aircraft engine with a large cooling fan and oil radiators. The tank was modified with a spaced-out suspension that provided a more stable platform for the 76mm gun, reduced ground pressure and better traction. With the arrival of the M4A1, the turret markings were changed to Arabic numerals in sequence from one onwards. (Artwork by David Bocquelet)

Pakistan also purchased 72 M36B2 through the Lend-Lease Program because its 90mm M3 gun provided superior firepower. In spite of the calibre of its gun, the M36B2 weighed less than 30 tons in part because the turret was open-topped and the front glacises plate and gun shield had 100mm of armour while the turret and the hull had a maximum of only 40mm. It had the same Grey Marine 6046 engine as the Sherman Mk.III as well as the same chassis and drive train and was also fitted with the spaced-out suspension of the Sherman E4 series. During the 1965 Pakistan-India War, one squadron in each M48 regiment had M36B2s. (Artwork by David Bocquelet)

110 M24 Chaffees replaced the armoured cars and the Stuart tanks as the principal reconnaissance AFVs in the Pakistan Army. It had two 44T24 V-8 Cadillac engines producing 220 hp at 3400 rpm and weighed only 20 tons due to a maximum thickness of 40mm of amour on the turret and a lightweight 75mm gun. It was the first US tank in which ergonomics were incorporated and catered for safety and comfort of the crew and ease of maintenance. (Artwork by David Bocquelet)

When the US Army started phasing out its M47 Medium Tanks in 1955, 304 were transferred to the Pakistan Army to equip its 1st Armoured Division. It was a large 40 ton tank with a height of 3.4 meters and its size belied the fact that the armour on the turret – though angled at between 30º to 60º - was only 100mm thick. It was armed with a 90mm gun and powered by a Continental V-12 twin turbo petrol engine coupled to a CD 850 automatic transmission. Its high fuel consumption limited its operating range to only 160 km which was further reduced under combat conditions. (Artwork by David Bocquelet)

With the 200 M48s that were supplied after the M47s, the Pakistan Army raised a light armoured division. In spite of being projected as a new design, in critical areas the performance of the M48 was no better than its predecessor. It had a lower power-to-weight ratio and the same stereoscopic range finder as the M47 which was difficult to master. It also carried 11 fewer rounds than the 71 that were stored in the M47. However, the turret of cast homogenous steel had a better ballistic shape and was slightly thicker. (Artwork by David Bocquelet)

The French AMX-13 light tank was named after its weight of 13 tonnes. It had an unusual and troublesome two man oscillating turret with a revolver type magazine. However, it had an excellent 75mm high-velocity gun derived from the German Panther tank and also adopted for the Israeli Super Sherman. A squadron strength of AMX-13s was captured by the Pakistan Army during the 1965 Indo-Pakistani War and promptly pressed in service in the camouflage pattern illustrated here. (Artwork by David Bocquelet)

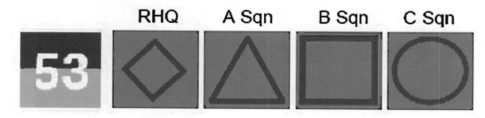

19th Lancers (British India Army)

3rd Indian Motor Brigade (British Army of India)

1st Indian Armoured Division (British Army of India)

8th Indian Division (British Army of India)

17th Indian Division (British Army of India)

Insignia of the Kohat Military District (British Army of India)

Insignia of the Peshawar Military District (British Army of India)

Insignia of the North Western Army, renamed into the Northern Command (British Army of India)

1st Armoured Division (Pakistan Army)

6th Armoured Division (Pakistan Army)

2nd Armoured Brigade (Indian Army)

4th Armoured Division (Indian Army)

17-Pdr anti-tank gun of the Anti-Tank Regiment. (Author's Collection)

Prime Minister Liaquat Ali Khan accompanied by General Akbar during a visit to the troops in Kashmir in 1951. (Author's Collection)

The fighting in Kashmir died down in winter, but in the early part of 1948, the Indian Army launched its spring offensive, and by June two divisions of the Pakistan Army were in action to stem the Indian advance. By April 1948, the Indians had two complete armoured regiments and one squadron of a third regiment in Kashmir. 7th Light Cavalry had two squadrons of armoured cars in Srinagar-Uri area, and its third squadron of Stuart tanks at Akhnur. Central India Horse had a squadron each at Jhangar and Naushera, and a third squadron near Jammu. Deccan Horse had a squadron minus of Shermans at Jammu and one troop at Chhamb.[89] Consequently, as the fighting intensified, in November 1948, 3rd Independent Armoured Brigade was placed under command of 7th Division. It concentrated in the area of Gujrat-Lalamusa with its three regiments – 13th Lancers, 19th Lancers, and Probyn's Horse. Probyn's Horse, which had moved from Lahore to Ojhri Camp and then just two months earlier on to Risalpur, now dispersed at a disued airfield near Gujrat. This gave ideas to Hesky Baig, its super-fit commanding officer. Every day, all the officers had to run 6 km around the airfield with Hesky in the lead. Mercifully, for Gul Hassan his daily runs ceased as his squadron moved to the border opposite Chhamb.[90] The deployment of a squadron opposite Chhamb was part of the safeguards that the army was taking against the possibility of an Indian winter offensive in Southern Kashmir

through what in operational terms was referred to as the Manawar Gap. The Manawar Gap referred to the approach that led down from the Chhamb Salient towards Gujrat and the Grand Trunk Road. A squadron of Deccan Horse had been moved across the River Chenab at Akhnur in early October 1948.

As part of the safeguards, the Guides moved from Kohat to the area of Nandipur, south of Sialkot. Having successfully cleared Dras and Kargil in summer, and opened up the line of communication with Leh, the Indians were now looking to recapture Bhimber and Mirpur thus threatening Pakistan's flank. The newly formed Directorate of Inter-Services Intelligence (ISI) with its first director, Shahid Hamid and Sahabzada Yaqub as its GSO-1, produced a number of appreciations on the Indian intentions. One great concern was the move of the Indian 2nd Independent Armoured Brigade that had arrived at Meerut from Ahmednagar in early 1948, and could threaten Pakistan. The day it left Meerut for a forward deployment, the ISI informed Prime Minister, Liaquat Ali Khan who addressed a public meeting that same afternoon, and showed his now famous fist to India as a mark of defiance.[91] It was this symbol of the fist that would be replicated in the insignia of the 1st Armoured Division when it was raised a decade later.

To respond to this threat, the Prime Minister chaired a meeting of the Joint Service Chief's Committee, and gave a free hand to the C-in-C for a counter-offensive, provided the advance bases from which the Pakistani forces operated continued to be in Azad Territories.[92] A plan for launching 3rd Armoured Brigade against the Indian Line of Communication in the area of Akhnur was approved, and the Prime Minister also discussed the offensive use of the air force in support of the brigade. The brigade moved to its forward concentration areas including 19th Lancers, 'which concentrated in Kotla – Bhimber area after a long night march in secrecy, and had assiduously camouflaged, and hidden its presence in that area by digging in tanks and obliterating all track marks'.[93] However, a UN commission, which was conducting negotiations on the settlement of the issue of Kashmir, was making good progress and the counter-offensive was cancelled. Finally, the two governments agreed to a ceasefire effective from 1 January 1949, but like the rest of the Pakistan Army, the armoured brigade remained on the border for the next six months.

5
THE CANTONMENTS NORTH OF RAVI

Around two hundred years ago, the British East India Company started using the term 'cantonments' for its military stations in South Asia. The earliest mention of cantonment occurs in the Bengal General Order of 1789 relating to Barrackpore. The order stated that 'no private bungalows or buildings could be erected within cantonment limits without permission of the Commander-in-Chief'. The term was specific to the sub-continent and described by the Oxford Dictionary as 'lodging assigned to troops or a permanent military station in India'. They developed as an enclave in a civil district, self-contained and in varying degrees self-supporting.[1] The oldest and largest cantonments associated with the Indian cavalry were in Central India in stations like Secunderabad. With the campaigns in Afghanistan and the threat of the Russian bear looming over the Hindu Kush, more were established on the North West Frontier. One of the most famous of these was Mardan. Under the Kitchener reforms of 1903, most of the regiments of the Indian cavalry were grouped into brigades at Secunderabad, Poona, Sialkot, and Risalpur with only four retained as divisional cavalry regiments. However, some of these brigaded regiments were detached to serve in a number of large and small cantonments. On the eve of the Second World War, apart from being based at Lahore, Rawalpindi, Sialkot, and Risalpur, they were also stationed on the Frontier at Quetta, Lorelai, Bannu, Kohat, and Peshawar. At Independence, the bulk of the armour was stationed north of the Indus, but the operational environment dictated a gradual shift into the Punjab. By the early 1960s most of the regiments based in forward garrisons like Sialkot and Lahore, and in the new cantonment at Kharian which was constructed by the US Army Corps of Engineers,

The Guides at Mardan

Mardan was one of the earliest cantonments in North Western India and synonymous with the Corps of the Guides. Following the defeat of the Sikhs and the establishment of British rule at Peshawar, in 1851, the Corps went to restore law and order in the plains of Yusufzai. After being constantly on the move for three years, the commanding officer of the Corps decided to construct a permanent home 'to give shelter to 876 wild men and 300 wild horses,'[2] and selected a site for a fort at Mardan. Its construction in 1854 was under the close supervision of Colonel Hodson[3] and 'the Hoti-Mardan Fort became not only the home of the Guides, but also the symbol of British power on the wild borders of Yaghistan, the land of everlasting conflict and of unending vendettas'.[4]

The Guides was initially garrisoned inside the fort, which was shaped like a five-pointed star: the design replicated on a smaller scale the European forts of that era. As the surrounding area was pacified and irrigated by the Lower Swat Canal, the

The garden of the Guides Mess at Mardan, in 1908. (Author's Collection)

cantonment spread out around the fort and became green. Mardan remained as the home of the Corps of Guides for 90 years but, 'in 1939 came the fateful order, long rumoured, that Mardan was to be given up and that the Corps of Guides would resolve into separated component parts'.[5] The breakup of the last of the composite corps in the British India Army was a result of the Chatfield Report published in 1938, which focused on the modernisation of the British India Army. The Guides Cavalry moved to Quetta where it was mechanized, and the Guides Infantry to the Khajuri Plain near Peshawar. When the Guides vacated Mardan, the cantonment was taken over by the school of the RIASC.

After Independence, Mardan was occupied by the Punjab Regimental Centre, which moved from Sialkot and the Auchinleck Lines in Jhelum. All that is left as a reminder of the Guides at Mardan is the church with its graveyard and the Kabul Memorial.

The Risala at Risalpur

Close to the time that Younghusband wrote about Mardan, another cantonment was being established nearby and would be associated with the cavalry for the next 43 years. Until 1903, all troops in the region were part of the Peshawar Military District but following the Kitchener reforms of the British India Army, a regular division was formed at Peshawar designated as the 1st (Peshawar) Division.[6] Its infantry brigades were based at Peshawar and Nowshera, but there was no accommodation for the cavalry brigade, for which land was purchased east of the River Kabul. Being very close to Nowshera, it was initially named the Nowshera Cavalry Cantonment. However, to avoid any confusion with the Nowshera Cantonment, the name was changed to Risalpur and notified in the Indian Army Order of August 1910.[7] This name was considered suitable, as it was synonymous with the Urdu word *risala* meaning cavalry. The cavalry brigade was designated as the 1st (Risalpur) Cavalry Brigade, and a major part of the accommodation including the officer's mess was constructed between 1916 and 1920. By this time, Risalpur had grown and possessed an airfield from where the Royal Flying Corps operated.[8]

Pay-Day of the Armoured Brigade's Signal Company, 1946. (Author's Collection)

Entrance to the Meena Bazaar during the Armoured Corps Week at Risalpur in 1950. (Author's Collection)

At the outbreak of the Second World War, the brigade consisted of 16/5th Lancers and Probyn's Horse at Risalpur, and the Guides and 5/12th Frontier Force at Mardan. Following Independence, Probyn's Horse, and 13th Lancers were the only regiments of the brigade based at Risalpur. With the Pakistan Air Force Academy in the process of being established, there was probably a shortage of space because the 3rd Self Propelled Artillery Regiment was at Mardan, and a regiment of the Frontier Force Rifles at Malakand. The third tank regiment – i.e. 19th Lancers – was based at Peshawar.[9]

In 1952, its accommodation was taken over by the Centre and School of the Military Engineers, which was earlier based at Sialkot.

Thus after 55 years, Risalpur ceased to be a cavalry cantonment.

The New Home of the Armoured Corps

Around the same time as Risalpur wound down as a cavalry cantonment, the significance of Nowshera in the annals of the Pakistan Armoured Corps ascended. It initially consisted of two villages, located on opposite banks of the River Kabul – Nowshera Khurd and Nowshera Kalan. During the operations against the Sikhs at Peshawar, the surroundings of Nowshera formed a base for the British Field Army. In 1848-49, the British started constructing a cantonment on the western bank of the river in a sandy plain, three miles in diameter. The area was surrounded by low hills on all sides except the north, which was open towards the river.[10] It had a strategic location astride the Grand Trunk Road at the junction of an important artery that branched north to Risalpur and onwards to Mardan, Swat, Dir, and Chitral.[11] Following Independence and the subsequent war in Kashmir, the 2nd (Nowshera) Brigade, re-designated as the 103rd Infantry Brigade, moved to Kashmir and Nowshera was no longer a permanent station for combat units until the armoured corps started expanding in the 1950s.

Since it had been a large station for gunners, at Independence Nowshera should logically have become the home of artillery and accommodated both the Centre and School. However, to create an additional vacancy for a full colonel, the British artillery officers seconded to the Pakistan Army decided to locate the Centre at Campbellpur (renamed as Attock), and the School at Nowshera.[12] When the Pakistan Armoured Corps started expanding in 1955-56, some regiments were raised and stationed at Nowshera. It was also the station of choice for the raising of the 6th Armoured Division. With the support of the Armoured Corps Centre, 29th Cavalry was also raised at Nowshera before the 1971 War, and many years later all the regiments raised for Saudi Arabia were assembled here.

The Cavalry at Rawalpindi

It was obvious at the General Headquarters that Risalpur was too far north a placement for its only armoured brigade. During the Kashmir War and the subsequent 'emergencies', the units of the brigade shuttled back and forth between Risalpur, and their concentration areas in the surroundings of Gujranwala and Gujrat. Consequently, after the 'Fifty-one Flap' the 3rd Independent Armoured Brigade did not move back to Risalpur, but was re-located to Rawalpindi. Though it remained here for only four years, Rawalpindi has a unique place in the post-Independence history of the armoured corps that it was the first station where an armoured division was raised.

The history of Rawalpindi (fondly known as Pindi), is spread over several millennia.[13] By 1911, the place was, 'chiefly notable as the largest military station in India, and the key to the British system of defence upon the North-West Frontier'. The garrison consisted of one regiment each of British and native cavalry, two regiments each of British and native infantry, one battery of horse and one of field artillery, an ammunition column of field artillery, and two companies of sappers and miners. Following the Kitchener Reforms of the British India Army in 1903, Rawalpindi became the headquarters of the 2nd (Rawalpindi) Division. More importantly, it was the headquarters of the Northern Army whose area of responsibility stretched over 2,500 km from the North West Frontier Province all the way to Bengal.[14] The Northern Army consisted of five divisions and three brigades. In 1920, the Northern and Southern Army were split into four commands and the headquarters at Rawalpindi was re-designated as Northern Command. Northern Command was re-formed again as North Western Army in April 1942 but reverted to its earlier title in November 1945. In 1947, the headquarters of Northern Command became the headquarters of the Pakistan Army.

The army transformed the village of the Rawal into the third largest urban centre in Punjab, next only to Lahore and Amritsar.[15] The cantonment had a population of 40,000, and was developed on the grid pattern that the British generally applied to the planning of their military stations in India. One of the first of two regiments to be mechanized was based at Rawalpindi: in 1938, Scinde Horse shed its horses after a mounted parade; inspected by the C-in-C and converted to a frontier regiment. While the regiment headquarters was at Rawalpindi, the squadrons were deployed in Razmak, Bannu, and

The Nowshera Club. The note on the original post card showing this photograph stated: 'Not so nice as it looks here as the foliage is always covered in dust'. (Author's Collection)

Wana. Scinde Horse remained at Rawalpindi until the end of 1941 and then moved to Syria to serve with the PAIFORCE. Skinner's Horse also mechanized at Rawalpindi and in 1940 left for operations in Sudan. It was replaced by 18th Cavalry, which arrived from Merut. It was the third regiment to be mechanized at Rawalpindi and then left for North Africa as part of the 3rd Indian Motor Brigade.[16]

During the latter part of the Second World War, Rawalpindi was one of the training bases for the Indian airborne forces. A parachute brigade, which formed the nucleus for the 44th Indian Airborne Division, was located here in 1944, and carried out jumps from the Chaklala Airfield. A year before Independence, 3rd Cavalry that had been re-raised as an airborne reconnaissance regiment for the airborne division, came to Pindi to complete its parachute training. It remained here until Independence and was garrisoned a little outside at Ojhiri Camp, on the road to Murree. After Independence, this camp was briefly occupied by 11th Cavalry, which arrived from Secunderabad and was placed under 7th Division as its reconnaissance regiment.

During the Kashmir War of 1948, its importance grew as alongside the establishment in Bhara Kohu (ten miles further on the road to Murree); it was the main supply depot for the forces operating in northern Kashmir. Subsequently, an infantry regiment of the Azad Kashmir Forces was also based here, with a recruit training centre for its regiments. In 1956, the headquarters of 4th Armoured Brigade was also raised at Ojhri Camp, but after two months it moved to Mansar Camp near Campbellpur.

The six years between 1952 and 1958, were Rawalpindi's heydays as a post-Independence cavalry station. Of course, the army headquarters was based at Rawalpindi, and there were other static establishments like the Central Ordnance Depot, the Central Workshops, and the Royal Army Service Corps Centre at Chaklala. However, the only combat elements were from the armoured corps and black berets abounded particularly in West Ridge. The Calcutta Office had been vacated by the headquarters of 7th Division and at the end of the emergency of 1951, it was occupied by the headquarters of 3rd Independent Armoured Brigade. It also had the distinction of being the first premises to house the headquarters of the 1st Armoured Division when it was raised. 19th Lancers was located at Palmer Lines, next to the railway station with the officer's mess in a grand old building

An aerial view of Risalpur Cantonment taken in 1935 from an altitude of 9,800ft. The cavalry lines occupied the left portion of the cantonment. (Author's Collection)

Tanks of 3rd Armoured Brigade based at Risalpur crossing the River Kabul at Akora Khattak during a bridging exercise in 1951. (Author's Collection)

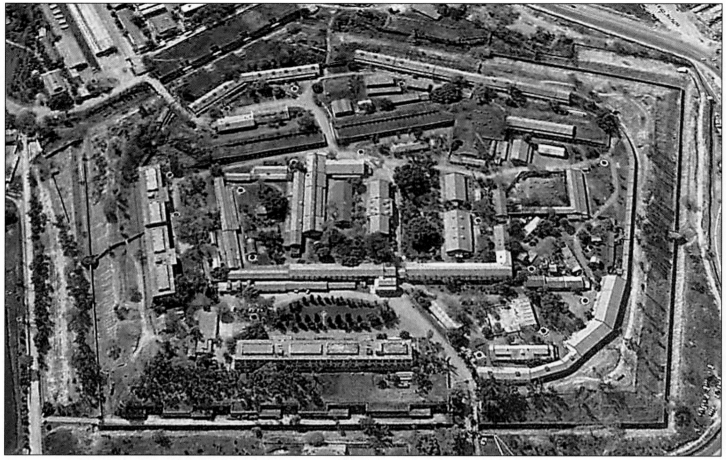

Constructed in 1883, the Arsenal at Rawalpindi was a major supply depot for the Northern Command of the British India Army. (Author's Collection)

at 274 Peshawar Road. 13th Lancers was accommodated in former barracks of the Royal Artillery close to the R.A. (Royal Artillery) Bazaar, which were a distinct improvement to their accommodation in Risalpur particularly so because it had electricity.[17]

When 1st Armoured Division started relocating to Kharian, Rawalpindi ceased to be station for armoured regiments.

The Brigade at Mansar Camp

As the armoured corps started expanding in the mid-1950s, Rawalpindi and Nowshera became congested. The spill over was accommodated in a camp near the village of Mansar that lay roughly halfway between Rawalpindi and Nowshera. Mansar lies on the Grand Trunk Road close to the historic fort of Attock, and is the western most village of an area known as the Plains of Chach. At the early stages of the Second World War, the British established a camp near Mansar for Italian POWs captured in Africa. About a 100,000 were transferred to camps in India, which were spread through the length and breadth of the sub-continent from Yol in Assam to Bangalore, Malir, Quetta and in North Western India. They were generally well administered and the POWs were even issued currency.[18] While many other POW camps were sited close to cities like Bhopal and Bikaner, some like Mansar Camp were located at a distance from an urban sprawl and for that reason, the quality of accommodation was better. Following the war, Mansar was a transit camp for British troops on their way home and a British Other Rank recollected that, 'We found the camp very clean and comfortable compared to some we had been in'.

At Independence, Mansar Camp accommodated a large colony of refugees but after they were settled elsewhere, it was transferred back to the military. In 1956, the 4th Armoured Brigade shifted in from Rawalpindi to await the construction of new cantonment at Kharian.

The brigade found Mansar a peaceful station and though the buildings were temporary wartime structures, they were fairly comfortable and sufficient for the personnel and their families. It also had a variety of terrain for training. However, geographically Mansar was not a safe location for the armoured brigade. Over the centuries, the Indus has been prone to flash floods often caused by a combination of heavy rains and snowmelt.

Gifts from the US Army Corps of Engineers

In 1955, the US Joint Chiefs of Staff included Pakistan in the list of countries to benefit from the Direct Forces Support Program. This program was designed to overcome the deficiencies of the armed forces of regional allies and the US undertook a number of construction projects for Pakistan's military. These projects were assigned to the US Army Corps of Engineers, which during the Cold War was also active in Libya, Turkey, Saudi Arabia, and Iran. The actual work fell to the Mediterranean Division of the Corps of Engineers and its Trans-East District, which set up an office in Karachi as well as a laboratory for testing construction materials.

That year, Soviet leaders made a state visit to Afghanistan, and granted a loan equivalent to $100 million, of which $40 million was for arms. The competition between the two superpowers for influence in the region had intensified, and the US Department of Defence designated the construction program in Pakistan as a Crash Program, and assigned the highest priority to improving an existing airfield at Mauripur.[19] The MAAG, which had been in Pakistan for a year and had yet delivered no visible sign of US assistance, also pressed for quick action by the Corps of Engineers.[20] The largest project that the Trans-East District undertook was a new army cantonment at Kharian to accommodate 18,500 troops of a corps headquarters and an armoured division.[21] [22] Initially the Pakistan Army wanted their Military Engineering Services (MES) to construct Kharian with funding provided by the US Government. However, it was realised in time that the scale of the project was beyond their capability, and the army requested the Americans to construct the cantonment.[23] The cost estimate in 1955, was around $30 million, which included $8 million for family housing, which was never built by the Americans. However, by 1958 the US Government had spent $65 million, which based on a US Inflation Rate of 3.65 percent per year comes to approximately $572 million for a similar project in 2015.[24] In rationalising the cost of construction of the cantonment at Kharian, the US Department of Defense stated 'that the policy in 1955-56 was … to attempt to give the Pakistan Armed Forces facilities, which would be a credit to them and to the United States'.

Another major base became the Kharian Cantonment: originally a small and insignificant village on the Grand Trunk Road somewhere between Jhelum and Gujarat. Its only claim to fame was that from here a road led off west to Chillianwala, the famous battlefield of the Anglo-Sikh War, and to the village of Phalia, which may have been where Alexander the Great erected a monument to mark the grave of Bucephalus, his favourite horse. In the context of a conflict with India, Kharian was poorly located with the River Chenab separating it from the likely area of operation of the armoured division in the Sialkot

Construction of Kharian Cantonment at its early stages. In the foreground is the colony constructed for the engineers. In the background is the iconic water tank. (Author's Collection)

Brigadier Ghaziudin Hyder, Commander of the 5th Armoured Brigade, briefing Field Marshal Ayub Khan on a Crash Program for construction of married accommodation at Kharian, 1961. Seated, from left to right were: Major-General Andwar (E-in-C), Genral M. Musa (C-in-C), Field Marshal Ayub Khan and Major-General Sahabzada Yaqub Khan (GOC 1st Armoured Division)

Sector, and further south. However, it was not against India that the US was undertaking this construction program. Some villages at the construction site were relocated, however; their mosques and graveyards still exist within the cantonment boundaries.

Work on Kharian Cantonment began in 1956, and international companies like Gammon, General Electric and Caterpillar participated. Temporary housing for the engineers was constructed within the precincts of the new cantonment and 24 km away at Lalamusa. The initial problem was finding an adequate supply of water.[25] For this

reason, alongside the construction of temporary accommodation for the contractors, one of the first projects was to drill for water on the Bhimber Nallah near the village of Guliana, and the construction of the large iconic water tank. The Suez Crisis of 1956 closed the Canal and lengthened the supply line for imported materials, slowing construction at both Kharian and the Mauripur Airbase, which was concurrently being expanded. The Trans-East District also found itself competing for supplies with the Pakistan Government. In the late 1950s, the government was constructing a number of major irrigation

the northern end. A modern sewage treatment plant was installed at the southern end, and the American engineers claimed that the wastewater was potable.[26]

Interestingly, the General Headquarters was of the opinion that it would have been cheaper in both initial outlay and subsequent maintenance, if all future troop housing projects were undertaken on specifications and pattern prevalent in the Pakistan Army. However, this view, which was communicated to the MAAG, was probably not inspired by a desire to save American dollars, but was an effort to divert funds towards constructing accommodation for the families. This was a serious issue at Kharian and Multan, and since the start of the negotiations, Pakistan had insisted on living quarters for the families of officers and soldiers as well as followers i.e. janitors, mess waiters, cooks, etc. It cited two basic reasons. Firstly, the Pakistan Armed Forces comprised entirely of career personnel who spent their lives in military service, and needed their families with them. Secondly, Kharian was located in an isolated and sparsely populated area where no off-the-post housing was available.[27]

Major-General Sarfraz presiding over a meeting of military and civil administrators on imposition of Martial Law in 1958. (Author's Collection)

By April 1960, 1st Armoured Division had occupied the cantonment. Fifteen percent of the troops were still under canvas, but a year later, the contractor completed all the remaining accommodation for the division. It took two more years for the accommodation to be constructed for the headquarters of I Corps and the corps troops. The cantonment had a rectangular shape and in the centre was a large open space of 1,500 meters by 700 meters for training and sports. A landing strip was also cleared for light aircraft. Around this open space were the accommodation, vehicle garages, and other facilities. Placing this large field in the centre was impractical. It stretched the cantonment and getting from one end to the other without a vehicle was time-consuming. The cantonment was divided into a number of blocks with the officer's messes, and the Bachelor Officers Quarters (BOQs) at the

Field Marshal Ayub Khan and General Musa inspecting soldiers' family accommodation constructed under a crash program at Kharian. On the right is E-in-C General Anwar. (Author's Collection)

projects and had requisitioned 70 percent of the country's cement. In spite of these delays, work progressed well and within a year, the contractor had completed over 350 buildings. It included a centrally air-conditioned state-of-the-art hospital that like other features of design and construction at Kharian became a trendsetter. To provide good drainage for both the rainwater and the sewage, the cantonment was sited in a manner that the southern end was 60 meters below northern and southern ends.[28]

Following the 1965 War, 1st Armoured Division moved south to Multan and 6th Armoured Division shifted into Kharian, but it could occupy only half the cantonment since space had to be made for the 9th Infantry Division.[29] The latter was re-raised to complement the armoured division on the ORBAT of I Corps. As a result the cantonment was divided with the two divisions on either side of the large ground in the centre. In addition, the headquarters of I Corps with most of its appendages also moved into Kharian. Initially the armoured division was not cramped for space as it only had the 7th Armoured Brigade, which had been raised in the field, along with some artillery and service support units. However, shortly after the division arrived, orders were issued in October 1966 for the raising of 8th Armoured Brigade and an artillery brigade.

Lieutenant-General Bakhtiar Rana, Commander of the I Corps at the inauguration of Kharian Club, in 1964. (Author's Collection)

Three years later, a light armoured brigade with the numerical of '9' was added to the ORBAT of the division. By now, the cantonment was getting cramped, but fortunately, in 1969, the corps headquarters and its appendages moved to the colony that was vacated by the consortium which had constructed the Mangla Dam.

The Border City of Sialkot

Established as a cantonment 1849, Sialkot was the first station in British India to garrison an armoured division. It appears in historical records as one of the oldest cities in Northern India with a past that stretches back three millennia. The British annexed the city in 1849 after the Second Anglo-Sikh War, but the main garrison was 40 km to the west at Wazirabad. The foundations of the Sialkot cantonment were laid in 1849, and the troops shifted in from Wazirabad in 1852. During the events of 1857, when the British and some native troops left to join the columns marching towards Delhi, the remaining troops rebelled, but most of the Europeans survived inside the old Sialkot Fort. After the restoration of order, Sialkot continued as a cantonment housing both cavalry and infantry. Following the Kitchener Reforms of the British India Army, the 2nd (Sialkot) Cavalry Brigade was formed at Sialkot in 1903 consisting of the 17th Lancers (Duke of Cambridge's Own), 6th King Edward's Own Cavalry, and 19th Lancers (Fane's Horse).[30] The brigade was the cavalry formation of the 2nd (Rawalpindi) Division, but in 1914 it was sent to the Western Front in France as part of the 1st Indian Cavalry Division, landing at Marseilles in October 1914. Between the two World Wars, Sialkot was regularly used by the cavalry and remained as the primary station for the 2nd (Sialkot) Cavalry Brigade with one regiment stationed at Rawalpindi. By the 1920s it was a fairly large cantonment covering eight square kilometres. Apart from the cavalry, it also had a battery of horse artillery with its ammunition column, a battalion of British infantry, two battalions of native infantry, and engineer and transport

units. It also had two hospitals, one for British and the other for Indian troops.[31] At the beginning of the Second World War, the 1st Indian Armoured Division was formed at Sialkot in 1940 with the 1st Armoured Brigade raised from the headquarters of the 2nd (Sialkot) Cavalry Brigade. It consisted of two armoured regiments – Royal Deccan Horse and Probyn's Horse (which was located at Risalpur). 19th Lancers also joined the division at Sialkot as its reconnaissance regiment. The 3rd Indian Motor Brigade, which fought against such desperate odds in North Africa was also raised here in 1940. Two of its regiments, 2nd Lancers and 11th Cavalry mechanized at Sialkot, and 18th Cavalry at Rawalpindi. Thus, at its peak there were two formation headquarters and four armoured and motorised regiments at Sialkot. However, the motor brigade mobilised in December 1940, and departed for North Africa. In April 1941, anticipating a move to the Middle East, the headquarters of the armoured division, and the armoured brigade moved to Malir. [32] [33]

As the Pakistan Army tried to establish a semblance of order after Independence, being a large cantonment Sialkot drew in active formations and units, as well as static establishments. The 12th Frontier Force Regimental Centre was already located at Sialkot and in August 1947, the Regimental Centres of 15th and 16th Punjab moved in from Ambala. In November, the Engineer Centre was established at Sialkot with the Muslim elements of three Engineer Centres located in British India. The School of Military Engineering was established alongside, and the two had a single commandant. With the escalation of the conflict in Kashmir, the 2nd (Nowshera) Brigade (re-designated as 103rd Brigade) arrived at Sialkot in December 1947 with four infantry battalions. It was placed under command the headquarters of 10th Division located at Lahore. Two months later, 6th Lancers equipped with armoured cars arrived from Kohat. Prior to the Second World War, 6th Lancers had served in Sialkot for nine years but this time after a brief stay, it was re-located to Lahore. Since Sialkot was too

The C-in-C inspecting the M24s of the 15th Lancers after the regiment arrived at Sialkot, in 1956. (Author's Collection)

Mileage Marker at Sialkot, as seen in 1900. (Author's Collection)

of troops and armour in the garrison. 15th Division was raised at Sialkot in the mid-1950s and 15th Lancers, the reconnaissance regiment of I Corps moved to the garrison. By 1965, Sialkot had nothing less than four armoured units, one each for its four infantry brigades defending the Ravi-Chenab Corridor – 20th Lancers, 25th Cavalry, 31st Tank Delivery Unit, and 33rd Tank Delivery Unit.

25th Cavalry was raised as the integral armoured regiment for 15th Division at Kharian in 1962, and moved to Sialkot. Raised at Rawalpindi as the reconnaissance regiment for I Corps, 20th Lancers moved into the Harding Lines in Sialkot in 1963, which it occupied for the next nine years. From here, it moved out to fight both the 1965 and 1971 Wars. 31st TDU was raised in Nowshera in 1964, and defended Sialkot during the 1965 War. It was re-designated as a cavalry regiment after the war, remained at Sialkot, and fought the 1971 War as part of 8th Independent Armoured Brigade. 33rd TDU was raised at Kharian in 1964, moved to Sialkot before the 1965 War, and fought at the famous Battle of Chawinda. Re-designated as 33rd Cavalry it formed part of Task Force Chengez in the 1971 War, and fought in the Shakargarh Sector. It remained at Sialkot for 18 long years from 1965 to 1983. Another regiment, which also spent a long period in Sialkot, was 32nd Cavalry. It moved to Sialkot in 1966 and remained there for the next 17 years. During the two wars, troops were in combat with the Indians practically at the doorsteps of the city, but in both the wars, the Indians did not make a serious effort to capture it. In 1965, the Indian 26th Infantry Division with one tank regiment launched an attack opposite Sialkot, but in their war accounts, there are diverse views on whether the city was an objective to invest or capture. In 1971, while the Indians captured the weakly defended Phukhlian Salient, they made no effort to threaten the city. However, since in both the wars, the Indians launched their main offensive in the Ravi-Chenab Corridor, Sialkot has continued to be a garrison for a number of armoured regiments.

close to the border, the Regimental Centres subsequently moved to Jhelum, and when the armoured brigade shifted from Risalpur to Rawalpindi, the Engineer Centre and School occupied the vacant accommodation. Sialkot is only 11 km from the border with India, and as it developed into a major manufacturing town and its strategic importance grew, there was a corresponding increase in the strength

6

THE EQUIPMENT UNTIL 1965

During the course of the Second World War, the British India Army was not at a priority for equipment, and the war surplus American tanks and vehicles that were available at the end of the conflict were a bonanza. However, much of this equipment was on the verge of obsolescence, and though the situation did marginally improve, the IAC continued as a mixed force of discarded Churchills, Shermans,

Stuarts, and armoured cars. It was the same mixed configuration (fortunately less the Churchill tanks) that the Pakistan Armoured Corps acquired as its share, and struggled to keep combat worthy through the lean years after Independence. Soon after Independence, there were overtures to the US for military equipment, but it took a concentrated effort of five years by the political and the military leadership to convince the Americans to open the gates. In the decade of the 1950s, two clear stages are identifiable in equipping the armoured corps, the first of which was the endeavour to make it into an all-track force. It was achieved in 1952 by purchasing through the US Lend-Lease Program, better model Shermans as well as M36B2 tank busters. The second stage was to modernise the equipment, which was partly accomplished through the first US Military Assistance Program (MAP) that commenced in 1954, but was terminated during the 1965 War.

The Lean Years

At independence Pakistan inherited 162 Sherman medium tanks, and 135 light armoured vehicles consisting of M3 Stuarts, Humbers, and Daimlers.[1] The light tanks and armoured cars were largely with the light armoured regiments that were attached to the infantry divisions, while the Shermans equipped the regiments serving with 3rd Armoured Brigade. Even at its prime during the Second World War, the Sherman was a second runner to German tanks due to weaker amour protection, and inferior armament. However, it was easy to manufacture in automobile plants converted to producing tanks and easily operated by conscripted soldiers with a short training spell. Compared to the large German tanks, the Sherman was nimble, reliable, and had superior gun controls. It was also one of the most produced tanks of Second World War, only out-manufactured by the Soviet T-34.

There were many variants of Shermans supplied by the US to its allies during the war. The British identified them by mark numbers – the US M4 became Mark I, the M4A1 the Mark II, and so on.[2] The variants in service with the armoured regiments of the British India Army were the Sherman II, III, and V in which the basic difference was the engine.[3] All were armed with a 75mm gun that had its origins in the famous French *Canon de 75-modèle 1897* of the First World War.[4] [5] The field gun origins of the 75mm guaranteed that for its calibre, the high explosive round was very effective. This was one of the reasons why the Sherman could effectively support the infantry in Burma. At the opening stages of the Second World War, the doctrine of the US Army emphasised the role of tanks in support of infantry. Since the high explosive round was considered more important, parallel developments were not carried out on an armour-piercing round.[6] Its M61A1 Armour Piercing Capped round with a muzzle velocity of 620 m/s could penetrate only 94mm (3.7 inches) of armour plate, and that at ranges under 500 meters. While this performance was acceptable by the standards of 1942, it was totally inadequate in the latter years of the Second World War against superior German Tiger and Panther tanks. Due to its limitations, the 75mm was replaced by the 76mm M1 Gun with better types of ammunition that doubled the penetration power. With all its drawbacks, in the hands of a well-trained crew, the 75mm gun was accurate.

At Independence, the Pakistan Armoured Corps had two variants of the Sherman – the Mark III powered by the GMC marine diesel engine, and the Mark V powered by the A57 Chrysler multibank. Both were born out of the necessity for a compact, rear-mounted engine for the Sherman that could be developed and produced in the shortest possible time. The Grey Marine 6046 engine consisted of a twin-engine pack of diesel engines used on trucks and naval landing craft. The twin pack generated 375 horsepower at 2,100 rpm, which gave the tank a better road performance than the Chrysler multibank. However, the complex twin-engine layout, and sensitivity to dirt made it unreliable and the US Army issued this variant only to its training regiments. The majority were supplied to Commonwealth armies (including the British India Army), and Russia under the Lend-Lease

program. The A57 Chrysler multibank engine, which powered the Sherman Mark V, had a more novel design by coupling five engines, each with five cylinders to a common crankcase. The result was 25 cylinders, with a combined output of 370 horsepower at 2,400 rpm. Chrysler claimed the A57 could still move the Sherman even if 12 out of its 25 cylinders were knocked out. Each sub engine was geared to a common ring gear in the central crankcase, and a single central shaft handled all the output.[7] Obviously, the engine had five distributors and five carburettors, and it was a nightmare for the field mechanics to synchronise all five engines.[8] Until better facilities were established by the Americans, the 501 EME Workshop at Rawalpindi was the only installation of the Pakistan Army that could carry out base repair and overhaul of the armoured fighting vehicles and their engines.

Probably the best-remembered equipment of the Sherman was the Wireless Set No. 19, jointly developed in 1940 by the British War Office's Signals Experimental Establishment and Pye Radio. For tanks supplied by the US to Commonwealth Forces, companies like Canadian Marconi and RCA Victor manufactured an improved version in Canada.[9] When introduced during the North African Campaign, the No. 19 was a great success and was installed in AFVs, Bren Gun Carriers and command vehicles, as well as operated from ground stations. It was very versatile and could act as a relay station for retransmitting messages for long-range communication, and could also transmit Morse signals. Apart from the principal high frequency (HF) transmitter/receiver, the No. 19 packed a very high frequency (VHF) set for communication within a tank troop and an inter-communication set for the tank crew. The entire regiment, close to a hundred wireless stations in all, was tuned onto a single high frequency. It would take the Regiment Signal Officer (RSO) over half an hour to be satisfied that all sets were tuned on the designated frequency. The final communication check with the regimental commander listening-in, was a tense period for the tank commanders and their wireless operators. On the call of 'Hello all stations, how do you hear me? Over', the stations replied in a numerical order and woe betide the jittery operator who did not wait for his turn, and jammed the net. There was a lag of a few seconds between pressing the button to transmit and the set actually going into a 'send' mode. From the strength of the signal and the background noise, an experienced RSO could not only determine how well a sub-station was tuned, but also a fault in a wireless set.

Operating on a single frequency had an advantage; everyone from the tank commander upwards knew what was happening. The downside was an element of over-control by the commanding officer, and the need for strict wireless discipline to ensure that the stations were not jamming each other. To avoid a rap on their knuckles, troop leaders and tank commanders learnt to make short and crisp transmissions. During the 1965 War, regimental frequencies were abandoned, because unintended jamming disrupted command and control. Communication between the squadrons and the regiment headquarters was re-established through a rear-link.[10] The rear-link was a vehicle with two wireless sets manned by the squadron second-in-command, one operating on the frequency of the squadron and the other of the regiment. It relayed orders, messages, and information, and while it was not an ideal alternative, it did allow the squadron commander more independence. The US Army overcame the problem with the SCR-508/528 range of FM wireless sets used during the Second World War and the concept was incorporated in the subsequent GRC series. Compared to the VHF wireless sets that later generation tanks were equipped with, the HF band of the No. 19 could operate over far larger distances. In the late 1950s, a squadron of 11th Cavalry attached to the Infantry School at Quetta was in communication with the RHQ

A foreign military delegation inspecting an early model Sherman. The turret number designates this vehicle as belonging to the second troop of the A Squadron. (Author's Collection)

The C-in-C General Gracey at the Nowshera Ranges in 1948. (Colonel Pir Abdullah Shah Collection)

At Independence, the only other tank in service with the Pakistan Armoured Corps was the M3A1 Stuart, which operated with the light armoured regiments as well as the reconnaissance troops of the armoured regiments. Its early variants were one of the first tanks in the US Army during the Second World War. Weighing in at 14 tons it was armed with a 37mm gun, which was also fielded in the anti-tank role in 1940. The tank had a large magazine of 103 rounds but the 37mm ammunition had serious limitations. The armour piercing shot could penetrate only 60mm (2.4 inches) at zero degrees inclination at 460 meters, and the high explosive shell carried a very small charge of 36 grams of explosive. However, its secondary firepower was good with three Point 30 Browning machineguns; one coaxial with the gun, one on top of the turret in an anti-aircraft mount and the third mounted in the hull and called the bow-gun. Like some of the Sherman versions, the early Stuarts were powered by a radial engine designed for aircraft. A cartridge, resembling a shotgun round, was fired electrically to start the engine. The gasses pushed a piston, which turned a gear and cranked the engine fast enough for it to start. If the engine did not start, another cartridge had to be inserted. The output shaft of the radial engine sat high and consequently the propeller shaft to the front transmission ran well off the hull floor. To create space in the fighting compartment the turret was raised, giving the Stuart a high profile. A crew of only two in the fighting compartment was a significant weakness, with an over-taxed commander attending to the wireless, observing the terrain, locating and indicating targets to the gunner and reloading the

in Peshawar using Morse over a distance of 600 km.[11] The No. 19 did not only equip the armoured regiments. It was the principal wireless set for communication up to the division headquarters, but by the mid-1950s was no longer considered reliable.

gun. In its anti-tank configuration, the 37mm gun with a well-trained crew, could achieve a rate of fire of 25 rounds per minute, but not in the two-man turret of the Stuart tank.[12] On the positive side, the crews of the M3 Stuart liked its speed and mechanical reliability.[13] The only time that the Stuarts were in combat with the Pakistan Army was during the 1965 War when they were issued to a tank delivery unit. In one bold action, a single Stuart commanded by Saeed Tiwana played havoc with an Indian Gurkha battalion that was attempting to recapture a village after the ceasefire. By daybreak he had captured 57 POWs including two officers, and was awarded a Sitara-e-Jurat for this feat.

The US Lend-Lease Military Equipment

The initial request for economic and military assistance by the Quaid was rejected by the US because of the Kashmir War.[14] However, the US Government did indicate that the Congress was expected to pass an Enabling Act that would allow it to provide Pakistan military supplies from its stockpiles.[15] A second formal request was made by Prime Minister Liaquat during his tour of the US in 1950. Bashir Ullah Khan Babar of Probyn's Horse was ADC to the Prime Minister during this tour. It seemed that the US was now prepared to supply the M24 Chaffee tanks of Second World War vintage but up-gunned with a 76mm weapon. In return, the US wanted Pakistan to participate in the Korean War with a minimum of a brigade. This conflicted with Pakistan's interests and there was an impasse.[16] The Pakistan Government was reluctant to reduce internal forces by sending troops abroad. The nation was also not satisfied with the handling of the Kashmir issue by the UN. In the early 1950s, Pakistan was eyeing the latest equipment that was emerging on the US inventory, but as Mr Abol Hassan Ispahani, Pakistan's Ambassador in the US warned, it was too far away. Replying to a letter from the Defence Secretary Iskander Mirza soon after the visit of Prime Minister Liaquat, the ambassador stated, 'As for the 200 latest type tanks, your optimism really startles me. Those are still on the top-secret list and have not yet been made available to even the Atlantic Pact countries.'[17] The Top Secret tank Ambassador Ispahani was referring to was probably the M41 Walker Bulldog that was subsequently unveiled at a ceremony attended by President Truman at the Aberdeen Proving Grounds in 1951.[18]

In 1951, Pakistan became eligible for purchasing military equipment through the US Lend-Lease Program.[19] The US had large surplus stocks from the Second World War, which could be reconditioned to a high level of their functional efficiency, and they were providing it to favoured nations at 10 percent or less of its original value. By 1952, there was a stalemate in the Korean War and the US was re-evaluating Pakistan's role in countering the Communist threat to the Middle East as well as providing a base for air operations against the Soviet Union and China.[20] General Ayub Khan was now in command of the Pakistan Army, and he started

The squadron's 'rear link': two Wireless Sets No. 19. (Author's Collection)

The crew of an M3 Stuart light tank of the recce troop from an armoured regiment. (Author's Collection)

playing the anti-communist card both in terms of the domestic situation[21] as well as defending the Middle East's oil resources.[22] Due to the global cotton boom, Pakistan's economy was doing much better, and it could afford to purchase through the Lend-Lease Program. Following a number of meetings between Pakistan's Ambassador Mr Ikramullah, and the US Administration, a list was drawn-up with the office of Military Assistance at the Pentagon headed by Major General George Olmsted.[23] [24] However, final approval was still pending, and a concentrated push was required to obtain the equipment.

In 1952, Syed Shahid Hamid, the Master General Ordnance (MGO), travelled to Washington to accelerate the release of military hardware through the Lend-Lease Program. Prior to his departure, the Defence Secretary Iskander Mirza and the US Defense Attaché to Pakistan briefed Shahid Hamid. The Defense Attaché told him that if he played his cards well, Pakistan might be able to procure what it wanted. However, the first meeting that the MGO had with Olmsted in Washington did not have a positive beginning. Olmsted aggressively informed the MGO that 'You [Pakistan] are forty-first in the queue'. After a frank and hard discussion that lasted the full day, Olmstead conceded that he was willing to support Pakistan's request, but would have to convince others like the Secretary of State, Dean Acheson. Shahid Hamid stayed in Washington for two and a half months, and while Olmstead worked his end to build a positive lobby, he arranged for the MGO to address groups of officers at the State Department. Shahid Hamid also addressed a committee of the State Department, which apart from a number of admirals and generals, included Henry Byrode, the Assistant Secretary of State for Near East, South Asia, and African Affairs. The lobbying paid off and finally Olmsted had the approval to discuss the cost of the equipment Pakistan wanted to purchase. The sum presented was more than the MGO was allowed to commit, and Olmsted generously agreed to reduce the price further from 10 to seven percent.[25] Consequently, Pakistan was able to purchase equipment worth $26.5 million under the reimbursable clause of the Lend-Lease program.[26] It included 352 Sherman medium tanks, and 75 M36B2 motor gun carriages along with their ammunition and spares.[27] Starved of equipment and struggling to keep its Second World War vintage AFVs serviceable, this purchase was a shot in the arm for the Pakistan Armoured Corps.

Pakistan selected the E4 variant of the Sherman, retrofitted with a 76mm gun.[28] When this gun was first installed in the M4 during the Second World War, the weight unbalanced the turret. The barrel also protruded too far forward, making it difficult to transport, and on undulating terrain it had a tendency to hit the ground. Consequently, the length of the barrel was reduced by 30 cm i.e. from 57 to 52 calibres, which decreased its performance by 10 per cent. However, the gun could still penetrate 9cm of armour at 1,000 meters, which was roughly double the performance of the earlier 75mm gun. This penetration was achieved with the High Velocity Armour Piercing (HVAP) ammunition, which contained a core penetrator of tungsten surrounded by a lightweight aluminium body, giving it a higher velocity at impact and more penetration power. The larger charge required to propel the 76mm round created a strong blast at the muzzle end that kicked up dust and obscured vision. This was partly reduced by fitting a muzzle brake, which directed the blast sideways, but in the dusty and dry conditions that the Pakistani armour operated in, the tank commander and gunner had to work hard to acquire a target for a quick second shot.

The Sherman was tall for its size and weight, and did not provide a very stable firing platform. The weight of the breech and barrel of the 76mm gun further exacerbated issues of balance as well as the recoil, which had to be absorbed by a relatively light tank. A partial solution to this problem came from an unexpected direction. The Sherman could be fitted with two types of tracks; rubber and steel. The rubber tracks were more suitable for roads, but provided less cross-country traction. On the other hand, the steel tracks gave good traction but were much heavier. The compromise solution was a rubber track with end-connectors that extended out 10 cm (4 inches). To allow the use of extended end connectors on both sides of the track, the suspension system had to be spaced out from the vehicle's hull. It not only improved the ground pressure by almost 30 percent, bringing it below 12 psi, it also extended the relatively narrow track-width of 42 cm to almost 60 cm. This resulted in an increase in the width of the tank from 2.7 meters to over 3 meters, and provided a broader and consequently more stable platform for absorbing the recoil of the main gun. Fortunately, most of the E4s supplied to Pakistan were modified with extended end-connectors.

The Sherman E4 was powered by a Continental R-975 9 Cylinder Radial, which generated 450 horsepower at 2,000 rpm. It was superior in performance to the engines fitted in the Sherman III and V, and installed only on the variants supplied to US forces during the Second World War. It was an air-cooled aircraft engine and as there was no slipstream or propeller, a cooling fan was attached to the power output shaft and surrounded by a shroud. The fan sucked air through the fighting compartment to cool the oil radiators, and then propelled it into the engine compartment. While in summer, it provided a welcome draft for the crew, in winter it was painfully uncomfortable for the tank commander standing in the hatch. The cold air entered from his collar and exited through the cuffs of the trousers, freezing everything in between![29] A recurrent problem was adjusting the ignition timing of the two large magnetos installed on all aircraft engines of its type. It required taking out the R-975 engine – a time consuming process that needed half a day for a team of four technicians assisted by the crew.

The Pakistan Army re-fitted most of these Sherman E4s with the Set No. 19. However, there were not enough in stock and some Shermans retained the SCR 508 wireless set, which was probably one of the most famous wireless series used by US forces in the Second World War. It was a short-range vehicle mounted FM radio that operated in the frequency range of 20-28 Mhz, and a command tank had two BC 603 receivers, two BC 604 transmitters, and a BC 605 interphone amplifier for communicating within the crew. It excelled any tactical communication equipment possessed by either the Germans or the Allied nations, and remained free of the static and interference that bedevilled the AM radios. However, the preselected channels were difficult to tune. Before 38th Cavalry went into operations in Rahim Yar Khan in 1971, a special team had to be brought in from the School of Signals at Rawalpindi to assist the regiment in tuning the sets.[30] Another difficulty that tank crews encountered was the placing of the SCR 508 inside the tank. Being a large set there was insufficient space to install it in the turret where it could be monitored by the tank commander and the wireless operator. Instead, it was in the hull next to the co-driver who was not trained as a wireless operator.

The army also purchased 75 M36B2s Gun Motor Carriage because their 90mm M3 gun provided even greater firepower than the Sherman M4A1. The US Army also called them TDs for Tank Destroyer while in the Pakistan Armoured Corps they were called Tank Buster. It had been fielded in the anti-tank role during the latter stages of the Second World War to defeat the larger German tanks. In spite of the calibre of its gun (which was later installed on the M47 and 48s), the M36B2 was a light tank (weighing less than 30 tons) because it had only limited armour plating for protection from artillery shrapnel. The front glacises plate and the gun shield had up to 100mm (4 inches) of armour, but the rest of the turret and the hull had only 40mm (1.5 inches) or less. In the earlier versions, the turret was open-topped to save weight, and provide better observation. Subsequent versions, like the ones supplied to Pakistan, had a thin folding armoured roof for protection from shell fragments which was raised a couple of inches above the turret, to provide a visibility of 360º. It had the same Grey Marine 6046 engine as the Sherman as well as the same chassis and drive train and was also fitted with the spaced-out suspension of the Sherman E9 series.

The Pakistan Armoured Corps did not like the tank. Yahya Effendi, who served in a squadron of M36B2s during the 1965 War, recollects that: 'It was an awkward fighting vehicle in every sense. The synchronisation of the engines was a nuisance for the mechanics, and while driving, an inexperienced or flappy driver could smash the single plate clutch by sudden release, thus immobilising the vehicle.'[31] The Pakistan Army initially planned to deploy them in the anti-tank role with the infantry divisions. The regiments of M36B2s were organized into four squadrons, one each to support the three infantry brigades and the fourth as division reserve. Each squadron had three tank troops of four tanks each making a total of 48 tanks, and six Bren Gun Carriers were used for command in the regiment and squadron headquarters.[32] However in exercises like VULCAN and

M36B2 being rafted across the River Jhelum during the NOVEMBER HANDICAP Exercise. Notable is the raised turret roof of this vehicle. (Author's Collection)

NOVEMBER HANDICAP held in the 1950s, a bad precedence was set by using them in offensive operations. In the early 1960s, all three armoured regiments of 6th Armoured Division were equipped with two squadrons of M47/48s, and one of M36B2s which suffered heavy casualties. Of the 11 M36B2s of the squadron of 11th Cavalry that were in the Chhamb offensive on 11 September 1965, most broke down in the first few hours, and only two survived the action.[33] Brought back to strength when the regiment reverted to the armoured division, the squadron of M36B2s was decimated by the Centurions of Hodson's Horse at Phillaurah. The M36B2s of the Guides Cavalry and 13th Lancers fared only slightly better. After the 1965 War, the M36B2s were withdrawn from the regiments, but during the 1971 War they were hastily issued to independent squadrons and again suffered badly.

The First US Military Assistance Program

The equipment purchased from the US through the Lend-Lease Program started arriving in 1953, and provided a welcome injection of much needed hardware. The Pakistan Army stationed officers in the US for inspection and during several visits to the US, the MGO himself checked the equipment entering the pipeline.[34] Though second-hand, the tanks had been overhauled and succeeded in making the armoured corps into an all tracked force. This purchase by Pakistan probably diluted the resistance of the US for providing military assistance. None-the-less, a concentrated push was still necessary by both the Defence Secretary, Iskander Mirza, and the C-in-C, General Ayub Khan. Following some high level meetings both internally and with the Americans, the gap between what the United States was offering and what Pakistan wished for slowly narrowed.

The Pakistan Army was aware that accepting aid from the US would bind the country into an alliance and all lieutenant colonels and above serving in the general headquarters were asked for their

opinion.[35] There is no information on the consensus, but in 1954, Pakistan signed a military assistance agreement with the US. The same year the relationship was further sealed with Pakistan joining the South East Asian Treaty Organisation and a year later, the Central Treaty Organisation. The United States initially agreed to $171 million in direct military aid, and it seems that expectations of further assistance were not high. The minutes on the Second Conference of Commandants of GHQ Training Establishments, 1955 records that: 'The Conference was warned to be on guard against loose talk regarding United States Military aid. It would not automatically solve all our problems for us, nor would the consequent expansion do more, in the first instance, than make good deficiencies in existing formations'.[36] The actual extent of US military assistance was kept a closely guarded secret,[37] but it ultimately spilled over $600 million administered through the MAAG in Pakistan. In material terms, the share of the Pakistan Armoured Corps was 504 medium tanks and 220 light reconnaissance tanks out of which the first consignment of 110 M24s started arriving in 1956. The 504 medium tanks were received over a period of eight to nine years ending in 1963, and the 110 remaining reconnaissance tanks were never delivered.

The M24 Chaffee replaced the armoured cars and the Stuart tanks as the principal reconnaissance AFV. The basis for the development of the M24 was the shortcomings of the M3 and the M5 Stuart light tanks that were identified during the Second World War, and a great deal of thought was put into its design. It had wider 40 cm tracks for improved mobility, and a relatively low silhouette to enable it to remain undetected. It was also the first US designed armoured vehicle in which ergonomics was incorporated. The design catered for the safety and comfort of the crew and ease of maintenance, e.g. a large access hatch for the loader eased ammo loading and other maintenance chores. In addition, the driver's hatches were not only larger than on previous light tanks, they also rotated and could remain

An M24 demonstrating its fording capability during a visit by General Ayub to the 15th Lancers at Sialkot in 1956. (Author's Collection)

open irrespective of the position of the turret and gun. The tank was powered by two 44T24 V-8 Cadillac engines, which produced a healthy 220 hp at 3,400 rpm, but the cruising range of the tank was only 160 km. The power of the two engines was handled by twin hydromatic (automatic) transmissions, combined into a synchromesh transfer case, which gave eight forward and four reverse speeds. The reverse speed of 30 km/h enabled the tank to rapidly disengage and seek cover. Since its role demanded a high degree of agility, every effort was made to keep the weight of the vehicle under 20 tons. The glacis plate was only 2.5cms thick (but sloped at 60 degrees from the vertical), and the maximum armour anywhere on the tank was just 4 cm. This proved as a serious drawback in the combat environment of the latter part of the Second World War, and during the 1965 War. It was also under-gunned with a lightweight 75mm gun that had a thinly walled barrel, which was derived from the gun used in the B-25H Mitchell gunship bomber. Theoretically, the gun had a maximum rate of fire of 20 rounds per minute, but at that rate, the light gun tube would have heated up quickly and not lasted long.

Though the tank had been fielded in the closing stages of the Second World War, for the Pakistan Armoured Corps, it was the first relatively modern tank that came into service. Probably for this reason, it impressed some of the officers including the Director Armoured Corps, Sahabzada Yaqub who considered it 'as the tank then best suited to our needs'.[38] Sahabzada was probably influenced by his course at the École Superieure de Guerre'. Though the French were equipped with the M47s, they favoured the mass employment of light tanks, which depended for their protection on speed, manoeuvrability, and low silhouette and were fitted with a high velocity gun. This concept translated into the design of the AMX-13, and its variants. During the 1965 war, the Indian regiment in Chhamb was equipped with the latter tank. The Armoured Corps Centre and School quickly geared up for training on the M24s. Colonel 'Bob' Babur who was commandant of the Centre and School during this period recollects that 'a very impressive demonstration was held at the Ranges for an American team [from the] USMAAG, and they were impressed by

the efficiency of our *Jawans* [soldiers] in handling them'. There was also a variant of the M24 supplied to the Pakistan Army for air defence of its armoured forces. Designated as the M19 Gun Motor Carriage, it had two 40mm Bofors guns or four Point 50 Brownings mounted on an open turret.[39]

The first medium tanks received by the Pakistan Army under the US MAP were 304 M47 Pattons. The M47 was fielded by the US as an interim solution for a new post Second World War medium tank by placing a new turret with a 90mm M3 gun on the hull of the M26 Pershing tank. The manufacture of M47s commenced in 1951, but by 1953 they were being replaced by M48s and by the time they entered service with the Pakistan Armoured Corps in 1957/58, they had been declared obsolete in the US Army. The M47 was a large tank with a height of 3.4 meters that towered above its adversary, the T-54, being developed on the other side of the Iron Curtain. It had a combat ready weight of 44 tons, but with its Continental V12 twin-turbo petrol engine delivering 810 hp, it had a power-to-weight ratio that was better than the T-54. For the tank crews of the Pakistan Army, graduating from the Sherman series to the M47 was more than a generation leap. Its engine was coupled to a CD 850 automatic transmission, and after the dry clutch and manual gearbox of the Sherman; the M47 was a pleasure to drive aided no less by a joystick instead of long control sticks in earlier tanks. Its torsion bar suspension and eight large shock absorbers (four on either side) enabled it to glide over obstacles. It also had some interesting features like a control with which the tank commander could override the gunner's inputs as well as elevate and traverse the main gun.

The M47 had its drawbacks; its size belied the fact that the armour on the turret though angled between 30 to 60 degrees, was only 100mm thick, and with a 'gas-guzzling' engine, it had an operating range of only 160 km. Under combat conditions, this range reduced dramatically, and was of major concern to the regiments equipped with these tanks in the 1965 and 1971 War. Samiuddin Ahmed, who commanded a squadron in 24th Cavalry at Khem Karan in the 1965 War, recollects that during operations, the amount of fuel in the M47s was a constant source of concern to the crews, and was the primary reason that the regiments had to pull back to leaguer and replenish every night.[40] The biggest issue faced by not only Pakistani tank crews, but also tankers from 26 other nations equipped with M47s, was operating the Stereoscopic Rangefinder. It was supposed to improve the probability of a first-round hit, but proved difficult to use.[41] The gunner had to align the marks on a diaphragm in the eyepieces with the image of the target. Since these marks were more distinct than the image of the target, it was difficult to determine when they were at the same apparent distance. Its working and operation was difficult for the Pakistani gunners to understand, and since it required about a thousand practice rangings, the range finder was never mastered.[42]

M47 tanks of the 32nd Cavalry at the Republic Day Parade at Rawalpindi in 1968. (Author's Collection)

After completing the delivery of the M47s, the Americans also supplied 200 M48s. They had entered service with the US Army in 1953, and the Americans claimed that the M48 was a completely new tank design with a new turret, a redesigned hull and an improved suspension. It was the first US medium tank that had a crew of four, and the first to mount the Point 50 Browning on a rotating ring with hand wheels for elevation and traverse. The turrets of both the M47 and M48 were cast homogeneous steel with the latter having marginally thicker armour, and a dome shape that offered improved ballistic protection. However, after experiencing the 1965 War, the Pakistani tank

Front suspension of an M48 tank showing the combination of shock absorbers and torsion bars that gave a smooth ride. (Author's Collection)

crews were of the opinion that the armour of the M48 could be more easily penetrated and referred to it as *shisha* (glass).[43] In spite of being projected as a new tank design, in performance and other critical areas, the M48 was no better than the M47. It weighed about the same as its predecessor, but had a lower power-to-weight ratio and the same stereoscopic range finder that was difficult to operate. Due to problems with the track compensating idler spindle, the early model M48 supplied to Pakistan suffered with breakdowns in transmission, suspension, and tracks being thrown. The M48 also had the same 'gas-guzzling' engine which limited its operational range and there was an opinion within the Pakistan Armoured Corps that 'the US had not provided Pakistan with the diesel powered M48, which had more power and range, thus reducing its cruising range and consequently its offensive capability.'[44] Both the M47 and M48 had the same 90mm gun that had been the primary US anti-aircraft gun during the Second World War. To that extent, it shared a similarity with the famous German 88mm Flak, but had not been as extensively employed in

the anti-tank role as the dreaded 'eighty-eight'. A distinctive feature of the 90mm gun was the T-type muzzle break, which was supposed to, but did not reduce the recoil of the gun to any appreciable extent. However, it did deflect some of the blast to the sides, thereby cutting down on obscuration of the target after firing. The M48 carried 11 fewer rounds of ammunition than the 71 carried by its predecessor, and the principle armour defeating ammunition was the HVAP. It had a muzzle velocity of 1,235 m/s, which was far better than the 1,000 m/s of the 100mm D-10 gun fitted on the T-55. One disturbing aspect of the M48 was that 24 of its 62 main gun rounds were stored in the turret as well as the entire ammunition for the heavy and medium machineguns. 19 rounds of 90mm ammunition were stowed to the left of the driver with a further 11 rounds to his right, eight horizontally on the turret floor, 16 stowed vertically around the turret ring and the remaining eight for ready use in the turret. It made the Pakistani crew in the turret nervous as they felt they were sitting on a potential volcano if the tank was hit.[45]

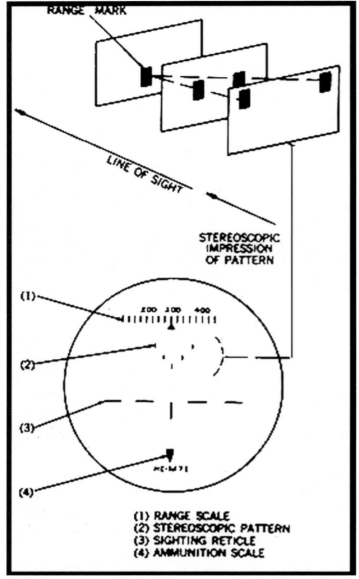

(1) RANGE SCALE
(2) STEREOSCOPIC PATTERN
(3) SIGHTING RETICLE
(4) AMMUNITION SCALE

Schematic layout of the Stereoscopic Rangefinder. (Author's Collection)

The biggest concern that the Pakistan Army had regarding the M47s/48s was their weight which hampered operations in the irrigated plains of Punjab.[46] A major exercise was conducted by the army in 1962 to assess the cross-country performance of the tanks in which the results were disappointing.

Of interest is a comparative assessment of the mobility of the M47/48 against the T-59 that entered service with the Army after 1965. In spite of its relatively smaller size and lower weight, the cross-country performance of the T-59 was not significantly better than the M48. In the early 1980s, one of the corps carried out tank-going trials through areas that had been deliberately inundated for various lengths of time ranging from a few days to a month. The two tanks that were tested were the T-59 and the M47Ms, which had been upgraded by the Iranians with a Continental AVDS-1790-2A supercharged diesel engine generating 690 hp at 2,800 rpm. While the M47M with its better power-to-weight ratio surged through with its boat shaped front rising like a prow of a ship, the T-59 with its 520 hp engine struggled through some of the worst patches that were inundated. However, the army did not consider this an issue when the T-59s entered service.

Just as the M47/M48 was a quantum leap for the Pakistan Armoured Corps over the Shermans, so also was its AN/GRC wireless set.[47] The first introduction that the crews of the corps had

to the Angry series (as they were known in the US Army), came with the M24 Chaffee. The development of the GRC was the result of a careful analysis of the operations of wireless equipment used during the Second World War. The biggest advantage that it provided was a high degree of flexibility in managing the communication within the regiment by segregating that of the squadrons. However, it was only the experience of the 1965 War, which compelled the armoured corps to discard the single frequency regiment net. Another major advantage that the GRC series provided was inter-arm communication. The GRC-3/4s were for armour units (20.0–27.9 MHz); the 5 and 6s were for the artillery (27.0–38.9 MHz); and the 7 and 8s were infantry sets (38.0–54.9 MHz). Because of an overlap in the frequencies used by each arm, both the infantry and armour could call for artillery support, but armour could not call infantry and vice versa. For this a separate radio set, the AN/VRC-10 (the vehicle born version of the PRC-10 which was an infantry man-pack set), was installed in tanks and vehicles. The infantry could communicate through a call box that was conveniently located at the rear of the hull that hooked into the interphone unit of the tank crew.

Another wireless set that greatly improved command communication at the tactical level was the Telefunken AN/GRC-9 that was a high-powered set operating in the medium frequency range. It was an improved version of the BC-1306 that had been well proven during the Second World War. It came in many configurations, but the one used by the armoured corps were installed in both jeeps and Dodge trucks, and greatly improved communication for the rear link particularly in the regiments equipped with Shermans. It had a welcome range of 30 to 50 km, and when hooked onto a loudspeaker the sound carried to a distance of 80 meters 'loud and clear'. It was a very popular set and the ambition of every wireless operator in the regiment was to man a GRC-9.[48]

While converting to the American equipment, the army received little assistance from instructors from the US. 'An American team came to the Armoured Corps Centre to teach a group of officers, and NCOs the driving of the American tanks. The Americans taught us how to start, drive and maintain the tanks, they admitted that they did not know the technical aspects of the tank and were not bothered to know them'.[49] Detailed knowledge was acquired from attending technical courses in the USA. These courses were a welcome change, because until then the only technical and tactical courses that officers of the Pakistan Armoured Corps could attend abroad were at the Armoured Corps School at Bovington, UK. A number of majors and captains from armour, but some also from the Corps of Electrical and Mechanical Engineers (EME) attended the Armor Motor Officers Course at the US Armor School in Fort Knox, Kentucky. This course was the equivalent of the Technical Officers Course conducted at the School of Armour at Nowshera. Shamim Manto, who attended this course along with officers from 12 countries, recollected that 'it was very well organized with modern training aids.'[50] While the knowledge acquired by the Pakistani officers was beneficial to the corps in general, within the regiments the officers and the crews mostly taught themselves using the excellent sets of Technical Manuals (TMs) provided with the equipment.[51] These TMs, which covered the entire range of equipment including rifles, machineguns, wireless sets, jeeps, trucks, guns and tanks, were exceedingly well compiled, and liberally illustrated with detailed drawings and photographs. Apart from instructions related to the operations of the equipment, there were separate TMs on the maintenance and repair of systems, and assemblies like engine and clutch, hull and suspension, hydraulics and fuel, as well as spare parts lists, etc.

In addition to delivering 110 M24s, the United States had agreed to subsequently supply another 110 light tanks, and offered the M41 Walker Bulldog. In all likelihood, this was the Top Secret tank that Mr Ispahani, Pakistan's Ambassador in the US had referred to. When it was unveiled in 1951, it was heralded as 'a revolution in US tank design … the world's best light tank'.[52] It was the first US tank to be built around a gun instead of an engine and weighed 23 tons. It was well armed with a newly developed and accurate high-velocity 76mm gun that was stabilised both in the vertical and horizontal plane. It replaced the Chaffee in the US Army and by the late 1950s it was being supplied to a number of allies. It would have been provided to the Pakistan Army, but the armoured corps was looking for M48s to replace the Shermans. Consequently, a case was made for more M48s, which the Americans refused. What the Pakistan Army did not appreciate was that the

An M32 ARV being demonstrated to King Hussein of Jordan in 1953, in Peshawar. (Author's Collection)

dynamics of the supply of equipment from the US had changed. The American administration had entered the Kennedy era, and one of the main changes that occurred was that Military Assistance Programs had been taken away from the Department of Defense. It was now re-designated as Foreign Military Sales (FMS) Programs and brought under the purview of the Department of State to fit within the larger dimensions of foreign policy. In addition, following the Indo-China War, there had been a shift in the relations between the United States and India, which had an adverse effect on military assistance to Pakistan. Consequently, the armoured corps neither received any more M48s, nor the M41 Walker Bulldog that the US had offered. The quantity and type of tanks (and other equipment) being supplied by the US to Pakistan was kept a closely guarded secret and the Indians were under the impression that the M41 was in service with the Pakistan Army. The Operation Order of the Indian 1st Armoured Brigade found in the tank of the CO of Poona Horse in the 1965 War, states the possibility of some Pakistani regiments being equipped with the M41.

A common feature of all American AFVs of that era was the Browning machinegun: the M1919A4 Point Three 'O' and the M1921 Point Five 'O'. The Point 50 Browning was employed in the anti-aircraft role while the Point 30 Browning was fitted both as the coax and hull mounted machine guns. The crews of the Pakistan Armoured Corps were well familiar with these weapons from the days of the Sherman and Stuart tanks. The Point 30 Browning machine gun had been in service for many decades. Owing to its reputation as a simple, robust, and reliable weapon, the Browning gas/blowback design was in use with the US military from the First World War until Vietnam, a span of over 50 years. However, the Point 30 Browning had a slow rate of fire of 400–600 rpm, and lacked a quick-change barrel. It was also heavy with a weight of 13.5 kg (31 pounds), and equally heavy recoil.

In comparison, the German MG 42 that saw extensive service during the Second World War, had an impressive rate of fire of 1,200 to 1,500 rpm and weighed 2 kg (4.4 pounds) less than the Point 30 Browning. Its drawbacks were sensitivity to dust and comparative expense to manufacture.

Browning's other contribution to the American military arsenal was the Point 50 machinegun. Its official designation was 'Browning Machinegun, Cal .50, M2, HB, Flexible' but US troops called it the 'fifty-cal', and Pakistani soldiers continuing the British practice, called it the Point 5 'O'. Its design also dated back to the First World War, and it was actually a scaled-up version of the Point 30 machinegun, even using the same GO – NO GO gauges for adjusting the timing and headspace. During the 1965 War, the Point 50 was often the only air defence weapon available to the armoured troops, and was quite effective against low flying Indian aircraft. As the leading elements of 1st Armoured Division were transiting in the bridgehead on the second day of the 1965 War, three Indian Mystere aircraft made the mistake of making a low-level pass over the mass of tanks and vehicles trying to cross the BRBL Canal. They ran into a hail of fire of hundreds of Point 50 machineguns of the armoured and artillery regiments and the engineer battalions. Abdul Mokeet Khan observed this spectacle while his squadron of 15th Lancers was trying to cross the obstacle. 'The sky became ablaze with tracers travelling in all directions and one aircraft was shot down.'[53] The credit for the kills achieved by the Point 50 was a consequence of its ammunition, which excelled in its long range accuracy, external ballistics, stopping power, and lethality. The Point 50 could achieve a cyclic rate of 450-550 rounds per minute, but sustained fire at that rate would shoot out the barrel within a few thousand rounds, requiring replacement. Consequently, the actual rate was anything less than 40 rounds per minute.

The US military assistance package also delivered a fleet of vehicles

T-16 Bren Gun Carriers of the 19th Lancers during field training in 1955. The T-16s were equipped with wireless set No. 19s and issued to the armoured regiments to train the crews and conserve real tanks. (Author's Collection)

M4A4E9 Sherman tanks acquired under the US 'Lend-Lease Program' in 1954. (Author's Collection)

on a ring mount which gave the logistic echelons an effective cover against low flying aircraft during the 1965 and 1971 Wars. The M34 remained the backbone of the cargo lift capabilities of the Pakistan Army for over 30 years; and was subsequently upgraded with a diesel engine. There was also a 5-ton version that was a multitask vehicle for command posts, to carry bridging pontoons, and tow artillery guns. For the armoured corps the most important 5-ton version was the M62 Wrecker Crane. It was built jointly by International Harvester and Diamond T, and represented one of the best examples of robust US military technology. It was virtually a mobile mini workshop equipped with welding equipment, an air compressor for pneumatic power tools, a winch with a capacity of 10 tons, and a boom that had a maximum lift of 9 tons and could extend 2.5 meters out. It was ideal for removing/replacing tank engines, and was the pride and joy of the Light Aid Detachments who referred to it with the simple title of 'the breakdown'. The Light Aid Detachments were from the Corps of Electrical and Mechanical Engineers and were attached to each armoured regiment. A similar organisation with the reconnaissance regiments were designated as Light Workshops.

that enabled the armoured regiments, to effectively support the tanks. All were upgrades of designs that had matured during the Second World War and included the Jeep M38A1, the M37 ¾ ton Dodge Truck and Ambulance, and the M34 Truck Cargo 2½ ton and 5 ton. The vehicles had a 24-volt electrical system, which was a big relief to the regiments. The previous vehicles of British origin only had a 12-volt system, and the batteries for the wireless sets had to be recharged by old charging engines that were notorious for not operating properly when most required.[54] The M34 2½ ton was a very robust vehicle and was called Reo by the crews of the Pakistan Armoured Corps after the name of the US Company that first manufactured it. It had a 6x6 drive train that operated on a ratchet system and automatically engaged when the vehicle required additional traction. Thirty were allotted to each armoured regiment, and every fifth truck carried a Point 50

With all that the US provided through the military assistance package, one critical piece of equipment that was not supplied was an Armoured Recovery Vehicle (ARV) capable of operating with the heavyweight M47/48s. The only ARV in service with the armoured corps was the M32, a limited number of which had been purchased through the Lend-Lease Program. The M32 was built on the chassis of the Sherman by removing the turret and installing a heavy-duty winch with the capacity to pull 30-tons, which was insufficient for the M47/48s. The winch could be attached to a load in the front or rear, over the crane or direct. The crane was an A-frame that was mounted on the front of the hull, but folded back for travel. The operations of the crane were limited as it could neither swivel nor extend forward or backwards with a load. The M32 version with the Pakistan Armoured Corps had an 81mm mortar mounted on the hull front, just ahead of the turret, to lay down obscuring smoke while carrying out recovery in the combat area. The scarcity of ARVs, which extended into the 1970s, was to some degree offset by using the winch of the versatile M62 Wrecker Crane. With an 80 meter cable and a load capacity of 20 tons (that could be increased by the use of pulleys to give a mechanical advantage that could double or triple the pull), the winch could recover a tank.

Another handicap faced by the armoured corps was the limited overhaul facilities established for the 'M' Series tanks. Under the US Military Assistance Program, a tank workshop was established adjacent to the 502 EME Workshops at Rawalpindi, which was capable of overhauling engines and conducting base repair. While the EME technicians at the tank workshop did a good job with the engines, the rest amounted to little more than the cosmetics of repainting the tank, outside and inside including all those parts not to be painted like wiring, grease points, etc. None-the-less, it was a major improvement over what had existed before, but nowhere close to the tank rebuild factory established by the Chinese many years later.

7
EXPANSION AND TRANSFORMATION UNTIL 1971

At its birth, the Pakistan Armoured Corps was beset with a myriad of problems across the spectrum of leadership, manpower, and equipment. The fact that the regiments absorbed and bonded the officers and soldiers of very diverse backgrounds is a tribute to the highly motivated though relatively inexperienced leadership, as well as the regimental culture inherited from the British Army of India. Eight years later, these regiments were again under stress as they transferred complete squadrons to the first of the many new raisings. The first major expansion of the corps was a consequence of military assistance from the United States that enabled the army to restructure and develop a new war fighting doctrine. In the process, the armoured corps underwent a transformation into a relatively modern force. Within 10 years of the commencement of the military assistance, the corps had also tripled in size with a structure that could boast of a heavy and light armoured division as well as an adequate number of regiments for the infantry divisions. As a result, it not only achieved parity with the Indians in the number of regiments, it was 10 years ahead in its organisational structure. However, after the 1965 War, the balance shifted in favour of the Indians and though more armoured regiments were sanctioned for the Pakistan Armoured Corps in the desperate months before the 1971 War, they were raised on a shoestring.

The Early Years

In comparison to the millions of refugees who abandoned their hearth and homes at Independence and migrated across the Divide, the breakup of the regiments and the transfer of squadrons pale into insignificance. However, it must have been heart wrenching for the officers, as well as the rank and file to turn their backs to a lifetime of association, and service to a badge and regiment to which they had owed blind allegiance. The Pathan Risaldar Major of Scinde Horse, Niaz Muhammad Khan was so torn by the decision to leave the regiment and serve in Pakistan that he did not sign his papers until the time of departure of the squadrons, and that too on the urging of his commanding officer. Until the end, he maintained that he had enlisted with the Scinde Horse, and that was where his loyalty lay. He sought consolation in the motto of the regiment: 'Man dies but the regiment lives.'[1]

Though most of the rank and file came *en bloc* as squadrons, the transfer of personnel to the regiments at Independence was not entirely a neat affair. The principal reason was that Muslims were over-represented in the IAC, and many trickled in from the centres, schools, and other installations. In addition the headquarters squadrons in the armoured regiments before independence were of mixed composition, and their Muslim personnel had to be adjusted. Finally, the last minute change of heart by some of the squadrons added to the number. Consequently, regiments ended up with more than their entitled manpower e.g. in 11th Cavalry:

> The Hindustani Mussalman element of the original PAVO Cavalry (11th FF) who in SECUNDERABAD had opted for service in INDIA and stayed back in SECUNDERABAD, later changed their minds and arrived in PAKISTAN on 13 November 1947. The Hindustani Mussalmans of 3rd Cavalry and the Long Range Squadron who were to be absorbed in the Regiment joined in dribs and drabs, and most of them had arrived by December 1947. Due to the influx of a large number of Hindustani Mussalmans, an additional holding squadron was raised as a temporary measure, and called 'D' Squadron. This squadron was further swollen when the Muslim Rajputs of Skinner's Horse joined us on 20 February 1948.[2]

Certainly, the other five regiments faced similar problems and absorbing squadrons into the regiments created friction. When Gustasab Baig brought the Muslim squadron of Deccan Horse from Secunderabad and joined Probyn's at Lahore, he also brought its *maulvi* (religious teacher). There could be only one *maulvi* in a regiment of the Pakistan Army and Probyn's insisted on retaining its own. However, Probyn's relented when Gustasab threatened to take his squadron elsewhere.[3]

Within the emerging Pakistan Army, the 'class' had little relevance except for ensuring a percentage of recruitment from different areas and provinces. Similarly, the class-based grouping of companies and squadrons was also irrelevant. However, it was not until 1956, when Pakistan became a republic, that class-based staffing of squadrons was discarded and the manpower amalgamated within the regiments. Following Independence, not all the regiments were assembled with squadrons of different classes. 6th Lancers comprised entirely of Punjabi Muslims and the Guides Cavalry was predominantly a Pathan regiment. Whether single class or mixed, the fact that the manpower flowed in from many regiments, made the task of giving them a common identity more difficult. However, many from the rank and file were veterans of the Second World War with a high sense of duty and motivation, and rapidly became part of the new team.

The regiments also did not differentiate between the originals and the new entrants. The first Risaldar Major of 11th Cavalry after Independence was Habib Khan previously of Skinner's Horse. Similarly, '19th Lancers honoured the regiment [CIH] and the man himself by accepting as its risaldar major the Gakkhar, Ali Musa Khan'.[4] Ali Musa was a highly decorated VCO who had served with distinction in CIH in North Africa, Italy, and Greece.[5] He was an imposing figure and his citation for MBE describes him as 'a great personality with unflagging zeal'.[6] Apart from the manpower, the regiments also had a very mixed trove of officers. Only four accompanied 13th Lancers from Secunderabad – Akram, Bokhari, Cardoza, and Zaheer. Aslam Khan, Durrani, Umar Khan, and Ayaz Faruki joined the regiment from Scinde Horse; Khatttak from 18th Cavalry, Nawaz and Qamar Zaman from 3rd Cavalry; Shahzada Alam and Ghafoor Khan of Hoti from 16th Cavalry; and Bashir from 2nd Royal Lancers. Similarly 11th Cavalry arrived from Secundrabad with only two officers, Masud Khan in command and Hafeez ur Rehman who was holding the dual post of second-in-command and adjutant. Muhammad Yaqub Khan came later from Secunderabad with the rear party.[7] The Guides had only four original officers in the regiment.

The headquarters of 3rd Armoured Brigade, which the Pakistan Army inherited at Independence was previously the 254th Indian Tank Brigade. At the end of the Second World War the 254th had moved 4,400 km from Burma to Risalpur and on the restructuring of the IAC, it was re-designated as the 3rd Armoured Brigade. With the turmoil that the newly born Pakistan Army faced at Independence, it was fortunate that the armoured brigade headquarters was well established at Risalpur as a subordinate formation to the Peshawar Military District. It had arrived at its peace station proudly wearing the shoulder flash of the Fourteenth Army and allowed to bring the brigade commander's staff car as well as the two AEC Armoured Command Vehicles (ACV) of the 'G' Command and 'Q' Command that had served the brigade throughout the Burma Campaign.[8] These command vehicles carried the names of two famous battles – Imphal and Kohima – that had changed the course of the war. The ACVs were subsequently transferred to the headquarters of 1st Armoured Division and retired after they had been used in Exercise TEZGAM in 1960. The first Pakistani officer to command the 3rd Armoured Brigade was K.M. Idris and his brigade major was Muhammad Azim Khan, 6th Lancers, who held this post until late 1950. They both had the privilege of receiving the Quaid on his visit to the brigade on 13 April 1948. On this important event the Quaid was accompanied by his sister, Mohtarma Fatima Ali Jinnah and Brigadier Gimson, the advisor at GHQ on the armoured corps. For the address by the Quaid, the brigade was arrayed on one of the many large aprons at the Risalpur airfield. It was a short speech, but eloquent as the Quaid was, he stated everything that needed saying. He even touched on the uniqueness of the armoured brigade: "Your brigade is the only one of its kind in the Pakistan Army, in fact in the whole of the Muslim world. This unique distinction that you enjoy is a befitting compliment to the biggest Muslim state."

Ironically, in spite of the Quaid's recognition of the significance of the armoured brigade, the government was considering its disbandment on the plea that the Army could neither afford such expensive equipment nor maintain it satisfactorily.[9] In an effort to reduce expenditure on the Army, release commenced on a large scale from the end of 1947 and continued for six months.[10] In his address to the Armoured Corps Centre the Quaid sympathised with the soldiers

under release, saying that though many did not wish to go "…but it is unavoidable. After all great wars, it is necessary to reduce the Army to its peacetime strength, and all cannot remain."[11] However, the Kashmir Conflict put an end to the release of personnel, and any thoughts on disbanding the only armoured formation possessed by the Pakistan Army and at that time by the entire Muslim world.

Of the six tank regiments allotted to Pakistan, Probyn's Horse, 13th and 19th Lancers, were designated as medium armoured regiments. They were equipped with Shermans, and were part of the armoured brigade. When the Guides at Kohat came under command the freshly raised 9th (Frontier) Division, it was also equipped with Shermans though it was still designated as a Heavy Armoured Regiment because of the Churchill tanks it was equipped with at Ahmednagar. 6th Lancers and 11th Cavalry were designated as light armoured regiments equipped with a mix of Stuart tanks and Daimler armoured cars, but retained the organisation of a reconnaissance regiment. 6th Lancers briefly moved to Sialkot in 1948, and was then allocated to 10th Division at Lahore, while 11th Cavalry was placed under command of 7th Division whose headquarters was located at Rawalpindi.[12] The organisations of the medium armoured regiments, and the light armoured regiments were the same that existed during the Second World War. They were large in terms of manpower and equipment, and reflected the manner in which they operated during the war. Their squadrons were organised to operate independently; the squadrons of the light armoured regiments because of their role of reconnaissance; and the tank squadrons because in Burma the armour mostly fought in half squadrons and tank troops in support of infantry.

Each tank regiment had a mixed bag of 60 medium tanks, consisting of two squadrons of Sherman V (M4A4s with the Chrysler multi-bank engine) and one squadron of Sherman III (M4A3s with the twin General Motors marine diesel engine). These Sabre Squadrons (the term was a carryover from the horse mounted days), were organised into four troops with four tanks each. The headquarters troop had three tanks (squadron commander, squadron second-in-command and the Forward Observation Officer), making 19 tanks in total. In addition, the squadron had one tank dozer and one armoured recovery vehicle. The squadron also had a large administration troop with three 15 cwt (3/4 ton) trucks and fourteen 3 ton Lorries. Consequently, the squadron had 150 all ranks which compared to the present organisation was much larger. The regiment headquarters had three tanks; one each for the commanding officer, the second-in-command and the battery commander. The headquarters squadron consisted of a reconnaissance troop of four Stuart tanks and six scout cars, and an Inter-communication (IC) Troop of eight jeeps fitted with wireless sets. The IC troop provided a command link with the squadrons when they were operating at a distance or independent to the regiment. The commanding officer was also authorised a staff car which was invariably a dilapidated Chevrolet. The total manpower authorized to the regiment was over 600 personnel, which included a female nurse for the families of the Other Ranks.

To supervise the maintenance of 68 tracked vehicles (designated as 'A' vehicles), and close to an equal number of trucks and jeeps (designated as 'B' vehicles), was not easy, particularly since the equipment had seen better days and spares were in short supply. It had to maintain and find spares for three different types of tank engines; the Chrysler multi-bank and the General Motors twin diesel engine installed in the Shermans; and the twin Cadillac engines on the Stuart V. Most of the trucks were started by a hand-crank and one of the rules imposed by I.U. Babar commanding 13th Lancers, was that if vehicle did not start on the third hand-crank, the driver was punished with 28 days of rigorous imprisonment.[13] To conserve transport, all

'B' vehicles were jacked up in the garages except those detailed for garrison duties. The 'A' and 'B' vehicles were driven for 8 km every month to ensure that they were in running condition.[14] The squadrons of the reconnaissance regiment had a headquarters and five troops and as with the armoured regiments, a sizable number of trucks for administrative support. Two troops had three armoured cars, the third had three Stuart tanks, and there were two rifle troops, which were carried in 15 cwt. trucks for dismounted action. The inclusion of in-house infantry made the reconnaissance squadron a versatile and flexible sub-unit capable of operating independently.[15] It could create self-contained detachments of a combination of sabre and rifle troops depending on the given mission; such sub-unit groupings were called link troops. The headquarters squadron had a supporting role with a signal and administrative troop.

For quite some years after Independence, the armoured corps suffered from an acute shortage of spares and replacement engines. When Wajahat Hussain, the ADC to the C-in-C, General Gracey on his own initiative put in a request for an engine to replace the one in the Chief's Cadillac staff car, he was informed that it would have to be taken out of the only Stuart tank that the army had in reserve. When Gracey heard about this he said to his ADC: "By the way Wajahat. I appreciate your concern for my Cadillac engine. Desmond mentioned it to me. Don't worry about changing it. I am quite used to pushing vehicles as I did a lot of it during the war; it does not bother me."[16] There are conflicting accounts about the number of tanks that were serviceable in the early years but Shahid Hamid, who was appointed as the Master General Ordnance in 1951, states a figure of 35 in the armoured brigade.[17] The Defence Committee chaired by Viceroy Mountbatten was responsible to oversee the agreed distribution of stores, arms and ammunition between the Pakistan and Indian Armed Forces, but nothing was moving. Field Marshal Auchinleck, who was a member of the committee, was very sympathetic to Pakistan and his efforts finally succeeded. On receiving a message that a ship was bringing stores from India, General Gracey personally went to Karachi to receive it, but was greatly disappointed to find that the Indians had shipped spares for Churchill tanks (which the Pakistan Army did not possess), as well as junk from the Second World War.[18]

Ultimately, the government was confronted with the reality that with the existing shortages of spares and equipment, the army was incapable of defending the country. The case was presented to the Defence Committee chaired by Liaquat Ali Khan and the cash-starved government reluctantly agreed to release funds.[19] A purchasing mission was sent abroad and with an improved state of spares, the army felt confident enough to demonstrate the prowess of the armoured brigade to the first royal head of state to visit Pakistan. The young Shahinshah Reza Shah Pahlavi wanted to improve Iran's armed forces. On a visit to Pakistan in 1951, he was taken to various formations and training establishments.

Ali Musa Khan, OBI, IDSM, MBE, Risaldar Major of CIH and 19th Lancers. (Author's Collection)

The armoured brigade, now commanded by Haji Iftikhar, gave an excellent demonstration at the Nowshera Firing Ranges in which 19th

The Quaid arriving at Risalpur to addres the PAF Academy and 3rd Armoured Brigade in 1948. (Author's Collection)

A Sherman being loaded on a Diamond T tank transport which remained in service well into the 1960s. (Author's Collection)

that had a capacity of 18 tons.

Ideally, the armoured brigade should have been garrisoned even further south than Rawalpindi, but there was no cantonment up to Lahore except for Jhelum where the headquarters of I Corps was in the process of being raised. Sialkot, where the 1st Indian Armoured Division had been raised during the Second World War, could have accommodated the brigade, but it was too close to the border. In the days of British India, Rawalpindi was a large garrison and there was sufficient accommodation for the regiments of the armoured brigade, though most of it was close to 70 years old. Late in 1952, the Guides Cavalry also joined the brigade at Rawalpindi and the presence of officers from four armoured regiments must have added a great deal to the vitality and social life of the station.

A year after the brigade had settled at Rawalpindi, it received a much-needed relief. The Sherman M4A1E4s and M36B2 Tank Destroyers, that had been purchased from the US under Lend-Lease arrived and were issued to the regiments. The E4 variant was a welcome replacement to the Sherman IIIs and Vs, which were under-gunned, underpowered veterans of the Second World War, and at the fag-end of their serviceable life. 19th Lancers was the first regiment to receive the E4s followed by Probyn's Horse, and 13th Lancers. The Guides deposited their obsolete tanks, and converted to the M36B2 Tank Destroyer with its 90mm gun.[24] The army now took a bold step by raising a second armoured brigade at Peshawar that was designated as the 100th Armoured Brigade. Its headquarters was converted from the 100th Infantry Brigade, which before Independence had been the Peshawar Brigade and commanded by some famous officers of the British India Army, including Field Marshal Claude Auchinleck.[25] The brigade was placed under the 9th (Frontier) Division, which was a skeleton formation with a dual task of an administrative sub-area. The two light armoured regiments, 6th Lancers and 11th Cavalry were converted into Sherman regiments and along with 9th Frontier Force formed part of the brigade. The brigade headquarters along with 11th Cavalry was based at Nowshera. The other two units i.e. 6th Lancers and 9th Frontier Force Battalion were based at Peshawar and Malakand respectively. Apart from these regiments and a workshop company, the brigade had little else in the way of combat and service support, and was disparagingly called the 'undy fundy brigade'.[26] In due course the regiments reorganised themselves (by adopting the TO&E of armoured regiments) and converted to tanks, but to change their mind-set from reconnaissance to armour operations took time. From the time that Martel's recommendations had been implemented in late 1942, the most skilled recruits went to the tank regiments and the less skilled to the reconnaissance regiments.[27] This may have been one of the reasons for the weak performance of the brigade when it participated in Exercise AGILITY, a major army exercise. It was only when the brigade was commanded by Gul Hassan that the tank troops and squadrons were put through a rigorous program of field training, and became comfortable in conducting armour operations.[28]

Lancers conducted an attack on two axes while firing on the move. The Sherman was a relatively large tank with a weight of 33 tons and the Shah, who was himself an armour officer, was most impressed.[20] He complimented the armoured corps and later joined the officers for lunch on the banks of the River Kabul. The mess *shamiana* (canopy) in the regimental colours of 19th Lancers and replete with the fine silver trophies of the Armoured Corps Centre and the Guides, presented a beautiful spectacle. The lunch was organised by Wajahat Hussain, who had the privilege to brief the Shah on the history of each piece of silver including the Inter-Regimental Polo Cup that was the centrepiece of the Guides collection.[21] Prior to the Second World War, the Guides Cavalry had won the cup for three years running. However, at Independence, the Indians objected to the cup being taken to Pakistan. The case was referred to Field Marshal Auchinleck who gave the final verdict in the regiment's favour.

In 1951, there was another confrontation with India known as the Fifty-one Flap, and the army was deployed in its battle locations with the armoured brigade spread between Gujranwala and Gujrat. The Guides was up-front at Nandipur northwest of Gujranwala. These were difficult times for the nation and the army. The threat was dangerous and the coffers were bare, but spirits were high. During a durbar, Lieutenant Colonel Abbas Durrani CO Guides informed the regiment that there was no money to pay the troops. A VCO stood up and said: "We will get money from home but will not stop working."[22] When the time came for the Army to return to barracks, it was decided to relocate the armoured brigade from Risalpur to Rawalpindi, as it was far closer to the operational area. In spite of the best efforts of the Army Ordnance to provide sufficient spares, the brigade was hard pressed to keep their vintage vehicles running. Probyn's Horse and 19th Lancers, which were located the furthest away at Gujranwala were the first to move back and the Grand Trunk Road was littered with their vehicles to Rawalpindi.[23] The backbone of the brigade's capability to transport tanks by road was a small number of American Diamond T tractors with trailers. Like the tanks, the transporters had seen extensive service during the Second World War. They were initially manufactured by the Diamond T Company in Chicago for the British Army in North Africa and were so successful that they were inducted by the US Army and supplied to all its allies. The tractor could pull a trailer load of 54 tons, and it was also fitted with a winch

However, it was unfortunate that these two regiments, which had such a store of experience in reconnaissance during the Second World War, were converted to tank regiments and the army had to subsequently raise reconnaissance regiments afresh. There had been a strong rivalry between the tank and light armoured regiments; and though the latter was looked down upon, in pre-Independence India, 'they proclaimed with a great deal of pride that reconnaissance tasks were closer to the classic cavalry role'.[29] Now that the role of the light regiments was changing and they were converting onto tanks, this rivalry faded.[30] Not everyone within the army was in favour of grouping all the armoured regiments under armoured brigades. The

The new M4A1 Shermans with the 76mm gun at a ceremonial parade in West Ridge, Rawalpindi. (Author's Collection)

commanders of the infantry divisions, like Major General Habibullah, were of the opinion that their formations needed an integral tank regiment. His agenda point for discussion recorded in the notes for a C-in-C's conference in March 1956 stated: 'Without a tank regiment, the infantry division lacked the power to counter-attack. Bearing in mind the shortage of armour available to this country, it was considered that one medium tank regiment per infantry division was preferable to an independent armoured brigade. However, it could comprise of a lesser number of tanks'.[31]

Expanding the Corps

By the middle of the 1950s, Rawalpindi was a busy station professionally as well as socially, and with a major US Military Assistance Programme under negotiation, it was also buzzing with political activities.[32] At the end of 1953, an Army Planning Board under Major General Yahya Khan was established along with US advisers, to deliberate on the reorganisation of the Pakistan Army, its plans and commitments. An American Military Survey Mission arrived in February 1954 and three months later, the US and Pakistan signed a Mutual Defence Agreement. The US had initially offered to assist Pakistan in equipping four infantry divisions and one armoured brigade but under this agreement, they included an armoured division.[33] The US Military Assistance Program (MAP) divided the army into two entities – the MAP forces and non-MAP forces. US military assistance was earmarked exclusively for units designated as MAP forces, which were to be deployed to protect the western approaches to the country and for intervention in the Middle East in accordance with US requirements. Military aid supplied under the program was not to be used by non-MAP forces i.e. those deployed against India, such as troops on the Kashmir border, the Indian border in general or in East Pakistan.[34]

By October 1954, a US Military Assistance Advisory Group (MAAG) was established within the headquarters of the Pakistan Army, and their families were accommodated in Chaklala. Though the agreement was signed in May 1954, the first consignments of a 110 M24 Chaffee light tanks did not start to arrive until the middle of 1955. They were relics of the Second World War and the C-in-C, General Ayub Khan complained to the US about the war surplus being diverted to Pakistan.[35] However, the fact is that the M24s were a significant improvement on the armoured cars and Stuart tanks that had previously been in service with the light armoured regiments. Instead of raising fresh reconnaissance regiments, the army decided to convert three machinegun battalions from the Punjab Group into armoured reconnaissance regiments.[36] It was a bad decision for obvious reasons, and Anthony Lumb who was assigned the unenviable task of converting the first battalion, soon reported that it was unachievable.[37] The General Headquarters relented and instructions were issued to the armoured corps in January 1955 for raising two reconnaissance regiments: 12th Cavalry and 15th Lancers. The organisation of these regiments was basically the same as the earlier reconnaissance regiments except each squadron consisted of three troops of tanks (instead of armoured cars) and two rifle troops.

The corps preferred to use the term 'reactivation' because both these units had existed on the ORBAT of the British India Army. 12th Cavalry was the product of the amalgamation of 22nd Sam Browne's Cavalry (Frontier Force) and 25th Cavalry (Frontier Force) in 1921. 17th Cavalry and 37th Lancers (Baluch Horse) were amalgamated to form 15th Lancers. In 1937, these two regiments along with 20th Lancers were converted into training regiments. 12th Cavalry became the training depot for the 2nd Indian Cavalry Group at Ferozepur and the 15th Lancers for the 1st Indian Cavalry Group at Jhansi. 12th Cavalry was reactivated at Rawalpindi, and subsequently moved to Sialkot as the reconnaissance regiment with I Corps. However, operationally it was under command 8th Division to cover the large frontage assigned to the formation. It inherited not only the seniority and battle honours of Sam Browne's Cavalry; it also adopted the title of PIFFERS. PIFFER is an acronym adopted by a group of regiments who trace their lineage back to the Punjab Irregular Frontier Force, which was raised in 1851 to protect the northwest frontier of British India. The claim to this title was reinforced by the fact that while it

M24 Chaffee light tanks of 15th Lancers. (Author's Collection)

received one squadron from 6th Lancers, the other two were from the Guides and 11th Cavalry, both PIFFER regiments. 12th Cavalry also inherited the regimental silver of Sam Browne's Cavalry that was in possession of the Armoured Corps Centre and had been brought from Babina as part of the share of the Pakistan Armoured Corps.

The regiment was fortunate on its reactivation on two accounts; firstly by receiving three intact squadrons along with their officers from old and established regiments; and secondly by having Muhammad Asghar Khan who had already commanded 19th Lancers, as its first commanding officer. Asghar was an outstanding officer and sportsman, who had fought with 19th Lancers in Arakan, Burma. He used to start his day by cycling into the unit every morning at 5.30 a.m. for the physical training period, and maintained a strong grip on the regiment. Within two years, he had energised the regiment to a standard that in 1959, it wrested the championship of the Armoured Corps Week from 6th Lancers who had been the winners since Independence.[38] 15th Lancers was reactivated at Nowshera by Bashir Ahmed and like 12th Cavalry it received a squadron each, but from the three other regiments; Probyn's Horse, 13th and 19th Lancers. It took the seniority and battle honours of the pre-1947 15th Lancers, and many years later added the title of Baloch to its designation because of its historical links with 37th Lancers (Baloch Horse).[39] It was initially assigned as the reconnaissance regiment for 9th Division, but subsequently moved to Sialkot under command of 15th Division.

The next regiment reactivated was 20th Lancers. It was raised as a reconnaissance regiment in June 1956 on the ORBAT of 1st Armoured Division at Rawalpindi. Its first commanding officer was Nasrullah Khan, a Kaim Khani of exceptional temperament and a great sense of humour. He had been commissioned from IMA, fought in the Second World War and had already commanded Probyn's Horse. The background of 20th Lancers was similar to 12th Cavalry and 15th Lancers. It was a product of the amalgamation in 1920 of the 14th Murray Jat Lancers and 15th Lancers (Cureton Multanis). In 1937, it became the training regiment for the 3rd Indian Cavalry Group at Lucknow, and in 1940 it was converted into a training centre. With this lineage, it took the seniority and battle honours of its pre-

1947 predecessor. The 'senior six' regiments had received a big setback when they shed complete squadrons for the raising of 12th Cavalry and 15th Lancers, for example. Probyn's Horse lost some of its best sportsmen to 15th Lancers.[40] Consequently, on their protest, the policy was drastically changed and when 20th Lancers was reactivated, these regiments were allowed to post personnel of their choice from different grades of service. The quality of manpower that 20th Lancers received was obviously just average. The regiment was initially issued with M36B2s that were transferred from the Guides Cavalry, and were showing their age. However, in 1959, it was re-equipped with Chaffee tanks, and after serving seven years with the armoured division, it moved to Sialkot where it fought in the 1965 War.

4th Cavalry was the first 'new' armoured regiment added to the ORBAT of the Pakistan Army. For many years to come it was the only regiment that was allotted the number of a regiment that had gone to the share of the Indian Army (Hodson's Horse), but this regiment did not use '4' in its title. 4th Cavalry was initially named as 4th Risala. However, 'Risala' did not conform to the existing titles of cavalry or lancers. Muhammad Nawaz Khan of Kashmir War fame raised it at Nowshera in 1956 and Sikander (Sikku) Khan designed the badge.[41] The regiment was actually born as an *ad hoc* headquarters under Nawaz who had been tasked to monitor the army exercise AGILITY. Nawaz was a legend, and though he had spent most of the Second World War in the RIASC, he was recognised for his knowledge of armour tactics. However, he had a loud voice and rough manners,[42] and was retired prematurely, because he had strong disagreements with his GOC.[43] Like 20th Lancers, the regiment was greatly handicapped in its raising both in terms of manpower and equipment. It was initially equipped with the old Sherman Vs and IIIs that had been pulled out of storage and like 20th Lancers, the manpower it received were mostly 'discards'. Only a dominating personality like Nawaz, who had earlier commanded both 6th and 13th Lancers, could mould the regiment into a strong team in spite of all the problems, but it required some draconian measures. On a charge which involved a serious dereliction of duty, a group of three JCOs and twenty-two NCO/ORs were sent on compulsory retirement within 24 hours.[44] During the next five years, 4th Cavalry shuttled between Nowshera, Peshawar, and Mansar Camp and in the process was re-equipped with two squadrons of the 'newer' Sherman M4A1s and one squadron of M36B2s. Finally, it converted onto the M47 tanks and joined 1st Armoured Division at Kharian.

The British India Army had practically no experience in employing armoured divisions. To support the war effort, orders were issued in India at the early stages of the Second World War, for the raising of four armoured divisions. However, only one headquarters was raised which served under the PAIFORCE and was employed in an auxiliary role for protecting the oil fields and maintaining internal security in Palestine.[45] The focus of the Army in India had shifted towards training and equipping armoured brigades for operations in Burma.[46] Given this background, it is not surprising that the Pakistan Army was reluctant to accept the offer by the US of an armoured division. According to a report by a US Congressional Committee, the Pakistan Army was…

inclined to have tanks scattered in relatively small units at various locations [while the US believed] that a tank force organised as an armoured division concentrated at a single location would be more economical and more effective.[47]

The aim of Exercise AGILITY conducted in 1956 was to determine how relevant such a heavy armoured force would be in Pakistan's operational environment. However in what may have been a case of 'the cart before the horse', the decision by the Pakistan Army to accept an armoured division may well have been influenced not by appreciating the strategic and operational role played by a large mechanized formation, but by the American offer to construct a modern division-size cantonment at Kharian.

The raising of the 1st Armoured Division with a balanced structure was a quantum leap both for the Pakistan Army as well as the armoured

Brigadier Yahya Khan receiving Brigadier-General Saxton (first head of the US MAAG in Pakistan) at Chaklala, 1954. (Author's Collection)

corps placing it ten years ahead of the Indians.[48] It was conceived as a heavy armoured division, not on the US Army pattern of floating combat commands, but the more rigid organisation of brigades that the Pakistan Army was familiar with. Apart from one heavy and two light armoured brigades, it had an artillery brigade, an armoured reconnaissance regiment, a self-propelled air defence regiment and all the trappings of the combat support and logistics units. The mailed fist in its insignia resembled that of the British 6th Armoured Division, but for the 1st Armoured Division it symbolised the fist that Prime Minister Liaquat Ali Khan showed in a speech in Karachi in 1951, in defiance of India's military build-up. The black background signified the colour of the belt and beret and was surrounded by the red and yellow colours of the Pakistan Armoured Corps.[49] It was probably one of the first insignias of the Pakistan Army that was round in shape. Prior to becoming a republic; the shoulder patches were of the pattern inherited from the British India Army, and resembled the shape of the Crusader shields. In 1956, the Pakistan Army decided to adopt a round shape that reflected Islamic Heritage. The first General officer selected to command the armoured division was Haq Nawaz. He was from the Punjab Infantry and had earlier commanded 9th (Frontier) Division in Peshawar. Though he had been Brigadier General Staff of I Corps during NOVEMBER HANDICAP, he had no practical experience in the handling of armour formations. The corps was already stunned by the abrupt and unceremonious retirement in early 1956 of Lieutenant General Yusuf, who was a thoroughbred and hard-core armour officer and felt that the selection of Haq Nawaz was prompted by other considerations. General Ayub thought that the corps was getting out of step and Haq Nawaz, who was a tough commander, was the right choice to bring it in line.[50]

GHQ had given the armoured division a blank cheque, and it selected the old office of the Department of Military Accounts at Rawalpindi for its headquarters. Reluctantly, the headquarters of 3rd Armoured Brigade moved out to West Ridge where its regiments were located. Until the army was reorganised in 1962/63, the most

senior staff appointment in the division headquarters was of a Grade 1, and Haq Nawaz selected Gustasab Baig who had been with him in Peshawar to fill in the slot. It was a good choice since Gustasab (also known as Gussy) was an exceptional officer, who had also served as the brigade major of 3rd Armoured Brigade. He was well respected in the corps for his dedication and professional competence. Gustasab reported to the division on 1 March 1956, and within six months had organised and operationalised the headquarters. 3rd Armoured Brigade was absorbed into the armoured division and 4th Armoured Brigade was raised at Ojhri Camp on the outskirts of Rawalpindi in March 1956 with administrative support provided by its two armoured regiments – 13th Lancers and Probyn's Horse. By now, Rawalpindi was getting too congested with the headquarters of three armoured formations, and five armoured and reconnaissance regiments. Consequently, the headquarters of 4th Armoured Brigade was temporarily based at Mansar Camp, awaiting the completion of accommodation at Kharian. By the end of June 1956, it was joined by its regiments from Rawalpindi and the first brigade commander, Sahabzada Yaqub Khan took command in September 1956. A third armoured brigade, 5th Armoured Brigade, was raised later when the division moved to Kharian. The presence of the armoured division at Rawalpindi in 1958 was timely and convenient. Since it was practically the only major formation in the area between the Indus and the Jhelum, it played an important role in the Martial Law of 1958 by briefly taking over the administration of the Rawalpindi Division.[51]

The formation of an armoured division was the first step that the Army took towards creating a combined arms mechanized force. Concurrent to the raising and reequipping of the armoured regiments, between 1956 and 1957 the 1st and 7th Frontier Force were motorised. In the process, these battalions encountered the same problems that the cavalry faced when it was mechanized at the outbreak of the Second World War and had to conduct cadres to train the soldiers on mechanical transport, communication, and anti-tank weapons. Gradually more Frontier Force battalions were added to the list and in 1960, the 7th Frontier Force was the first to be equipped with M113 armoured personnel carriers and designated as an armoured infantry battalion. The selection of the Frontier Force Regiment for providing battalions for conversion to armoured infantry was due to the shared historic links with some of the cavalry regiments like the Guides, 11th, and 12th Cavalry that dated back to the PIFFERS. However, the fact that General Musa had worn the badges of the Frontier Force Regiment may also have been a factor. The pace at which the US provided APCs was not as fast as tanks and artillery. In the 1965 War, of the five Frontier Force battalions with the armoured divisions, only two (7th and 10th Frontier Force) were equipped with M113 APCs. The remaining three (1st, 9th, and 14th Frontier Force) were still motorised.

The issue of M47s to the regiments of the armoured brigades commenced while they were at Rawalpindi. When Wajahat Hussain joined the regiment on his return from Staff College in 1956, he found;

a completely changed atmosphere with the induction of the US Aid. This was generating a great activity in the intensive conversion … to new and better equipment. Undoubtedly, it was a great improvement in the regiment's capabilities. In its wake, going through the complicated American maintenance system, along with constant inspection and monitoring by members of the US MAAG Group, who were located next door, right in the middle of GHQ, they were constantly breathing down our necks.[52]

Technically, the role of the MAAG in Third World nations allied with the US was to assist in the training of conventional armed forces. However, the MAAG in Pakistan not only wielded great influence, they also supervised at every level. When officers returned from courses in the US, the MAAG even tried to control their postings on the pretext of properly utilising the aid.[53]

The Americans revamped the system of maintenance by introducing to the army and the armoured corps the concept of Centralised and Squadron Maintenance Teams (CMTs & SMTs). Every vehicle in the regiment had to be serviced and inspected by the SMT every month, and once a quarterly by the CMT. The record of inspection was entered in a document titled AB406. Apart from an annual inspection that could last over three days, they periodically visited the garages with gauges in-hand.[54] The Digest of Service of 7th Frontier Force records two inspections conducted in March 1961 and February 1962. A JCO of the Guides who served as a driver on a M47 recollects that, 'What irritated the inspectors from the US MAAG was that the Pakistani tank crews locked the pick axes, shovels, crowbars, sledge hammers, etc. inside the tank for safe-keeping instead of strapping onto their brackets outside'. Occasionally, the visits by the members of the MAAG could turn unpleasant. Colonel Hollingsworth was a highly decorated and experienced cavalry officer who got along very well with the officers of the armoured division at Kharian but could be very abrasive.[55] During an inspection of 19th Lancers at Kharian, he cross examined an inexperienced troop leader on the maintenance of the M47 tank. When the troop leader replied incorrectly, Hollingsworth started shouting, "These chaps are f….ing up these tanks," and after an argument with Nasrullah, the commanding officer, he stormed out of the garages. Nasrullah had a mild temperament, but he was also a proud Kaim Khani and refused to allow Hollingsworth into the mess where he had earlier been invited for lunch. It created an awkward situation for the division headquarters and ultimately Nasrullah relented.[56] The MAAG in general was cooperative and on occasions supported the Pakistan Army in their hard task of obtaining from US Government the equipment it needed.[57] The MAAG also turned a

Major Hollingsworth, US MAAG. (Author's Collection)

blind eye to the syphoning-off of training ammunition by the army for building up its war reserves. While the ammunition for training was provided at a lavish scale, none was provided for operations. Therefore the army diverted 50 percent of the training ammunition into its General Staff Reserves, but gave a certificate that all the ammunition had been expended at the ranges. In fact the army did this for all types of ammunition for small arms, recoilless rifles and artillery.

The equipment arrived spasmodically and General Ayub complained to the Americans about the slow pace of delivery.[58] The Pakistan Army felt that neither was there sufficient quantity forthcoming for the army to be equipped quickly, nor was the aid planned equipment-wise or unit-wise so that uniformity could be maintained. This produced a great strain on the army, and affected its administration and operational efficiency.[59] On the other hand, the Americans understood that Pakistan was having difficulty in raising the additional forces to properly use all this equipment and that acceleration of deliveries would add to these difficulties.[60] The Americans had a point since providing equipment is only the first stage. Before a unit or formation is operational, crews have to be trained technically and tactically, maintenance procedures have to be streamlined spares and ammunition stocked and field exercises conducted. However, in spite of the slow pace of delivery, the Pakistan Army in general and more specifically the armoured corps were better-off in equipment, ammunition, and stores than they had ever been since Independence. Jeeps and trucks were plentiful, and there was even a helicopter for the GOC.[61] Zahir Alam recollected: 'In the armoured corps these were the days of plenty of everything, tanks, vehicles and ammunition. Captain Bunty Sarwar and I, when the range was allocated to the Centre for recruits training, sometimes used to draw half a truck of tank ammunition, take it on the ranges and fire it off, and there were no questions asked."[62]

Haq Nawaz only commanded the division for a year and, in 1957, Sarfraz Khan was appointed the second GOC of the division. He handed over the 3rd Armoured Brigade to Abdul Hameed Khan, another officer from the infantry. It was during the tenure of Sarfraz that the 1st Armoured Division occupied its permanent garrison at Kharian. In 1958, the accommodation at Kharian was only partially completed, but the locals were pilfering from the barracks that were

Nazir (G3I)   Shaukat (Hq sqn)   Riaz (SC Aq)   Zafar (G3O)

Ahmad (BM)   J.Zeb (Guides)   ghazi Hyder   H.Bukhari (13L)   Shabbir (2IC, IFF)   Najmi

Commanders and staff of the 5th Armoured Brigade, Kharian, 1964. (Brigadier 'Gussy' Hyder Collection)

ready. Therefore, on the request by the contractors, 3rd Armoured Brigade moved from Rawalpindi and 10th Frontier Force was the first to occupy the accommodation at Kharian. The next brigade to arrive was 4th Armoured Brigade from Mansar Camp.[63] As the accommodation neared completion, 5th Armoured Brigade was raised in Kharian in December 1959. Raja Ghaziudin Hyder was its first commander, and the units that formed part of this brigade were the Guides, 13th Lancers, and 1st Frontier Force. With the southward shift by formations and units of 1st Armoured Division, the 100th Armoured Brigade occupied Nowshera and Mansar Camp, and its armoured regiments started converting to the Pattons. Gul Hassan was commanding the brigade during this period and with his characteristic energy put it to work. Shortly after taking over the brigade, he conducted its first exercise with the Pattons in the area of Fatehjang west of Rawalpindi. He also led the brigade, when it performed the role of the enemy during Exercise TEZGAM. Initially 6th Lancers and 11th Cavalry received M47s transferred from regiments of 1st Armoured Division, where they had seen rough usage.[64] However, by 1963 the M47s were being replaced by new M48s, but since sufficient number was not available to equip all the armoured regiments of the brigade, the third squadron in each regiment was equipped with M36B2s. While both the AFVs used the same ammunition, mixing tanks of different roles and capabilities within a regiment proved to be a bad idea during the 1965 War.

In April 1964, the 100th Armoured Brigade was upgraded and named 6th Armoured Division. The number '6' was originally allotted to 6th (Bahawalpur) Division, which was raised from the Bahawalpur State Forces at Independence, but was disbanded in 1955. Abrar Hussain, who was appointed as the commander of the new division, replaced Riaz-ul-Karim who had commanded the armoured brigade after Gul Hassan. Abrar was one of the first IECO and his Indian Army number was IEC 14. He had been commissioned into

2/10th Baloch (later 7th Baloch), shortly before it surrendered to the Japanese at the fall of Malaya. Prior to surrendering, the battalion gave an excellent account of itself. Abrar spent three years as a POW, and in spite of extreme pressure refused to join the Indian National Army. Subsequently, the Japanese sent him along with 150 unruly Gurkhas as mine-breaching suicide troops on three successive island landings. Ultimately, the group was employed for building airstrips on a Pacific island led by their gallant commander, who 'remained defiant despite severe privations and cruelty by the Japanese'.[65] Abrar not only survived, but in 1945 also demanded and received the surrender of the thousand-strong Japanese garrison. In December 1945, an Australian force arrived on the island and was astonished to find it in Allied hands, even if the commander (Lieutenant Abrar) and his men were skeletons in rags, carrying Japanese weapons. For his exemplary conduct, personal bravery and strength of character, he was appointed as an MBE.

The Pakistan Army could not have chosen a more resilient commander than Abrar to lead the division during the 1965 War. He had a very positive attitude, was easy to work with, and raised the division with great care and attention to details.[66] The formation was structured as a light armoured division based on an American organisation and tactical concept, in which the division communicated directly with regiments without intervening brigade headquarters.[67] It had three armoured regiments (a fourth was added at the opening stages of the 1965 War), a lorried infantry battalion, a self-propelled artillery regiment, a medium artillery battery, an engineer battalion, and service support battalions.[68] The absence of a brigade headquarters subsequently led to speculation by military analysts that its organisation was influenced by the flexible structure of the Pentomic Divisions that the US Army adopted in the late 1950s for an atomic battlefield.[69] The assistant quartermaster, Sikku who eight years earlier had designed the emblem of 1st Armoured Division,

AMX-13s of the 1st Independent Armoured Squadron at Bhimber in 1969. These tanks were captured from the Indians in 1965. (Author's Collection)

Lieutenant-Colonel Ghazziudin Hyder, 19th Lancers, explaining the organisation of an armoured regiment to a delegation at Rawalpindi, 1954. (Author's Collection)

Corps, with the army and the corps implementing the lessons that flowed out of Exercise TEZGAM. A major change that had occurred earlier when the MAP equipment started arriving was the reduction in the tank strength in the regiments from 64 to 54. After TEZGAM it was decided to make the structure of the regiment more agile and the number of tanks was further reduced to 44. While the reduction was generally accepted in the armoured corps, what was debated was the organisation of the tank squadrons into three troops of four tanks rather than four troops of three tanks. Under the US influence, the corps had earlier experimented with and discarded a troop of five tanks.[70] Increasing the number of tanks in a troop reduced the flexibility of the squadron commander, and enlarged the responsibility of the troop leader, many of whom were JCOs. A lot was expected of the troop leader in charge of a four-tank troop. During operations, he was expected to form a base of fire with two tanks, and attack with the other two.[71]

The reduction in the number of tanks combined with the arrival of American equipment enabled the armoured corps to raise four additional regiments in 1962. Based on the 'New Concept of Defence' that had been formulated by the Army, these regiments were raised for the infantry division. The raising of 23rd and 25th Cavalry was assigned to the armoured division and 22nd and 24th Cavalry, the responsibility of the Armoured Corps Centre. 22nd Cavalry was raised by Yasin Khan at Nowshera as the tank regiment with 7th

also designed the emblem of the 6th. It had a black background, representing the color of the Prophet's flag. The horse symbolised *Buraq* a celestial animal that carried the Prophet Muhammad PBUH from Mecca to Jerusalem and back during the *Isra* and *Mi'raj* (night journey). The studs represented the seven heavens through which he passed for an audience with the Creator.

Fleshing Out the Structure
Following the raisings in 1955-56, there were no regiments added to the armoured corps for the next six years. However, in 1962 there was a burst of activity during Brig Bashir's tenure as Director Armoured

World War II-vintage 105mm Priest self-propelled artillery of the 1st Armoured Division on exercise in the Cholistan Desert in 1973. (Author's Collection)

Division, which was based in Peshawar.[72] It was initially issued M47s, but since 7th Division was operationally grouped with the 1st Armoured Division, they were replaced by M48s. 23rd Cavalry was raised with Shermans in Kharian by Ghulam Muhammad Khan and shortly after, it moved to Quetta as the tank regiment with 8th Division. 24th Cavalry was raised in Nowshera by Asghar Khan with M48s and subsequently joined 10th Division in Lahore. It was one of the first three regiments to receive Bengali Muslims in a sizable number. Finally, 25th Cavalry was raised (with M48s) at Kharian for 15th Division, which was responsible for the Sialkot Sector. Its first commanding officer was Nisar Ahmed Khan, known in the corps as 'Kaka' Nisar. He was retiring as a major, but with new regiments being raised, to the good fortune of the corps and

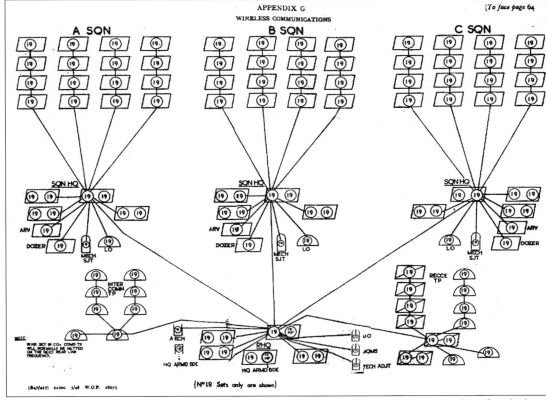

A communication diagram of an armoured regiment in the early 1950s – reflecting the large number of tracked and wheeled vehicles assigned to the unit. (Author's Collection)

the army, he was promoted to command 25th Cavalry. He had a good team of officers including squadron commanders like the lithe and suave Muhammad Ahmed, and the stout and tough 'Ginger' Raza, both from the Guides. The officers were complimented by equally good manpower with an entire squadron each from Probyn's Horse and 19th Lancers. However, what really made the difference in the performance of 25th Cavalry during the 1965 War was that it trained in the area where it subsequently fought. The army policy at that time was not to train closer to the border but Major General Yahya, the previous commander of 15th Division, decided that to familiarise the division with the terrain, it would conduct its field training within the operational area.[73]

Table 2: Number of tanks with the Pakistan Army at the eve of the 1965 War			
Type of Tank	Received from US	Issued to Units	Balance in Reserve
M24	110	105	5
M47	304	206	98
M48	200	196	4
M36B2	75	42	33
Sherman	352	213	139
Total	1041	762	279

These four were the last of the regular armoured regiments to be

General Musa, C-in-C Pakistan Army, reviewing M47 tanks of the 5th Armoured Brigade at Kharian. (Author's Collection)

raised prior to the 1965 War, but the Army needed more to support the New Concept of Defence that was being introduced in the early 1960s. By reducing the number of tanks in the regiments, equipment was available, but the army was restrained by the agreement with the US that limited the ceiling of the manpower that the US would support. To overcome this obstacle, the Army raised four Tank Delivery Units (TDUs) equipped with Shermans that had been replaced by the M47/48 in the regiments raised earlier.[74] Two TDUs were raised in 1963; 30th TDU by Sheikh Saifur Rehman to strengthen 10th Division at Lahore, and 31st TDU by Zahir ud din Ahmed, which was placed at Sialkot to reinforce 15th Division. A year later in 1964, two more TDUs were raised, both at Kharian. 32nd TDU was raised by Hashmat Ali Bokhari and in 1965 was with 11th Division south of Lahore. 33rd TDU was raised by Mervyn Cardoza, and fought in the Zafarwal/Chawinda Sector in the 1965 War. Each TDU had a nucleus (of two officers, three JCOs, and 51 other ranks), to be brought up to full strength on mobilisation. This strength of approximately half a squadron not only maintained all the equipment and stores authorised to an armoured regiment, but also periodically conducted an eight weeks refresher training course for groups of reservists organised as squadrons. It was a workable concept and when these regiments mobilised in May 1965, most of the reservists who joined the TDUs were already grouped and trained as squadrons. This is probably one of the reasons that in spite of the limitations of equipment and manpower, these TDUs performed well in the 1965 War and two of them were awarded battle honours.

From the time the Pakistan Armoured Corps started expanding

in 1955, within 10 years it had tripled in size, and could boast of 18 armoured regiments including the TDUs. Ten were equipped with Pattons, five with Shermans, and three with M24 Chaffee fielding a total of 762 tanks with 279 in reserve. The 98 M47s that are indicated in reserve is an enigma. It is the difference between the numbers received in the late 1950s and issued to the regiments prior to 1965. However three M47/48 regiments were re-equipped with old Sherman MIIs after the war. Across the border, India had been neglecting its armed forces during the 1950s, and had added only four regiments to its original 12, of which four (three were with the armoured division) had Centurions. Thus, the Pakistan Armoured Corps had not only achieved parity, but also surpassed it. However, it came with a price since a substantial number of officers as well as manpower transferred from the older regiments. For example, for the raising of the four regiments numbered 22nd to 25th the contribution of 6th Lancers was six JCOs, and 165 other Ranks.[75] This was nearly half the strength of the regiment, and only a few years earlier 6th Lancers had transferred a whole squadron to 12th Cavalry, as well as manpower to 20th Lancers. This large transfer of manpower must have affected the combat efficiency of all the regiments who contributed to the raisings of the new entries into the corps. It also affected the regiments in other unpleasant ways, for example, the Guides Cavalry lost its entire basketball team to 22nd Cavalry.[76]

NOTES

Author's note

1   It was also called the Army in India a term which covered regular British and Indian troops; Auxiliary Forces (India), and Territorial Force units, reserves, and Indian State Forces when placed at the disposal of the Government.

Chapter 1

1   Palit, Major General D.K., *Musing and Memories: Vol (II)*. p.111-112.
2   *Skinner's Horse, From Gallops to Gear*. Sainik Samachar.
3   Barua, Pradeep P., *Gentlemen of the Raj: The Indian Army Officer Corps, 1817-1949*. p.98. Many British officers who were associated with the development of mechanized warfare had served in India. Major General Percy Hobo Hobart, the first commander of the permanent tank brigade in the UK in 1933, served as an instructor at Quetta where he developed many of his radical views on armoured warfare. Lieutenant General Giffard Martel had also been a member of the Directing Staff at Quetta. Familiarly known as 'Q Martel' or just Q, he was a pioneering British military engineer, and tank strategist. General John Burnett-Stuart, one of the most influential British officers with regard to armoured warfare also spent considerable time in India. In 1925, General Chetwood (C-in-C India from 1930 to 1933) commanded one of the opposing forces in Britain's first exercise to test the new concepts of mechanized warfare.
4   Sandhu, Major General Gurcharan Singh, *The Indian Cavalry*. p. 425.
5   Chevenix-Trench, Charles, *The Indian Army and the King's Enemies 1900-1947*. p.137.
6   Chevenix-Trench, *The Indian Army*. p.137.
7   Sandhu, Major General Gurcharan Singh, *The Indian Armour. History of the Indian Armoured Corps. 1941-1971*. p.22.
8   'Army in India' was another term used for the British India Army. Sandhu, *The Indian Armour*. p.27.
9   Sandhu, *The Indian Cavalry*. p.426.
10 *History of 19th King George V's Own Lancers. 1921-1947*.
11 *Courses of Instruction, India, 1942, Pamphlet No 1, Fighting Vehicle School, Ahmednagar*. Logically the Germans and Japanese fell in the category of First Class Enemies and the Italians as Second Class.
12 11th Cavalry commenced mechanization on 23 September 1939 and sailed for Egypt on 6 April 1941.
13 Picken, H.W., *Nobody's Own: The History of the 3rd Cavalry and Its Predecessors, 1841-1945*.
14 Literal meaning is 'a man riding a horse'.
15 *Skinner's Horse, From Gallops to Gear*. op. cit.
16 Macmunn, Lieutenant General George, *The History of the Guides Part II 1922-1947*. p.102.
17 During the First World War, tank units of the British Army formed from the horse cavalry regiments had a far higher standard of maintenance than those which were not.
18 Macmunn, *The History of the Guides Part II 1922-1947*. p.102.
19 Sabre and Lance. Journal of the Pakistan Armoured Corps. Issue No IV. 1956.
20 *History of 19th King George V's Own Lancers. 1921-1947*.
21 Ibid, p.25. In British India, India Command was the name given to the general staff of the C-in-C, India.
22 To give an idea on the variety of equipment that the regiments had in the early stages of the war, in 1941, 6th Lancers was equipped with Light Morris Armoured Cars, the Guides with Marmon Herrington Armoured Cars and Armoured Carriers Indian Pattern, 11th Cavalry and 19th Lancers with Chevrolet/Fordson Trucks and Bren Gun Carriers and 13th Lancers with Chevrolet Crossley Armoured Cars. Probyn's Horse was the only regiment that was in the process of converting to Stuart Tanks.
23 *History of 19th King George V's Own Lancers. 1921-1947*. p.47. Some of these designations were subsequently changed e.g. the motor cavalry regiment were renamed as division reconnaissance regiments, and the light armoured regiments were renamed as armoured car regiments.
24 Khan, Brigadier Zaheer Alam, *The Way it Was*. p.42.
25 13th Lancers was operating with Scinde Horse, which was the other of the two regiments to be mechanized.
26 Other Ranks of armoured units while employed on road duties were issued with four bottles of mineral water per man per diem and ice at the scale of one maund (37 kg) per AFV.
27 The 3rd Indian Motor Brigade initially formed part of the newly raised 1st Indian Armoured Division.
28 Effendi, Colonel M.Y., *Punjab Cavalry. Evolution, Role, Organization, and Tactical Doctrine. 11th Cavalry (Frontier Force) 1849-1971*. p.69.
29 The early regiments that moved to North Africa had a reconnaissance troop of 50 motorcycles but it was disbanded because these two wheelers were found to be almost useless in the desert.
30 Effendi, *Punjab Cavalry*. p.71.
31 Sandhu, Gurcharn Singh, *I Serve. Saga of the Eighteenth Cavalry*. p.138.
32 Ibid, p.156.
33 Chevenix-Trench, *The Indian Army*. p.138.
34 Jeffrey, Alan and Rose, Patrick (ed.), *The Indian Army, 1939–47*. p.53.
35 Sandhu, *I Serve*. p.113.
36 Holder, Lieutenant Colonel Denzil, *Hindu Horsemen*. p.167.
37 Walker, pp.30-53.
38 *Military Training Pamphlet No 2 (India). Tank Hunting By Infantry. 1940*. p.5.
39 Sandhu, *I Serve*. p.118.
40 Chevenix-Trench, *The Indian Army*. p.151.
41 Effendi, *Punjab Cavalry*. p.81. In 1941, the terms 'harbour' and 'leaguer' were synonymous in British military terminology and did not have the same purpose as 'firm base', which was expected to represent a strong, fortified tactical deployment (see *Military Training Pamphlet No 1 (India). Armoured Units in the Field Part 2. General Considerations Common to both Armoured Regiments and Light Armoured Regiments 1941*).
42 Chevenix-Trench, *The Indian Army*. p.151.
43 Sandhu, *I Serve*. p.114.
44 *The Official History of the Indian Armed Forces in World War II. North African Campaign, 1940-1943*. When the Afrika Korps launched its offensive and threatened to encircle the British infantry division that by now was retreating from Benghazi, the race that ensued was grimly called the Benghazi Handicap by the British troops.
45 The Heavy Repair Depot at Chaklala was the forerunner of the 501 EME Workshop. Sandhu, *The Indian Armour*. p.23.
46 *Military Training Pamphlet No 21 (India). Notes for Junior Leaders. 1941*. MGS-M312 (N).
47 *History of the 17th (Poona) Horse*. p.60.
48 Ibid, p.59.
49 Coincidently, 32nd Lancers, a forerunner of 13th Lancers was one of the first troops to enter Bagdad during the First World War.
50 A 'flying column' is a small, independent unit capable of rapid mobility and usually composed of all arms. It is often an ad hoc unit, formed during the course of operations. Sandhu, *The Indian Armour*. p.129.
51 Macmunn, *The History of the Guides Part II*. p.102.
52 Pushto is the language spoken by the Pathans. Most probably it was the Pathan squadron of 13th Lancers. Khan, *The Way it Was*. p.42.
53 The Boys anti-tank rifle was replaced by the PIAT, a first generation anti-tank rocket launcher.
54 Effendi, *Punjab Cavalry*. p.177.
55 Fletcher, David, *Universal Carrier 1936-48: The 'Bren Gun Carrier' Story*.
56 Dominique Lormier: *Histoire de la France militaire et résistante, Volume 1*. Rocher, 2000.
57 General Messervy was the only officer of the British India Army to be given the command of a British armoured division. Messervy knew little about tanks and was not considered a great success in commanding an armoured division by either his subordinates or his superiors.
58 Effendi, *Punjab Cavalry*. p.91.
59 *History of the 17th (Poona) Horse*. p.59. There are others who claim to have used this statement in reporting the presence of large quantities of Axis armour south of Point 171. See Naravane, Major General A.S., *A Soldier's Life in War and Peace*. p.85-86.
60 After returning from captivity, Khan later served as Lieutenant-General and Foreign Minister of Pakistan. Two officers of 2nd Field Regiment, Indian Artillery who were also captured in this engagement were Major P.P. Kumaramanglam and Lieutenant Tikka Khan. Both rose to command their respective armies in India and Pakistan.
61 Sandhu, *The Indian Armour*. p.96.
62 *The Tiger Kills*. p.175.
63 Shergill, Lieutenant General M.S., *To Honour a Past*. U.S.I. Journal, No. 560 (April 2005 – June 2005).
64 Sandhu, *I Serve*. p.145.
65 Vaughan, Brigadier E.W.D., *A History of the 2nd Royal Lancers (Gardener's Horse), 1922 to 1947*.
66 *The Tiger Kills*. p.175.

67 Effendi, *Punjab Cavalry*. p.92.

68 *The Tiger Kills*. p.176.

69 Walker, pp.115-116.

70 Naravane, Major General A.S., *A Soldier's Life in War and Peace*. pp.85, 86

71 The debacle of the 3rd Indian Motor Brigade continued to remain in the memory of the armoured corps well into the 1950s. In a humorous, article *Exercise with Troops* written 17 years after the event, Fazle Haq comments on a justifiably nervous motor battalion commander defending against a tank attack, 'fully aware of the fate that overtook the motor brigades of the 8 Army at the hands of Rommel's Panzers'. Sabre and Lance. Volume 6. December 1959. p.10.

72 Reproduced from a captured German document: *Lessons from the African Theater of War*.

73 *History of the 17th (Poona) Horse*. p.62.

74 *The Tiger Kills*. p.311.

75 *Supplement to the London Gazette. 24 September 1942*. All these awards were given in a short spell of four days during the withdrawal to the Alamein position.

76 The Indian Distinguished Service Medal (IDSM) is equivalent of the Tamgha-e-Jurat.

77 DSM of 8152 I.O. Risaldar Mohd Rafiq Khan. 13th D.C.O. Lancers. The National Archives. Catalogue Reference: WO/373/21.

78 DSM of 1452 I.O. Daffadar Muhammad Bashir. 13th D.C.O. Lancers. The National Archives. Catalogue Reference: WO/373/21.

79 Khan, Brigadier Zaheer Alam, op. cit. p.70.

80 The brigade consisted of Skinners Horse and Central India Horse.

81 Russell, Jesse and Cohn, Ronald (ed.). *Marmon-Herrington Armoured Car*.

82 *History of the 17th (Poona) Horse*. p.58.

83 Macmunn, *The History of the Guides Part II 1922-1947*. p.128.

84 Randall Plunkett was decorated in 1930 while serving in the Northwest Province.

85 The Qattara Depression is a 7,000 square mile basin in which the surface consists of sand-encrusted saline lakes and marsh, small table topped hills and weird sand structures chiselled by centuries of wind. There are tracks through it, but difficult for even camels let alone tanks and wheeled vehicles, which stand a good chance of being bogged.

86 Young, *Rommel*. p.176.

87 Macmunn, *The History of the Guides Part II*. p.128. One member of 'B' Squadron who accompanied them during this entire period including the trek back, was the squadron mascot 'Dumba Singh'—born of a ration sheep while the squadron was in Kurdistan. It eventually returned with the squadron to India.

Chapter 2

1 The three regiments were 2nd Royal Lancers, 6th Lancers and Central India Horse.

2 Major General Martel was not new to India. He had been a member of the Directing Staff at Staff College Quetta in the late 1920s. As GSO3 to J. F. C. Fuller, he set out his wide-ranging ideas in a paper that profoundly influenced Fuller's thinking, which at the time simply regarded the tank as no more than a useful adjunct to infantry on the battlefield. In May 1940 during the Battle of France, Martel directed the tank attack on Rommel's 7th Panzer Division in the Battle of Arras in which the German frontline was driven back eight miles.

3 *Report on the visit by Lt. General G. Le Q. Martel to the Middle East, India, Burma and Tunisia*.

4 The basic pay was Rs.18 with an additional allowance of Rs.15 per month. Trade pay was over and above this.

5 General Headquarters India letter No 4405/I/S.D. (Armd. Tps) General Staff Branch. NEW DELHI, of 11 December. 1941. India Office Library and Records Reference IOR L/WS/I/448.

6 The organisation of the reconnaissance regiments differed according to the requirement of different theaters.

7 The IAC also contributed to the raising of the Corps of Indian Military Police (CIMP). A provost section was raised with soldiers of 7th Light Cavalry and 11th Cavalry in 1939 for the Force 4th Provost Unit, which accompanied the 4th Indian Division to Africa. In 1942, the CIMP was formally sanctioned by the government.

8 This was the origins of the Light Aid Detachment (LAD) which was subsequently authorized to every armoured unit and manned by trained EME personnel.

9 Major General Charles Gairdner was appointed as Major General Armoured Fighting Vehicles in India from December 1942 – February 1943. He was subsequently posted to Egypt as CIGS to C-in-C Middle East Forces from February – May 1943 and then returned to India as Director of Armoured Fighting Vehicles from August 1943 – November 1944.

10 On the Frontier, the Armoured Corps regiments continued to wear *Chappals* (sandals).

11 Sandhu, Major General Gurcharan Singh, *The Indian Armour. History of the Indian Armoured Corps. 1941-1971*. p.56. British tank pioneer General Percy Hobart introduced the black beret.

12 Chenevix-Trench, Charles, *The Indian Army and the King's Enemies 1900-1947*. p.223.

13 *Short History of the 6th DCO Lancers. September 1943-May 1945*. p.1.

14 Ibid, p.3.

15 Sandhu, *The Indian Armour*. p.151.

16 *The Tiger Triumphs. The Story of Three Great Divisions in Italy*. p.12.

17 Ibid, p.73.

18 Ibid, p.83.

19 Ibid, p.85.

20 Major General Dudley Russell was an officer of the Frontier Force Rifles. In 1936, he qualified as a higher standard interpreter in Pashto which resulted in his widely-used nickname of 'The Pasha'. He commanded the 6/13th Frontier Force during the campaign in Eretria in 1940.

21 Chenevix-Trench, *The Indian Army*. p.272.

22 Zaloga, Steven, *Staghound Armoured Car 1942-62*.

23 He was affectionately called 'Bingall'. After Independence, on the recommendation of Auchinleck, he was selected by Liaquat Ali to be the first commandant of the Pakistan Military Academy.

24 Ingall, Francis, *The Last of the Bengal Lancers*. p.98.

25 *Short History of the 6th DCO Lancers*. op.cit. p.40.

26 The German 88mm Flak 36 (commonly called the eighty-eight) was an anti-aircraft gun that was also used in the anti-tank role with devastating effect.

27 Ingall, *The Last of the Bengal Lancers*. p.100.

28 7th Armoured Brigade had to scuttle its 70 tanks because it could not ferry them back over the River Chindwin. Some accounts place the figure at 124 tanks.

29 The Burma Corps was the predecessor of the Fourteenth Army.

30 Crisp, Robert, *Brazen Chariots*. p.17-18.

31 *Report on the visit by Lt. General G. Le Q. Martel to the Middle East, India, Burma and Tunisia*.

32 Sandhu, *The Indian Armour*. p.179.

33 Ibid, p.179.

34 Effendi, M.Y. Colonel, *Punjab Cavalry. Evolution, Role, Organization, and Tactical Doctrine. 11th Cavalry (Frontier Force) 1849-1971*. p.105.

35 Sandhu, *The Indian Armour*. p.109.

36 *History of 19th King George V's Own Lancers. 1921-1947*.

37 The Sherman acquired its name from the British practice of naming American tanks after famous generals of the US Civil War.

38 Franz, Michael: *U.S. WWII M4/M4A1 Sherman Medium Tank*.

39 Sandhu, *The Indian Armour*. p.181.

40 Ibid, p.185.

41 Ibid, p.186.

42 Chenevix-Trench, *The Indian Army*. p.280.

43 Mclynn, Frank, *The Burma Campaign. Disaster into Triumph. 1942-1945*. p.417.

44 Military Training Pamphlet No15 (India). Inspection of Mechanized Units by Formation Commanders. Issued by General Staff India MGS-M252 (N).

45 Slim, Field Marshal William, *Defeat into Victory*. p.403.

46 Messervy was commissioned into Hodson's Horse and commanded 13th Lancers. At Independence, he was commanding Northern Command and was appointed as the first C-in-C of the Pakistan Army.

47 The fighter-bombers were on call from Cab Ranks, i.e. orbiting points close to the forward edge of the battle area. From these Cab Ranks, the Forward Air Controller could very quickly call on air support for any targets of opportunity or to counter threats to the troops in their area.

48 Perrett, Bryan, *Tank Tracks to Rangoon*. p.166.

49 *Japanese in Battle. 1st Edition*. General Headquarters, India. Military Intelligence Directorate 4/G.S.I. (T). May 1943.

50 *An account of the Operations in Burma carried out by Probyn's Horse during February, March & April 1945*. p.4.

51 All these attacks took place within a space of 36 hours, but obviously could not be sustained.

52 *An account of the Operations in Burma carried out by Probyn's Horse during February, March & April 1945*. p.12.

53 The reference to Ahmednagar is in the context of the tank firing ranges at this cantonment.

54 One of the tanks of Probyn's Horse taking part in this operation was named 'Clear-the-line' after the horse presented by Colonel Probyns' to the stud farm at Probynabad.

55 Sandhu, *The Indian Armour*. p.218-219.

56 Mclynn, *The Burma Campaign*. p.429.

57 Demi official letter dated 17 April 1945 from Lieutenant General F. W. Messervy, CB, DSO, Commander IV Corps to Brigadier C. E. Pert DSO, Commander 255th Indian Tank Brigade.

58 Demi official letter dated 10 April 1945 from General William Slim, DSO, MC, C-in-C, Fourteenth Army to Brigadier C. E. Pert, DSO, Commander 255th Indian Tank Brigade.

59 Slim, *Defeat into Victory*. p.480.

60 It was so poorly equipped that its fourth company used Stuart tanks abandoned by 7th Armoured Brigade in 1942 when it retreated across the Chindwin.

61 Lieutenant General Sir Oliver Leese, C-in-C, Allied Land Forces, South-East Asia.

62 Citation for Military Cross of 6274 I.O. Substantive Risaldar Abdul Razaq Khan, 16th Light Cavalry. Recommended 6th March 1945.

63 The landing was planned by Lord Mountbatten, Supreme Allied Commander South East Asia Command, who wanted a role in the recapture of Burma by organising a joint operation by land, naval, and air forces.

64 One squadron of 19th Lancers was equipped with Sherman Vs equipped with deep water equipment of the type used during the 'D' Day landing in France in 1944.

65 The emblem of the Fourteenth Army is still used by the brigade on its letterheads, invitation cards, etc.

66 Nath, Ashok, *Izza, Historical Records and Iconography of Indian Cavalry Regiments, 1750-2007*, p.285. The pre-1857 regular Bengal Cavalry Regiments were all disbanded or destroyed.

67 Rinaldi, Richard A, *Indian Army Airborne / Special Forces Units*. p.1.

68 *From Bitter Lakes to Bitter Thoughts. The Sabre and Lance. Journal of the Pakistan Armoured Corps. Golden Jubliee Issue*. 1997. p.53.

69 Because of the personality and appearance of the men, the acronym of GGBG popularly stood for: 'God's Gift to Beautiful Girls'.

70 *From Bitter Lakes to Bitter Thoughts*. p.53.

71 For a brief period the title of the Governor General's Body Guard was changed to Viceroy's Body Guard.

72 Nath, *Izzat*. p.413.

Chapter 3

1 Lord Roberts was C-in-C, India from 1885-1893. He did not consider Indians incompetent to be officers, but rather the reverse. Having in his youth seen what mutinous sepoys could do without officers, he thought it safer to keep all commissioned appointments in British hands, just in case, there was another mutiny or national rising of any sort. Heathcote, T. A: *The Military in British India: The Development of British Land Forces in South Asia, 1600-1947*. P.167.

2 The five Chiefs Colleges were Mayo College (Ajmer), Rajkumar College (Rajkot), the Daly College (Indore), Aitcheson College (Lahore) and Raipur College (Orissa).

3 Barua, Pradeep P., *Gentlemen of the Raj: The Indian Army Officer Corps, 1817-1949*. pp.9-10.

4 Notification was made in the London Gazette of 1 November 1946.

5 Mason, Philip, *A Matter of Honour*. p.456-457.

6 They were called VCOs because they received their commissions from the Viceroy and not from the British Monarch.

7 Sharma, *Nationalisation of the Indian Army*. p.52

8 Some elements from the RIASC known as Force K were sent to support the British Expeditionary Force in France in 1939. After most of the force (less the animals) was evacuated from Dunkirk, it served in Britain until 1944 and was subsequently redeployed in Burma.

9 Hussain, Hamid, *Panorama of Officers in the Pakistan and Indian Army*.

10 Connell, John, *Auchinleck. A Critical Bibliography*. p.947.

11 This is in reference to the three defendants who were tried by a joint court-martial for the most serious charge of "waging war against the King-Emperor" (the Indian Army Act, 1911, did not provide for a separate charge for treason) as well as murder and abetment of murder. The defendants were Colonel Prem Sahgal, Colonel Gurbaksh Singh Dhillon and Major General Shah Nawaz Khan.

12 11 years later in 1934, Lord Halifax, the Secretary of State for India officially defined Indianisation as: ' … the process of introducing Indians into the Commissioned ranks of the defence forces in India.'

13 Jeffrey, Alan and Rose, Patrick(ed.), *The Indian Army, 1939–47. Re-forging the Damascus Blade*. p.190.

14 Nath, Ashok, *Izzat: Historical Records and Iconography of Indian Cavalry Regiments, 1750-2007*. p.473.

15 Saddozai, Sardar Ahmed Shah Jan, *Saddozai Kings and Vaziers of Afghanistan 1747-1842*.

16 Afridi, Tariq, *Lt. General Mohammad Yousuf*.

17 Iftikhar Khan had five brothers in the army. The eldest was Major General Muhammad Akbar Khan, Pakistan's first general. To differentiate himself from the Major General Akbar who conducted operations in the first Kashmir War, he used the suffix of 'Rangroot' after his name. Major General Iftikhar's other brother were Major General Anwar Khan, the first Pakistani Engineer-in-Chief, Brigadier Muhammad Zafar Khan, Brigadier Afzal Khan (who was commissioned into 16th Light Cavalry but later attached to the Army Service Corps), and Brigadier Yousaf Khan.

18 Risaldar Major Raja Fazal Dad Khan, had three estates in Montgomery (Sahiwal), Chakwal and Lyallpur (Faisalabad), which were later divided among his nine sons.

19 Palit, Major General D.K., *Musing and Memories: Vol (II)*. p.109,

20 He was the brother-in-law of Muhammad Yusuf and the son of an honorary lieutenant.

21 N.A.M. Raza was the younger brother of N.A.K. Raza who was commissioned in 1927. They were from the Kizalbash tribe and their father had served in the Indian Police.

22 Palit, *Musing and Memories*. p.109.

23 Also amongst the Pioneers were General Muhammad Musa who was C-in-C of the Pakistan Army in the 1965 War, and Haji Iftikhar's friend Sam Manekshaw who commanded the Indian Army in the 1971 War.

24 Barua, *Gentlemen of the Raj*. p.61.

25 Effendi, *Punjab Cavalry*. p.66.

26 In that ironic twist of history, after losing an internal power struggle, Ayub sought asylum in India. In the Second Afghan War, 3rd Punjab Cavalry fought against the Afghans. Subsequently the 3rd and 1st Punjab Cavalry were amalgamated to form 11th PAVO Cavalry which Ayub's grandson el Effendi joined.

27 While in the Middle East during the war, el Effendi wore a signet ring presented to his grandfather by Queen Victoria. Engraved on the ring were the words, 'Enemy to Enemy, Friend to Friend'. See: *Punjab Cavalry*. p.96.

28 Muhammad Asghar Khan and Sahabzada Yaqub both passed out together from IMA and joined 18th Cavalry. However, the history of 18th Cavalry states that Sahabzada Yaqub was the only Indian officer to sail with the regiment to North Africa.

29 Sandhu, Major General Gurcharn Singh, *I Serve. Saga of the Eighteenth Cavalry*. Lancer International. p.114.

30 Nath, *Izzat*. p.511.

31 Sandhu, Major General Gurcharn Singh, *The Indian Armour. History of the Indian Armoured Corps. 1941-1971*. p.147.

32 Interview with Brigadier Amir Gulistan Janjua, Pakistan Armoured Corps.

33 Proudfoot, C.L., *We Lead: 7th Cavalry, 1784-1990*. p.57.

34 Proudfoot, *We Lead: 7th Cavalry, 1784-1990*. p.64.

35 Sandhu, Major General Gurcharan Singh, op. cit. pp.253-4.

36 Hesky Baig also served in Japan with the 7th Light Cavalry for a year.

37 Sandhu, Major General Gurcharn Singh, *I Serve. Saga of the Eighteenth Cavalry*. p.160.

Chapter 4

1 Sandhu, Major General Gurcharan Singh, *The Indian Armour. History of the Indian Armoured Corps. 1941-1971*. p.239. Having been shipped back to India some of the regiments were redeployed overseas for security duties.

2 Sandhu, *The Indian Armour*. p.240

3 Jeffrey, Alan and Patrick, Rose (ed.), *The Indian Army, 1939–47. Re-forging the Damascus Blade*. p.179.

4 Sandhu, *The Indian Armour*., op. cit. p.241.

5 Narrated by Riazul Haq who was in the entourage of General Zia ul Haq, President of Pakistan when he revisited this landing beach.

6 *The Cock Crows*, Newspaper of 23 Indian Division. Published October 1945. Extract reproduced in *Sabre and Lance*. Journal of the Pakistan Armoured Corps. Issue No 1. June 1953.

7 Sandhu, *The Indian Armour*. p.243.

8 Effendi, Colonel M.Y., *Punjab Cavalry. Evolution, Role, Organization, and Tactical Doctrine. 11 Cavalry (Frontier Force) 1849-1971*. p.135.

9 McMillan, Richard, *The British Occupation of Indonesia 1945–1946: Britain, the Netherlands and the Indonesian Revolution*.

10 There was strong public opinion in India against Indian troops being employed to fight the Indonesians. See: *Note on the Armed Forces by Jawaharlal Nehru to the Defense Member Baldev Singh, 12 September 1946*, contained in Auchinleck Papers (John Rylands University Library, Manchester) File LXXIII, MUL 1193.

11 Riza, Major General Shaukat, *The Pakistan Army 1947-49*. p.109.

12 Khan, Brigadier Zaheer Alam, *The Way it Was*. p.43.

13 Sandhu, *The Indian Armour*. p.243.

14 *Probyn's Horse Newsletter, 1946-1947*.

15 *Guides Regimental Newsletter, September 1946.* The American equipment was well kitted out and among many other refinements, there were small white bags of silicate for keeping items such as the wireless set free of humidity. Impressed by the equipment stowed in the tanks, a dry witted old Rajput soldier of Poona Horse picked up one of these bags and remarked, '*Chini bhi de rakha hai!*' (They've even placed some sugar). See *History of the 17th (Poona) Horse.* p.64.

16 The Churchill tanks were discarded by the Indian Army soon after Independence.

17 The deduction was made by Ashok Nath, an internationally recognized authority on the Indian Cavalry.

18 The last of the JCOs who had been trained as recruits at Lucknow and Babina, retired from the Pakistan Armoured Corps in the early 1980s.

19 Sandhu, Major General Gurcharan Singh, *I Serve. Saga of the Eighteenth Cavalry.* p.159.

20 Sandhu, *I Serve.* p.256.

21 Sandhu, *I Serve.* p.245.

22 *History of the 17th (Poona) Horse.* p.64.

23 Khan, *The Way it Was.* p.44.

24 Khan, Fazal Muqeem: *The Story of the Pakistan Army.* p.50.

25 Interview with Brigadier Said Azhar, Pakistan Armoured Corps.

26 Husain, Major General Syed Wajahat, *1947 Before During After.* p.94.

27 Interview with Brigadier Amir Gulistan Janjua, Pakistan Armoured Corps.

28 Sandhu, *The Indian Armour.* p.246.

29 In 1953, Probyn's farm was handed over to the army. See: *Sabre and Lance. June 1953.* In 1967, Probyn's Horse recovered 81 acres of land as compensation due to the efforts of Brigadier Agha Javed Iqbal. Ref: Interview with Lieutenant General Muhammad Amjad.

30 *Probyn's Horse Newsletter 1946-1947.*

31 Khan, *The Way it Was.* p.43.

32 Azhar, Brigadier Said, *Reflections of 19th Lancer's Days.*

33 Major Bernard Weatherill, who fought with 19th Lancers in Burma, owned the shop. He joined politics and rose to become Speaker of both the House of Commons and the House of Lords. However, he always carried a thimble in his pocket as a reminder of his humble background and the motto on his coat of arms states 'A stitch in time'. He was patron of the Indian Officers' Cavalry Association in UK and a recipient of the Hilal-i-Pakistan.

34 The share of the mess silver of the Corps of Artillery and of Signals was also shipped to UK on the plea that it had been contributed by British officers. See: Riza, Major General Shaukat, *The Pakistan Army 1947-49.* pp.160–161.

35 Interview with Colonel Samiuddin Ahmed, Pakistan Armoured Corps.

36 Major General Gwatkin had been on the roll of 19th Lancers and its predecessor 18th Tiwana Lancers for 40 years. He was a distinguished polo player and a recognised football player.

37 Interview with Colonel Samiuddin Ahmed, Pakistan Armoured Corps.

38 Sandhu, *The Indian Armour.* p.251.

39 The action at Gauche Wood occurred in France during the Battle of Cambrai 1917, when the 18th King George's Own Lancers attacked a German position dismounted.

40 Digest of Service of 19th Lancers.

41 *Reorganization of the Army and Air Force in India.* Report of a Committee set up by H.E. the Commander-in-Chief in India. Volume 1, New Delhi. Govt of India Press, 1945, p.224.

42 The other regiment that was to be disbanded was Central India Horse because it had a serious mutiny in 1940. Ref: Committee report on *Reorganization of the Army and Air Force in Indian.* p.224.

43 Macmunn, Lieutenant General George, *The History of the Guides Part II 1922-1947.* p.147.

44 These lavish celebrations on the eve of Independence were also conducted by other regiments of the British India Army. The Digest of Service of 7th Battalion (Cokes) Frontier Force Regiment records that their Indian commanding officer Brishwar Nath spent the Mess money on lavish entertainment thereby leaving only a paltry sum of about Rs. 5,000. Further the amount was locked up in Indian securities which could only be cashed at a devalued rate.

45 The phrase is related to the Continental Divide of North American that extends from the Bering Strait to the Strait of Magellan, and separates the watersheds that drain into the Pacific Ocean from those river systems that drain into the Atlantic Ocean.

46 Alan and Rose (ed.), *The Indian Army, 1939–47.* p.182.

47 Sandhu, *The Indian Armour.* p.247.

48 Alan and Rose (ed.), *The Indian Army, 1939–47.* p.182.

49 In 1922, the merger of 18th King George's Own Lancers (Tiwana Lancers) and 19th Lancers (Fane's Horse) formed 19th King George's Own Lancers.

50 During the Second China War, the regiment had established a China Fund subscribed to by the men. The sale of the loot was added to this money. The fund was used to establish the farm in 1860, and was replicated by many other Silladar regiments on a lesser scale. See: *A History of the XI King Edward's Own Lancers (Probyn's Horse)* by Captain E. L. Mazwell. Published 1914.

51 Interview with Lieutenant General Muhammad Amjad. Pakistan Armoured Corps.

52 *Ahmednagar to Nowshera,* The Sabre and Lance. Journal of the Pakistan Armoured Corps. Golden Jubilee Issue. 1997. p.31.

53 Babina was established in 1942 as a temporary camp with wartime hutted accommodation of bamboo and tin sheets. It was named after the Babina Forest adjoining the River Betwa south of Jhansi.

54 Risaldar Major Gulam Shah, who was a young sowar on the train, recollects that on instructions from Shahzada Alam, all the troops pointed their rifles from the windows of the train and were ready to shoot. In all his service, he has yet to see such a bold, courageous, and forceful junior officer. This information was provided by Captian Khalid Walid Awan, the grandson of the Risaldar Major who served in 15th and 19th Lancers.

55 *The Break from Babina,* The Sabre and Lance. Journal of the Pakistan Armoured Corps. Golden Jubilee Issue. 1997. p.27.

56 *Courage Amongst Carnage,* The Sabre and Lance. Journal of the Pakistan Armoured Corps. Golden Jubilee Issue. 1997. p.39.

57 Alumni Newsletter, Lawrence College Ghora Gali.

58 *History of the 17th (Poona) Horse.* p. 65.

59 Abhey Singh had served with the 18th Cavalry at the Battle of Ghazala and was captured along with Sahabzada Yaqub, Hissam el Effendi, and Tikka Khan. He was interned along with these officers in a POW camps in Italy, and also attempted to escape with Sahabzada Yaqub. After the War he was posted to Poona Horse, and brought the squadron of Kaim Khanis from Risalpur to Jhansi.

60 *The KKs of Poona Horse: Journeying from Jhansi,.* The Sabre and Lance. Journal of the Pakistan Armoured Corps. Golden Jubilee Issue. 1997. p.59.

61 General Messervy had served in Hodson's Horse, and commanded 13th Lancers prior to the Second World War.

62 Sandhu, *The Indian Armour.* p.247.

63 Alan and Rose (ed.), *The Indian Army, 1939–47.* p. 192.

64 Chevenix-Trench, Charles, *The Indian Army and the King's Enemies 1900-1947.* p.294.

65 Rikhye, Major General Indar Jit, *History of 6th Duke of Connaught's Own Lancers.*

66 Effendi, *Punjab Cavalry.* p.171.

67 *Courage amongst Carnage.* op. cit. p.38.

68 The British had nicknamed Dera Ismail Khan as 'Dera Misery Khan' because of its hot summers and isolated location.

69 Macmunn, *The History of the Guides Part II.* p.177.

70 Husain, *1947 Before During After.* p.127.

71 Rahmat Ali Khan was the son of Khan Quraban Ali Khan, former Indian Police, and the first Inspector General (IG) Police Punjab in August 1947, and also IG Police in NWFP in 1953. A year later he was appointed as Governor of NWFP where he served from 1954–55.

72 Riza, *The Pakistan Army 1947-49.* p.193.

73 Govind was the younger brother of the famous Zorawar Singh who had served with Gussy Haider in CIH in Italy and Greece during the Second World War. Govind had earlier been the ADC to General Auchinleck along with Lieutenant Colonel Syed Shahid Hamid who was the Private Secretary to C-in-C India.

74 Sandhu, *I Serve.* p.158.

75 Askari was wounded the same year he was commissioned into the 7th Light Cavalry in 1942, and spent rest of the war recuperating. He was demobilised after the war, but re-commissioned in 1948.

76 Macmunn, *The History of the Guides Part II.* p.155.

77 This plan, formulated in the early part of the twentieth century, advocated withdrawing all regular forces from tribal territory into outposts, or cantonments, along the administrative border. The un-administered districts would then once again become the responsibility of the local militias.

78 Macmunn, *The History of the Guides Part II.* p.259.

79 Husain, *1947 Before During After.* p.97.

80 Interview with Brigadier Said Azhar, Pakistan Armoured Corps.

81 Macmunn, *The History of the Guides Part II.* p.160.

82 Ibid. p.162.

83 Husain, *1947 Before During After.* p.54.

84 Ibid. p.72.

85 Sandhu, *The Indian Armour.* p.249.

86 Khan, *The Story of the Pakistan Army.* p.73.

87 Most of the account of the 11th Cavalry's operations during the Kashmir War is based on an unpublished narrative written by Lieutenant Colonel Nawaz Khan whose extracts have been reproduced in *Punjab Cavalry. Evolution, Role, Organization, and Tactical Doctrine. 11 Cavalry (Frontier Force) 1849-1971* written by Colonel M. Y. Effendi. However, some facts are substantiated from other sources.

88 Effendi, *Punjab Cavalry*. p.165.

89 Amin, Major Agha Humayun, *The War of Lost Opportunities (Part II)*.

90 Khan, Lieutenant General Gul Hassan, *Memoirs of Lt. Gen. Gul Hassan Khan*. p.85.

91 Hamid, Major General Syed Shahid, *Early Years of Pakistan*. p.70.

92 Zaheer, Hasan, *The Rawalpindi Conspiracy Case 1951*. p.169.

93 Interview with Brigadier Said Azhar, Pakistan Armoured Corps.

Chapter 5

1 Mazumder, Rahit K, *The Indian Army and the Making of Punjab*. p.61.

2 From the contents of a letter by Colonel Hodson to his father as quoted in *The History of the Guides Part I 1846- 1922*. p.286.

3 Lieutenant Hodson raised the Guides as its adjutant and commanded it at the age of 32 years as a brevet major from 1853-55. Accused of fraud he was dismissed from the Guides but was later cleared of dishonesty. In 1857, he raised a regiment of 2,000 irregular Horse that became famous as Hodson's Horse. The killing of the Mughal princes, his vengeful treatment of Indians, and unproved charges against him of looting, darkened his reputation. He died at the age of 37 years at Lucknow while storming the Begum Kothi. His last words were "I hope I have done my duty".

4 Younghusband, Lieutenant Colonel Francis, *The Story of the Guides*. Chapter: The Home of the Guides.

5 Macmunn, Lieutenant General George, *The History of the Guides Part II 1922-1947*. p.97.

6 *1st (Peshawar) Division*. Wikipedia.

7 *Risalpur Cantonment*. Global Security.Org.

8 During the First World War, the Royal Flying Corps established a base and a Fighter Conversion Centre at Risalpur. In 1919, two squadrons of the Royal Air Force were stationed at Risalpur from where they participated in operations during the Third Afghan War, and in Waziristan against the Faqir of Ipi.

9 Khan, Lieutenant General Gul Hassan, *Memoirs of Lt. Gen. Gul Hassan Khan*.p.84.

10 *Imperial Gazetteer of India, 1901. Volume 18*. p.417.

11 Ten miles to the east of Nowshera is Akhora Khattak, which was founded by the great grandfather of the famous Pashto poet and Pathan warrior, Khushal Khan Khattak.

12 Interview with Major General Kamal Matinuddin, Pakistan Artillery.

13 Archaeologists believe that a distinct culture flourished on the plateau of Rawalpindi as far back as 3,000 years. The material remains found at the site prove the existence of a Buddhist establishment contemporary to Taxila, but less celebrated than its neighbour does. It appears that the ancient city went into oblivion because of the Hun devastation.

14 *The Indian Army 1914*.

15 Mazumder, *The Indian Army and the Making of Punjab*. p.63.

16 Sandhu, Major General Gurcharn Singh, *I Serve. Saga of the Eighteenth Cavalry*. p.113.

17 *Sabre and Lance*. Journal of the Pakistan Armoured Corps. Issue No 1. June 1953.

18 When Italy capitulated in September 1943, the Italians were treated not as POWs but as internees, waiting to be repatriated once the war ended.

19 Mauripur was later renamed as Masroor Base Airbase.

20 Grathwol, Robert P. and Moorhus, Donita M, *Bricks, Sand and Marble. U.S. Army Corps of Engineers. Construction in the Mediterranean and Middle East, 1947–1991*. p.67.

21 *Report on U.S. Financed military construction at Kharian and Multan in West Pakistan*. p.1.

22 The major projects for the Pakistan Air Force were providing facilities and constructing/strengthening the airfields at Drig Road (Faisal Airbase), Sargodha and Peshawar. For the Pakistan Navy, the Corps of Engineers constructed a pier as well as ammunition storage facilities. They also constructed a new jet runway, corresponding taxiways, and support facilities at the Karachi civilian airport. A credit of $4.8 million was provided by the US Government for this project.

23 Interview with Brig. Amir Gulistan Janjua. Pakistan Armoured Corps.

24 *Report on U.S. Financed military construction at Kharian and Multan in West Pakistan*. p.18.

25 Grathwol and Moorhus, *Bricks, Sand and Marble*. p.103.

26 Interview with Brigadier Amir Gulistan Janjua. Pakistan Armoured Corps.

27 Grathwol and Moorhus, *Bricks, Sand and Marble*. p.10.

28 It was at Kharian that the army was introduced to and adopted the US Army terminology of BOQs (Bachelor Officers Quarters) and MOQs (Married Officers Quarters).

29 In 1947, the Peshawar Area was designated as the Peshawar (Frontier) Division and six months later numbered as the 9th (Frontier) Division. Disbanded in 1952/53, it was re-raised as the 9th Infantry Division in 1966 at Kharian.

30 Sialkot was one of the four stations of the cavalry brigades in India, the others being Risalpur, Meerut, and Secunderabad (Bolarum). The cavalry brigades had two Indian cavalry regiments and one British. The brigade stations were popular; less popular were those where regiments were individually garrisoned i.e. divisional cavalry regiments i.e. Quetta, Peshawar, Bannu, Kohat, Loralai, Dera Ismail Khan, Ferozepur, Jhansi, and Lucknow. However, some of the regiments with the cavalry brigades were stationed at Lahore and Rawalpindi. See: Sandhu, *The Indian Cavalry*. p.424.

31 *Gazetteer of the Sialkot District, 1920*. Lahore, Punjab Government. p.170-171.

32 During the war, 1st Armoured Division was renumbered as the 31st Indian Armoured Division. On return from the war, it was designated as the 1st Armoured Division and based at Ahmednagar.

33 Sandhu, *The Indian Armour*. p.36-47.

Chapter 6

1 Raza, Major General Shaukat, *The Pakistan Army 1947-49*. p.301.

2 Letters after the mark number denoted modifications to the base model: 'A' for the 76mm L/55 gun instead of the 75mm, 'B' for the 105mm M4 L/22.5 howitzer, 'C' for the (British) QF 17 pdr (76.2mm) gun, and 'Y' for the wider tracked HVSS type suspension.

3 *The AFV Database*. Article on the Internet.

4 The French Canon de 75-modèle 1897 field gun was also adopted by the US and used well into the Second World War as the 75mm M1897 field gun.

5 *75mm Gun M2/M3/M6*. Wikipedia.

6 Franz, Michael, *U.S. WWII M4/M4A1 Sherman Medium Tank*.

7 Edgar, Julian, *The Chrysler A57 Multi-Bank Engine. An amazing engine*.

8 Interview with Colonel Asmat Nawaz Janjua. Pakistan Armoured Corps.

9 Old tankers of the Pakistan Armoured Corps would recollect that the sets featured English/Cyrillic lettering on the front panel. The reason for this was that these sets were also supplied to the Soviet Army.

10 Interview with Brigadier Shamim Yasin Manto by A.H Amin. February 2002.

11 Using Morse, the No. 19 could communicate between the two wings of the country, a distance of over 2,300 km.

12 Some British units tried to fight with a crew of three in the turret of the Stuart tank, but it was very cramped.

13 The Indian Army used them with success in the mountains in Kargil during the Kashmir operations and also deployed them during the Indo-China Border Conflict of 1962.

14 Nawaz, Shuja, *Crossed Swords. Pakistan Its Army and the Wars Within*. p.94.

15 Nawaz, *Crossed Swords*.p.96.

16 *690D.95/5-1151: Telegram. The Secretary of State to the Embassy in Pakistan. Secret. Washington, May 11, 1951*.

17 Top Secret letter P.O. 75/50/13 dated Boston, Mass., 29 May 1950 from the Ambassador M.A.H. Ispahani to Colonel Iskander Mirza, Ministry of Defense, Karachi, Pakistan Army GHQ archives.

18 *The Best Light Tank. The Army uncovers its secret new T-41 for Truman*. Life. 26 February 1951. p.26.

19 Lend-Lease was a program under which the United States supplied its allies with material and equipment during the Second World War. The supply could be in the form of sales, transfer, lease, lend, etc. After the War, the US Congress did not authorize any free transfer, so the administration charged for the equipment, usually at 90 percent discount.

20 The British had constructed a large number of airfields in Northwestern India and the United States had developed a substantial air infrastructure at Karachi during the Second World War to support operations in the China- Burma-India Theater.

21 This is in reference to the Rawalpindi Conspiracy of 1951.

22 Nawaz, *Crossed Swords*. p.98.

23 *Memorandum dated 27 November 1951. 790D.5-MAP/11-2751. Office of the Assistant to the Secretary Defense for International Security Affairs*.

24 Major General George H. Olmsted was a strong negotiator and on retirement, became one of the Washington's wealthiest and most powerful businessman, managing a group that controlled banks and insurance companies.

25 Hamid, Major General Syed Shahid, *Early Years of Pakistan*. p.101.

26 Around the same period, India purchased military hardware and spares worth $36.3 million.

27 Nawaz, *Crossed Swords*. p.100.

28 In 1953, the Israelis were supplied with the M4A4 variant which were upgraded with a HVSS suspension, a Cummins V-8 460 horsepower (340 kW) diesel engine, and a French high-velocity 75mm gun. The Indians installed the same gun in two regiments of Shermans but the tank performed badly in the 1965 War.

29 Hamid, Major General Syed Ali, *Forged in the Furnace of Battle*. p.5.

30 Khan, Brigadier Zaheer Alam, *The Way it Was*. p.386.

31 Effendi, Colonel M.Y., *Punjab Cavalry. Evolution, Role, Organisation, and Tactical Doctrine. 11 Cavalry (Frontier Force) 1849-1971*. p.175.

32 *Notes for C-in-Cs Discussion on 19 Mar 1956*. Archives of Major General Syed Shahid Hamid.

33 Letter to the Editor on the *1965 War – The Sialkot Sector* by Lieutenant Colonel Yahya Effendi (Defense Journal, 1998).

34 Hamid, *Early Years of Pakistan*. p.101.

35 Mitha, Major General Aboobaker Osman, *Unlikely Beginnings: a Soldier's Life*. p.165.

36 *Report on the Second Conference of Commandants of GHQ Training Establishments 1955*. From the Archives of Major General. Syed Shahid Hamid.

37 Khan, Fazal Muqeem: *The Story of the Pakistan Army*. p.156.

38 Qayyum, Colonel Abdul, *Mosaic of Memories and Ideas. Sahabzada Yaqub Khan.*

39 The armoured division had one self-propelled light anti-aircraft regiment of four batteries, each with eight twin 40mm Bofors and eight Point 50 Brownings in quad mounts.

40 Interview with Colonel Samiuddin Ahmed, Pakistan Armoured Corps.

41 Stereoscopic range finders had been in service with the US Army during the Second World War. They suffered from the disadvantages that very few soldiers are able to see stereoscopically with sufficient exactness to obtain good results. Thus, the degree of accuracy obtained by a range-taker varied.

42 Interview with Brigadier Zahir Alam, Defense Journal.

43 Interview with Colonel Samiuddin Ahmed, Pakistan Armoured Corps.

44 Effendi, Colonel M.Y, *Punjab Cavalry. Evolution, Role, Organisation, and Tactical Doctrine. 11 Cavalry (Frontier Force) 1849-1971*. p.177.

45 Interview with Brigadier Muhammad Ahmed, Pakistan Armoured Corps.

46 Interview with Lieutenant General Hameed Gul, Pakistan Armoured Corps.

47 Khan, *The Way it Was*, p.81.

48 Hamid, *Forged in the Furnace of Battle*. p.35.

49 Ibid. pp.85-86

50 *Remembering our Warriors. Brig Shamim Yasin Manto*. (Defense Journal, February 2002).

51 Ibid.

52 *The Best Light Tank.*

53 Khan, Brigadier Abdul Mokeet, *Memoirs of 1965.*

54 Khan, *The Way it Was*. p.74.

Chapter 7

1 Jeffrey, Alan and Patrick, Rose (ed.), *The Indian Army, 1939–47. Re-forging the Damascus Blade*. p.193.

2 Effendi, Colonel M.Y., *Punjab Cavalry. Evolution, Role, Organisation, and Tactical Doctrine. 11 Cavalry (Frontier Force) 1849-1971*. p.141.

3 Interview with Brigadier Asmat Baig Humayun , Pakistan Armoured Corps.

4 Filose, Brigadier A.A., *King George V's Own, Central India Horse, Volume II*. p.359.

5 Ali Musa Khan earned an IDSM in North Africa during Operation CRUSADER in 1941, when CIH was serving with 4th Indian Division commanded by Maj. General. Messervy. He was the risaldar major of CIH for two and a half years and was awarded with an MBE for his services when the regiment was on Internal Security in Greece after the war. The history of CIH records that: 'Having seen every day of the war on service with the regiment [Ali Musa] was a tower of strength'.

6 Citation for MBE of 8305 I.O. Risaldar Major Ali Musa Khan. Central India Horse.

7 Effendi, *Punjab Cavalry*. p.140.

8 Brigadier Rawlinson, who had been appointed the first commander of 3rd Armoured Brigade, had been the Chief of Staff to General Slim. On his request, General Slim obtained permission from the headquarters in New Delhi for the brigade to continue to wear the insignia of the Fourteenth Army and bring the vehicles.

9 Khan, Fazal Muqeem, *The Story of the Pakistan Army*. p.59.

10 Khan, *The Story of the Pakistan Army*. p.59.

11 Address to the Armoured Corps Centre, Nowshera, by Quaid-i-Azam Muhammad Ali Jinnah on 13 April, 1948.

12 The two divisions not allocated armoured regiments were 8th Division at Karachi/Quetta and 14th Division in East Pakistan.

13 Khan, *The Way it Was*. p.48.

14 Interview with Lieutenant General Raja Saroop, Pakistan Armoured Corps.

15 Effendi, *Punjab Cavalry*. p.104.

16 Husain, Major General Syed Wajahat, *1947 Before During After*. p.109.

17 Hamid, Major General Syed Shahid, *Early Years of Pakistan*. p.87.

18 Husain, *1947 Before During After*. p.107.

19 Hamid, *Early Years of Pakistan*. p.85.

20 Interview with Brigadier Said Azhar, Pakistan Armoured Corps.

21 Husain, *1947 Before During After*. p.170.

22 Interview with Brigadier Jafar Khan, Pakistan Armoured Corps.

23 Khan, *The Way it Was*. p.54.

24 Ibid. p.56.

25 When the author was serving on the staff of 6th Armoured Division in 1973, he was in charge of the headquarters library which still held a large number of gazetteers from the era of British India related to the Northwest Frontier and Afghanistan. They had been inherited from its predecessor, the pre-Independence Peshawar Brigade.

26 Letter to the Editor by Colonel Yahya Effendi, Defence Journal, April 1998.

27 *Report on the visit by Lt. GeneralG. Le Q. Martel to the Middle East, India, Burma and Tunisia.*

28 Interview with Major General Khurshid Ali Khan, Pakistan Armoured Corps.

29 Sandhu, Major General Gurcharan Singh. *The Indian Armour. History of the Indian Armoured Corps. 1941-1971*. p.540.

30 Interview with Brigadier Amir Gulistan Janjua, Pakistan Armoured Corps.

31 *Notes for C-in-C's Discussion on 19 March 1956*. Archives of Major General Syed Shahid Hamid.

32 Husain, *1947 Before During After*. p.179.

33 Nawaz, Shuja, *Crossed Swords. Pakistan Its Army and the Wars Within*. p.97.

34 Alavi, Hamza: "*Pakistan-US Military Alliance.*" Economic and Political Weekly 33, no. 25 (1998): 1551-1557.

35 Nawaz, *Crossed Swords*. p.134.

36 The battalions were of the 15th Punjab Regiment, which was a machine gun regiment of four battalions: 1/15th to 4/15th. After the reorganisation of the army, these battalions were renumbered as 9th, 10th, 11th and 12th Punjab.

37 Interview with Brigadier Amir Gulistan Janjua, Pakistan Armoured Corps.

38 *Sabre and Lance*. Journal of the Pakistan Armoured Corps. 1958. p.32.

39 The system of grouping armoured regiments with the infantry groups is done to foster a better esprit de corps between infantry and armour, especially if particular units have fought together.

40 *Sabre and Lance*. Journal of the Pakistan Armoured Corps. 1958. p.29.

41 Sikku also designed the badges of a number of other armoured regiments including 22nd Cavalry, 25th Cavalry and 33rd Cavalry. He also assisted Akram Hussain Syed in designing the badge of 26th Cavalry.

42 Khan, *The Way it Was*. p.71.

43 Interview with Colonel Asmat Nawaz Janjua, Pakistan Armoured Corps.

44 Interview with Colonel Asmat Nawaz Janjua.

45 *The British-Indian Army's Four Armoured Divisions: A Debate.*

46 Barua, Pradeep P., *Gentlemen of the Raj: The Indian Army Officer Corps, 1817-1949*. p.118.

47 *Report on U.S. Financed military construction at Kharian and Multan in West Pakistan*. Report of United States Congressional Committee. March 1, 1961. p.2.

48 Until the 1965 War, the Indian 1st Armoured Division had a British Second World War organisation of a heavy armoured brigade and a motorised infantry brigade.

49 The insignia of the division was designed by Captain Sikandar Khan, 13th Lancers. See: *Regimental News. Sabre and Lance. Journal of Pakistan Armoured Corps*. Volume IV. 1956.

50 Interview with Colonel Asmat Nawaz Janjua. Pakistan Armoured Corps.

51 During the 1950s, the civil administrative division of Rawalpindi was very large. In the north, it rested on the River Indus and in the south; it shared boundaries with the Lahore and Multan Divisions along the River Chenab.

52 Husain, *1947 Before During After*. p.191.

53 Riza, Major General Shaukat, *The Pakistan Army War 1965*. p.47.

54 Interview with Brigadier Jafar Khan, Pakistan Armoured Corps.

55 During the Second World War, Hollingsworth was recognized by GeneralPatton as one of the two best armoured battalion commanders. He retired as a lieutenant Generaland was one of the 10 most decorated US General of all times. He headed MAAG Pakistan in its early years and had a reputation of being very abrasive when inspecting regiments. He could also walk into the office of the C-in-C at any time. In a condolence message on his death, Major General Shabbir Hussain Shah, EME, wrote, "I knew the General during his days in Pakistan as a young colonel in the USMAG. What a man! What a soldier! He was a true friend of Pakistan".

56 Interview with Colonel Samiuddin Ahmed, Pakistan Armoured Corps.

57 Khan, *The Story of the Pakistan Army*. p.157.

58 Nawaz, *Crossed Swords*. p.134.

59 Khan, *The Story of the Pakistan Army*. p.159. The MGO, Major General Syed Shahid Hamid had the prime responsibility to equip and supply the army. He negotiated hard with the Americans and consequently came under a direct attack by the US Ambassador.

60 Nawaz, *Crossed Swords*. p.134. General Sexton of the US Army was of the opinion that the flow of equipment into Pakistan was at a pace that allowed the Pakistan Army to absorb it.

61 Interview with General Jehangir Karamat, Pakistan Armoured Corps.

62 Khan, *The Way it Was*. p.84.

63 Interview with Brigadier Amir Gulistan Janjua, Pakistan Armoured Corps.

64 Effendi, *Punjab Cavalry*. p.176.

65 Citation for MBE of IEC 14. Lieutenant Abrar Hussain. 2/10 Baluch. The National Archives. Catalogue Reference: WO/373/104.

66 Interview with General Jehangir Karamat, Pakistan Armoured Corps.

67 Husain, *1947 Before During After*. p.210.

68 *Men of Steel. 6th Armoured Division in the 1965 War*. p.1.

69 The Pentomic Divisions were organised with five highly mobile battle groups (penta) with their slice of supporting arms and services that could function on an atomic or non-atomic battlefield. Command was exercised through task force headquarters to carry out a given mission with units designated before the battle. For more details see: Wilson, John B. Manoeuvre and Firepower. *The Evolution of Divisions and Separate Brigades*. Centre of Military History. United States Army. Washington, D. C., 1998. p.272-280.

70 Interview with Brigadier Muhammad Ahmed, Pakistan Armoured Corps.

71 Interview with Major General Inayat Ollah Khan Niazi, Pakistan Armoured Corps.

72 22nd Cavalry is the only armoured regiment which has a motto in English, 'Death or Glory', inscribed on it badge. The badge and shoulder titles were designed by Col. Sikku Khan who also designed the insignia of 1st and 6th Armoured Division.

73 Interview with Lieutenant General Farrukh Khan, Pakistan Armoured Corps. In 1962, General Yahya was commanding 15th Division in the Sialkot Sector. When leaving the division he predicted that the forthcoming battle would be fought at Chawinda. Consequently, when 25th Cavalry was ordered to move to Narowal during the 1965 War to counter a misreported threat, it was very perturbed at being dislocated. Interview with Brigadier Muhammad Ahmed. Pakistan Armoured Corps.

74 Musa, General Muhammad, *My version: India-Pakistan war, 1965*. p.26.

75 Khan, Brigadier M. Sher, *150 Years of 6th Lancers. A Regiment Par Excellence. A Brief Tribute Cum History*.

76 Interview with Major General Inayat Ollah Khan Niazi, Pakistan Armoured Corps.

ABOUT THE AUTHOR

Major-General Syed Ali Hamid
Born into a family with 150 years of tradition of soldiering, Syed Ali Hamid retired from the Pakistan Army after more than 50 years of service, more than half of this with the Pakistan Armoured Corps. He served with an armoured regiment during the Indo-Pakistan War of 1971, commanded a mechanized division, lectured for six years at the faculty of the Army Staff College and Pakistan's National Defence University, and developed a passion for military history. While extensively researching the history of the British India Army, and the military history of the Indian Subcontinent, he has published hundreds of articles in military magazines and journals, and several related books. This is his first instalment for Helion.